EMILY DICKINSON AND HYMN CULTURE

*This book is dedicated to the memory of
George Francis Balmforth –
Champion hymn-singer and Grandfather*

Emily Dickinson and Hymn Culture
Tradition and Experience

VICTORIA N. MORGAN
University of Liverpool, UK

ASHGATE

Published by
Ashgate Publishing Limited
Wey Court East
Union Road
Farnham
Surrey, GU9 7PT
England

Ashgate Publishing Company
Suite 420
101 Cherry Street
Burlington
VT 05401-4405
USA

www.ashgate.com

British Library Cataloguing in Publication Data
Morgan, Victoria N., 1975–
    Emily Dickinson and hymn culture: tradition and experience.
    1. Dickinson, Emily, 1830–1886 – Criticism and interpretation. 2. Watts, Isaac, 1674–1748 – Influence. 3. Women hymn writers. 4. Hymns – Metrics and rhythmics.
    I. Title
    811.4-dc22

Library of Congress Cataloging-in-Publication Data
Morgan, Victoria N., 1975–
    Emily Dickinson and hymn culture: tradition and experience / by Victoria N. Morgan.
        p. cm.
    Includes bibliographical references and index.
    ISBN 978-0-7546-6942-5 (alk. paper)
    1. Dickinson, Emily, 1830–1866—Knowledge—Hymns. 2. Dickinson, Emily, 1830–1886—Religion. 3. Dickinson, Emily, 1830–1886—Literary style. 4. Hymns, English—History and criticism. 5. Spirituality in literature. I. Title.
    PS1541.Z5M66 2010
    811'.4—dc22

2009036612

ISBN 9780754669425 (hbk)

Mixed Sources
Product group from well-managed forests and other controlled sources
www.fsc.org Cert no. SA-COC-1565
© 1996 Forest Stewardship Council
FSC

Printed and bound in Great Britain by
MPG Books Group, UK

Contents

Preface

Any writer who sets out to engage with questions surrounding spirituality has an especially challenging road ahead of them. There are multiple opportunities for forging ahead with one direction in mind, only to find there are an equal number of u-turns and changes in direction required. When Emily Dickinson is the primary companion on that road, the journey is even more surprising. She is, without doubt, one of the most rich and complex poets to read on the subject of spirituality. I set out on this particular road because I wanted to 'go' where she 'went'; to know some of what she knew. In some ways this is the journey 'to' nowhere, and Dickinson is instructive on this point ('Done with the Compass -/ Done with the Chart!' (Fr 269)). However imposed disorientation notwithstanding, the frequently recurrent images, rhythms and echoed voices to be found in Dickinson's poems suggested ways of looking at her vast corpus which highlight moments when tradition and experience on spirituality meet. At these moments the dialogism at work in Dickinson's poems is most effectively clear and it is also the most transformative. What followed was an investigation of the relationship between the expressions of spirituality in the poetry of Emily Dickinson and the representations of spirituality associated with the hymn culture she encountered.

Drawing upon contemporary women hymnists and the influence of the hymns of Isaac Watts, the book traces the dissent and challenge to the hierarchical 'I-Thou' model of relation found in traditional hymn address and shows how Dickinson engaged with it to produce her most spiritually probing and expansive poems. Watts's Dissenting position has been overlooked in previous discussions of Dickinson's use of the hymn form. Women hymnists contemporary with Dickinson, who also sought to redefine God in ways more compatible with their own experience, have similarly been ignored when considering the impact of hymn culture on Dickinson's poetry. This cultural context is further illuminated by the debates concerning alternative versions of the divine found in recent feminist theology. Like the redefinitions of the expectations surrounding hymns, these feminist debates centre around ideas of community and relation and so are employed in this book as a basis for the exploration of the emphasis on multiple and diverse relation in Dickinson's poetics.

The book is divided into three sections. The first section (Chapters 1, 2 and 3) is introduced with an outline of the scope of the book. This first section describes the history of hymn culture, analyses current debates about hymns and considers how hymnic space might be theorised. The second section (Chapters 4 and 5) examines the literary contexts and influences surrounding Dickinson's writing and engagement with hymn culture. This is exemplified by the work of Isaac Watts, Phoebe Hinsdale Brown and Eliza Lee Follen. The third section (Chapter 6, Parts 1 and 2, and Chapter 7) offers detailed analysis of a selection of Dickinson's hymnic poems, focusing on her use of bee imagery, the image which most closely aligns itself with hymn culture in Dickinson's poetics.

The conclusion the book reaches is that Dickinson's relation to hymnody is more wide-reaching, complex and subtle than criticism in this area has allowed. Far from being without a context, the radical re-visioning of the divine to be found in Dickinson's 'alternative hymns' can be situated within an engagement with a community of hymn writers. Moreover, the space which Dickinson's poems generate to accommodate this re-visioning can be seen in terms of a manipulation of hymnic space. In this, the book places readings of Dickinson's poems within important theological and historical contexts which have been previously overlooked. I hope what follows will go some way to stimulate new directions for interpretation and contribute to the ideological questions which currently surround Dickinson's poetics.

Acknowledgements

I would like to thank a number of people who have provided helpful comments, advice and discussion on various parts of this book at different stages; Jan Montefiore, Hester Jones, Jill Rudd, Dinah Birch, Philip Davis, Cora Kaplan, John Redmond and Ella Dzelzainis. Also Cristanne Miller, Ann Donahue, Juliet John and Paul Baines for their advice during the preparation of this book. I would like to thank the helpful staff at the British Library, the Sydney Jones Library, and St. Deiniol's Library, Hawarden. For friendship, support and encouragement throughout I would like to thank Roy Coleman. I would also like to thank Clare Williams, Leah Chidgey, Paul Jones, Will Rossiter, Laura Barlow and Catherine Jones. Also Joanne and Duncan for their support and for my nephew, Benjamin Morgan Priestley, who provided laughter and sunshine on days when Emily Dickinson came second. This book would not have been possible without the continued love, support and inspiration of my parents, Norma and Gregory Morgan.

All poems cited in this book are reprinted by permission of the publishers and the Trustees of Amherst College from *The Poems of Emily Dickinson: Reading Edition*, Ralph W. Franklin, ed., Cambridge, Mass.: The Belknap Press of Harvard University Press, Copyright © 1998, 1999 by the President and Fellows of Harvard College. Copyright © 1951, 1955, 1979, 1983 by the President and Fellows of Harvard College. Additional poems are reprinted by the permission of the publishers and the Trustees of Amherst College from *The Poems of Emily Dickinson*, Thomas H. Johnson, ed., Cambridge, Mass.: The Belknap Press of Harvard University Press, Copyright © 1951, 1955, 1979, 1983 by the President and Fellows of Harvard College.

The daguerreotype of Emily Dickinson used on the cover of this book appears by permission of the Trustees of Amherst College. I am grateful to Margaret Dakin at Amherst College Archives and Special Collections for her kind assistance in this matter.

List of Abbreviations

DCC E.A. Livingstone, *Concise Oxford Dictionary of the Christian Church*, 2nd edn (Oxford: Oxford University Press, 2000)

Fr *The Poems of Emily Dickinson: Reading Edition* (ed.), R.W. Franklin (Cambridge, MA: The Belknap Press of Harvard University Press, 2005)

HL Isaac Watts, *Horae Lyricae* (1706) as appears in *PW*

HSF Eliza Lee Follen, *Hymns, Songs and Fables for Young People*, 2nd edn (1831;Boston: W.M. Crosby and H.P. Nichols, 1851)

HSS Isaac Watts, *Hymns and Spiritual Songs* (1707) as appears in *PHSS*

L *The Letters of Emily Dickinson*, 3 vols, (ed.), T.H. Johnson (Cambridge, MA: The Belknap Press of Harvard University Press, 1958)

MWL Alfred Habegger, *My Wars Are Laid Away in Books: The Life of Emily Dickinson* (New York: Random House, 2001)

PHSS *The Psalms, Hymns and Spiritual Songs of the Rev. Isaac Watts, D.D. To which are added Select Hymns from other Authors; and Directions for Musical Expression* (Boston: Samuel T. Armstrong and Crocker and Brewster, 1832)

POD Isaac Watts, *The Psalms of David Imitated in the Language of the New Testament, and Applied to the Christian State and Worship* (1719) as appears in *PHSS*

PW *The Poetical Works of Isaac Watts, With a Memoir* (Boston: Little, Brown and Company, 1866)

RMB Benjamin Lease, *Emily Dickinson's Reading of Men and Books* (Houndmills: Macmillan, 1990)

SL *Emily Dickinson: Selected Letters*, (ed.), T.H. Johnson, eleventh printing (Cambridge, MA: The Belknap Press of Harvard University Press, 2002)

THJ   *The Complete Poems of Emily Dickinson* (ed.), T.H. Johnson,
            2nd edn (London: Faber and Faber, 1975)

VH   Asahel Nettleton, (ed.), *Village Hymns for Social Worship Selected
            and Original: Designed as a Supplement to Dr Watts's Psalms and
            Hymns* (Hartford: Printed by Goodwin and Co., 1824)

PART 1
Hymn Culture:
Tradition and Theory

Chapter 1
''Twas as Space Sat Singing to Herself – and Men –':
Situating Dickinson's Relation to Hymn Culture

> I have promised three Hymns to a charity, but without your approval could not give them - They are short and I could write them quite plainly, and if you felt it convenient to tell me if they were faithful, I should be very grateful [...].
>
> (November 1880, SL, p. 267)

In a letter to Thomas Wentworth Higginson in 1880, towards the end of her life, Emily Dickinson describes her poems as 'Hymns'. This emphatic choice of description employed alongside 'faithful' as a benchmark for quality in this letter is undoubtedly ironic.[1] Whilst calling into question the extent to which her gleefully unconventional poems deviate from traditional hymnody is humorous, there is also a genuine challenge being presented: How do these poems differ from traditional hymns and in what ways are they (un)faithful? Her use of the term connotes an irreverence for religious tradition and its expressive forms, but conveys equally, the serious import of her project. Her caveat 'They are short and I could write them quite plainly' confronts openly the expectations and parameters associated with traditionally sacred forms of writing, and the emphasis on 'plainness' in Puritan spirituality specifically. It also mirrors the cultural limitations imposed upon self-expression of the woman writer more generally in the mid-nineteenth-century. Dickinson's 'promise' of a voice which speaks from the margins, occupying only minimal space, is a flimsy veil indeed for what is a bombastic negative enquiry which assertively envisions her art as an alternative new form of hymnody, carrying with it a new kind of 'faith' altogether. The letter to Higginson quoted above witnesses the extent to which Dickinson conferred spirituality upon her writing, where the two are inextricably connected. Whilst calling her poems 'Hymns' operates upon the level of irony, it is undoubtedly also a sincere statement about her relationship with her art. In this letter, and in the poems she produced throughout her life, Dickinson is reclaiming the hymn. In conferring the status of hymns upon her work, and by making the connection between spirituality and

---

[1] Wendy Martin views Dickinson's reference to hymns in this letter as ironic because she perceives the poems Dickinson was offering to the charity as 'emphatically secular.' See *An American Triptych: Anne Bradstreet, Emily Dickinson, Adrienne Rich* (Chapel Hill: The University of North Carolina Press, 1984) p. 109.

writing explicit, Dickinson also aligns herself with other women hymn writers. Given her lack of concern with orthodox modes of publication, alluding to the inferior, 'acceptable' status of the female hymnist as opposed to poet was a risk that Dickinson was prepared to take.

As the following chapter will explore, most histories of hymnody will outline what is predominantly a communal practice which has served to redefine in different ways culturally agreed notions of the divine. It is also a practice which asserts a hierarchical model or mirror for human interrelation. Reassessing Emily Dickinson's engagement with the hymn genre and its associated imagery and assumptions, this book interrogates her critical engagement with religious orthodoxy by examining the symbolic value of the hymn as an ideologically loaded genre that always implies a representation of a speaker-God relation. The term 'religious orthodoxy' refers to the assumptions and practices surrounding Christian doctrine which are exclusionary and hierarchical and were familiar to nineteenth-century New England society, such as Calvinism's emphasis on Original Sin and an 'Elect' society. It also refers to the hierarchical depictions of the speaker-God relation to be found in religious culture more generally. This book argues that Dickinson's connection to hymnody is more complex than recent critical debate has allowed, and can be seen as producing not only subversion of patriarchal discourse on the divine, but also a re-envisioned and performative version of hymnic space in which an alternative mode of relation to the divine comes to the fore. In order to do this, the book provides detailed readings of carefully selected Dickinson poems alongside in-depth analysis of the form and imagery of eighteenth- and nineteenth-century hymns.

Many critics have compared Dickinson's verse form and imagery with those of the eighteenth-century hymn writer, Isaac Watts, arguing that any influence stems largely from Dickinson's dependence upon displaying an ironic distance from orthodox religion. Her connection to hymnody has always been analysed with regard to a male hymnist and in view of her being intrinsically antagonistic to the qualities connected with a particular kind of hymnody. As a result, the possibilities for a closer relationship between traditional hymnody and the articulation of spirituality in Dickinson's verse have been obfuscated. The fact that Dickinson was critical of American Evangelical Protestantism is in many ways a given. In contrast, this book aims to uncover the ways in which some of the conventions of traditional hymnody which are employed in Dickinson's poetry serve to convey an ideal space in which experience of spirituality is expressed and given a shape. These conventions will be explored in relation to the imagery and form to be found in Watts, but also those found in the work of contemporary women hymnists. In doing so it will challenge the tradition of reading Dickinson's poems as essentially atheistic and as gaining little more from hymns than an ironic distance from religious orthodoxy. It will also challenge the notion that Dickinson's work was produced out of a dedication to solitariness. Traditionally, the hymn is used to give voice to the imagined or real congregation alongside that of the hymn writer, while also conveying the expression of the writer's relation to God or the divine other.

A form of expression in which individuality *and* a sense of interrelation (such as a sense of community and social cohesion) are simultaneously articulated implies problematic obstacles that Dickinson's poetry engages with in different ways. If the speaker-God relation and notion of community expressed in traditional hymnody and religious discourse does not accurately reflect one's own experience of the divine, then other ways to express it must be negotiated. The notions of 'relation' and community are considered by feminist theologians as an alternative to an 'I-Thou' model of describing an individual's relation to the divine.[2] Dickinson's engagement with the hymn genre can therefore be seen through the dialectic between community and individuality that her poetics construct.

A word of caution: this book does not aim to reclassify Dickinson's poems as hymns, but rather, to explore the ways in which her relation to hymnody can be seen as profoundly informing the representation of spirituality in her work. It sees Dickinson's work as 'alternative hymns' in so far as they display a sophisticated manipulation of hymnic space which serves to incorporate the poet's own experience. In Dickinson's poems (more so than in work by many other poets) there is a sense of space in which the reader has scope to exercise her/his own imaginative processes. The sheer amount of wide-ranging criticism on Dickinson's work perhaps illustrates this point best; if one wishes to find a contradictory feeling or opinion expressed in Dickinson's work then examples are plentiful. It is not the intention in this book therefore, to present analysis of Dickinson's work overall, but rather to show how hymn culture influences particular aspects of her poetics. That is, the way in which some dominant modes of expression in her work, such as her use of the hymn form and of imagery of flight work to convey an alternative to the 'I-Thou'[3] model of address to be found in traditional hymnody and prayer. Dickinson's 'flood subject'[4] of immortality, together with the fluctuation between

---

[2]   As discussed in Chapter 3 and referred to throughout the book, the notion of 'relation' is used by theologian Elizabeth Johnson to connote the state of relation between the three elements of the Holy Trinity. This mode of relation or 'relatedness' which for Johnson is a model to describe a Christian way of life which does not reinscribe oppositional, patriarchal definitions of self and world and negotiates hierarchical structures, also has affinity with Daphne Hampson's notion of 'relationality' and Susan Welch's idea of 'community'.

[3]   The 'I-Thou' model of prayer is referred to throughout this book and is discussed further in Chapter 3, in relation to the hymn. The term is used by Daphne Hampson in *Theology and Feminism* (Oxford: Blackwell, 1990) (p. 169.) and draws upon Martin Buber's (1878–1965) *Ich Und Du* (1923; Eng. trans., *I and Thou*, 1937 and 1970). See E.A. Livingstone, *Concise Oxford Dictionary of the Christian Church*, second edition (Oxford: Oxford University Press, 2000) p. 84. Hereafter abbreviated to '*DCC*' followed by page number.

[4]   For example see Richard B. Sewall, *The Life of Emily Dickinson*, vol 2 (London: Faber and Faber, 1976) pp. 572, 690, 717. Dickinson describes the 'flood subject' of immortality in a letter to T.W. Higginson, see *Emily Dickinson: Selected Letters*, (ed.), T.H. Johnson, eleventh printing (Cambridge, MA: The Belknap Press of Harvard University Press, 2002) 9 June, 1866, p. 194. Collection hereafter 'SL', followed by page number.

religious faith and doubt often expressed in her poems, has been of special interest to critics. Indeed spirituality, and the various formalised and pre-established ways in which people express it, is a subject returned to again and again by Dickinson. In order to forge new critical inroads this book provides a historical, literary and theoretical basis through which to explore Dickinson's conspicuous interest in spirituality. It highlights connections between the space which Dickinson's poems allow and generate, and the space(s) which exists within the hymnic forms and imagery she chose to use. In this way the book will show how Dickinson's poems enact what they describe and will explore how they do that and to what radical effects.

The space which is made available in Dickinson's poems serves to accommodate, in a heterologous[5] way, both an individual subjectivity and also an 'open' space of relation with others by rendering the poem unbounded by the restraints and traps of linguistic and semantic definition. The notion of relation to others in Dickinson's work is both the imagined community, the state of being-in-relation, and also anticipated readers of her work. In this way, Dickinson, like mystical writers, offers versions of the divine to the reader in the ways which, somewhat ironically, mimic what might be said of God's offering of grace; with enough space between to create the freedom to choose. Dickinson's frequent rupturing of hymnic common metre and her use of imagery which recalls hymn culture serve only as markers for what is a much deeper engagement with the organising structures of orthodox religion. The 'speaker-God' relation in traditional hymnody is one such organising structure.

Although not formally aligned with a particular church or religious practices Dickinson's use of the hymn form and of biblical/Puritan imagery places her within a tradition of nineteenth-century women poets who negotiate space within traditional religious discourse in order to articulate their own version of spirituality. Cynthia Scheinberg and Linda Lewis have demonstrated the ways in which the work of Victorian poets such as Elizabeth Barrett Browning and Christina Rossetti utilise orthodox religion in their creative poetic processes to reformulate their own versions of spirituality.[6] Both of these women poets remained more aligned to particular religious affiliations than Dickinson (who famously refused conversion and formal connection with the Church). Their negotiation of religious discourse however has affinities with Dickinson's use of the hymn; working within orthodox religious discoursal space and radically reshaping and transforming it to

---

    5   The term 'heterologous,' from Michel de Certeau, *Heterologies: Discourse on the Other*, trans. by Brian Massumi (Minneapolis: University of Minnesota Press, 1986) is discussed in detail in Chapter 3.

    6   See Cynthia Scheinberg, *Women's Poetry and Religion in Victorian England: Jewish Identity and Christian Culture* (Cambridge: Cambridge University Press, 2002), hereafter shortened in parenthesis to 'Scheinberg', and Linda M. Lewis, *Elizabeth Barrett Browning's Spiritual Progress: Face to Face with God* (Columbia: University of Missouri Press, 1998).

accommodate their own (and by implication also others') experience of spirituality. Scheinberg argues that women poets such as Barrett Browning and Rossetti

> [...] should be read as creative agents of theological enquiry rather than merely passive recipients of a patriarchal tradition. Poetry was one of the most important generic sites in Victorian culture to accommodate this radical and public theological work of women - radical not in the sense that this theological poetry always positioned itself against traditional notions of gender or religion – but radical at the moment poetry provided a sanctioned public forum through which women could voice their theological ideas and participate in debates about religious, political and gendered identity. (Scheinberg, p. 4)

With this in mind, Dickinson's engagement with hymn culture can be seen as a deliberate attempt to emphasise the consideration of religious, political and gendered identity at work in her poetry more than as an attempt to disguise it within an acceptable mode of expression for a woman. Dickinson's use of the hymn form and of poetics of relation which invoke community can be seen as the representation and enactment of the 'alternative modes of literary values' (Scheinberg, p. 236.) in women's poetry. Scheinberg identifies these 'alternatives' as providing a resistance to the increasingly androcentric and theological 'generic patterns' in Victorian poetic theory:

> The alternatives to these generic patterns might position communal identity as more valuable than individual redemption, might posit multiplicity of perspectives and a community of voices [...] over unitary or monologic identity, might emphasise narratives of persistence rather than conversion or transformation, and might replace narratives of redemptive closure with narratives of perpetual hope. This list [...] is not meant to be conclusive, but rather only suggestive of a method that could challenge the often naturalised, universalised, and essentialised categories of 'great literature' through which certain theological assumptions are recast as 'aesthetic' values. (Scheinberg, p. 236)

Scheinberg's reading of Victorian poetic theory (as espoused by critics and poets such as Matthew Arnold) as androcentric and Christian, and her list of the alternative modes which she finds highlighted in women's poetry of the Victorian period is instructive. Such poetic 'alternatives' of multiple identities and deferred closure are immediately recognisable in Dickinson's 'modern' poetry.[7] However, Dickinson's use of the hymn form and the repeated attraction towards multiplicity *and* relation in her poetics suggests a challenge to the individualistic or 'monologic'

---

[7]   David Porter's *Dickinson: The Modern Idiom* (Cambridge, MA: Harvard University Press, 1981) describes Dickinson's spiritual doubt as pre-emptive of modernist decentredness, and in 'Searching For Dickinson's Themes' in *The Emily Dickinson Handbook* (ed.) by Gudrun Grabher and others (Boston: The University of Massachusetts Press, 1998) he connects her 'indefinite' self with Post-modernist literary theory, pp. 183–96. Grabher and others hereafter referred to as '*The Emily Dickinson Handbook*'.

identities which Scheinberg identifies in an increasingly theological Victorian poetics. It also suggests a radical reconfiguration of those theological and poetical structures.

In analysing Dickinson's relation to the hymn by establishing key aspects of contemporary hymn culture, and focusing on her use of bee imagery to exemplify her engagement with this culture in the final section, this book will demonstrate how her poems challenge the rigid parameters (and 'narratives of closure', Scheinberg, p. 236.) set by the Puritan Protestant work ethic and the assumptions about worthy production implicit in hymnody. It will illustrate how they display instead a mystical spirituality which opens up a space for ideas of community, revery and sexuality which challenge the exclusionary aspects of orthodox religion. It will also show how this spirituality and production of space has affinities with projections for the divine to be found in feminist theology as well as in philosophical discourses on the 'other.'[8] Such mystical spirituality can be seen through Dickinson's engagement with the modes of orthodox religion, namely through the interchange between God and speaker which the act of worship in hymns invokes. The nature of Dickinson's relation to orthodox Christian faith is a large subject to approach,[9] and any discussion of it involves at least a brief examination of religious culture in mid-nineteenth-century New England. Whilst the legacy of Puritanism showed itself during this period in conservative Evangelical Protestantism in the main, the creative change effected by the rejection of its values is visible in the minority movements that emerged. This study does not aim to pigeonhole Dickinson, or to consider whether she was ultimately a Puritan or aligned with a minority movement. Rather, it aims to examine the extent to which her use of such a religious culture, primarily through hymnody, provided her with an avenue to express a relation to the divine which, as in the mystical tradition, exists by evading such categories.[10]

Critical assessments of Dickinson's work which speculate about the poet's personal experience of religious faith and are predicated upon 'facts' or assumptions about her character (for example as an eccentric 'recluse') are unhelpful. They serve only to obfuscate her literary technique and to reinstate the binaries associated with religious discourse which her poetry necessarily suspends; such as

---

[8]   Feminist theologians Daphne Hampson and Mary Daly, as well as the theories of Luce Irigaray and Michel de Certeau will be discussed in relation to this, in Chapter 3.

[9]   The recent reprint of Roger Lundin's 1998 biography, *Emily Dickinson and the Art of Belief* (Michigan: William B. Eerdmans Publishing Company, 2004) and James McIntosh's *Nimble Believing: Dickinson and the Unknown* (Ann Arbour: University of Michigan Press, 2004) are evidence of the continuing interest in the subject of Dickinson's relation to orthodox religion and the nature of her spirituality.

[10]   For a recent discussion of Dickinson's relation to orthodox religion and the medieval mystical tradition, see Angela B. Conrad, *The Wayward Nun of Amherst: Emily Dickinson in the Medieval Women's Visionary Tradition* (New York: Garland Science, 2002) Conrad repositions the 'recluse' model of Dickinson within mystical tradition, associating this, and her preference for wearing white garments, with the lives of medieval mystics.

the distinctions between conformity and dissent, atheism and belief or chaos and design. Ambiguity and contradiction are always present in Dickinson's depiction of her relation to religious faith. Jane Donahue Eberwein argues:

> One can make whatever case one wants about Dickinson's beliefs or disbelief by selecting individual poems, letters, or even lines, but the way to reach insight is to look for long-term patterns in her religious references. Despite variations in tone and imagery, religion remained a centering concern for Dickinson from her first valentine with its comic references to Eden to her last letter [...].[11]

Eberwein's recommendation to look for 'long-term patterns' in Dickinson's corpus in order to gain insight is instructive. Her use of the hymn form, the use of bee imagery and the commitment to presenting a different relationality to the 'I-Thou' relation in traditional hymn address, which takes the form of a liberating space in her poetics, can be seen as 'long-term patterns' in Dickinson's work. David Porter's estimation of Dickinson's use of the hymn form epitomises the precedent which was set for criticism on this subject:

> [...] inherent in the hymn form is an attitude of faith, humility, and inspiration, and it is against this base of orthodoxy that she so artfully refracts the personal rebellion and individual feeling, the colloquial diction and syntax, the homely image, the scandalous love of this world, and the habitual religious scepticism.[12]

Whilst there is no doubt that Dickinson's rebellious use of hymns and paraphrases of Watts challenge religious orthodoxy, they also challenge the speaker-God relation that hymns present and represent. Although hymns can be seen as the expression of religious orthodoxy, and as reinscribing hierarchy, in Dickinson's poems the speaker-God relation becomes fluid, and hymnic space is reshaped to destabilise oppositional thinking. In this way, Dickinson's relation to the hymn genre precipitates the dialogical interplay in her poetry between orthodox religion and anti-linear, anti-hierarchical, mystical spirituality.

St. Armand argues that 'much of Dickinson's poetry was a continuing dialectic that used the imagery, premises and metrics of Puritan hymnology as a basis for a personal psalmody of questioning and protest.'[13] His term 'personal psalmody' locates Dickinson's creative process within a direct response to the Book of Psalms, and suggests a method and structure to her work which other critics

---

[11] Jane Donahue Eberwein, "Is Immortality True?': Salvaging Faith in an Age of Upheavals' in *A Historical Guide to Emily Dickinson* (ed.) Vivian R. Pollak (Oxford: Oxford University Press, 2004) pp. 67–102 (p. 70).

[12] David T. Porter, *The Art of Emily Dickinson's Early Poetry* (Cambridge, MA: Harvard University Press, 1966) p. 74.

[13] Barton Levi St. Armand, *Emily Dickinson and Her Culture: The Soul's Society*, 3rd edn (Cambridge: Cambridge University Press, 1989) p. 158. Hereafter referred to as St. Armand.

have been inclined to avoid. David Porter, for example, comments; 'For theme-seeking readers especially, Dickinson is not forbiddingly but, rather, *triumphantly* unmanageable.'[14] The meaning or main subject in Dickinson's poems can be especially difficult to pin down because of their combination of tight structure, complex syntax and seeming elusiveness. The complex and often apparently contradictory nature of her work makes any discussion of it challenging. We are given many paths to follow when exploring Dickinson's attitude to faith, and St Armand's term is useful for an inquiry into aspects of it which confront the ideas and images in hymns which she would have been privy to. It is in her attitude to the imagery and ideas implicit in hymnody, more than anywhere else, where we can see most clearly such 'questioning' and the approach of protest through the exploration of alternative possibilities which pervades so much of her work.

In highlighting the musicality in Dickinson's poems Valentine Cunningham asserts that she was an 'alternative hymn writer,' who wrote, like Christina Rossetti, 'in the mode most available to nineteenth century women poets.'[15] Indeed, the writing of congregational hymns initially became an acceptable form of expression for women, because it involved declarations of praise rather than espousing a complex theology and liturgical and poetic symbolism. However, Dickinson's use of hymnody does not appear to be born of necessity, given that she was not obviously aiming to publish her work and that she did not seem particularly interested in gaining critical acclaim or support from those around her. We know that in 1862, aged 31, she wrote to Thomas Wentworth Higginson, asking him whether he thought her verse 'breathed,' (SL, p. 171) but her interest in carving out a place for herself within the literary world seems to be very limited, and only several of her two thousand or so poems were published in her lifetime. Another point to remember is that Dickinson received a good level of education, and was perfectly capable of expressing complex theology and liturgical and poetic symbolism without utilising the hymn form or adducing a form of communal expression. Therefore, Dickinson's use of the hymn form was not born from a desire to offer acceptable, marketable verse, but rather, a decision to adopt the mode of traditional expression of spirituality in order to highlight its dissonance/resonance with her own experience. Moreover, a dialogic engagement with the imagery and ideas laid out in hymns can be seen as providing her with an ideal space in which to articulate her own sense of spirituality. This could be done whilst simultaneously offering comment upon the traditions and restraints of orthodox religious culture, such as Calvinism's hierarchical model of Election in which women were seen as being further away from God than men, and capable of only a vicarious experience of God.

---

[14]   David Porter, 'Searching for Dickinson's Themes' in *The Emily Dickinson Handbook*, pp. 183–96 (p. 196).

[15]   Valentine Cunningham, 'The Sound of Startled Grass', *The Guardian*, 19 October 2002. (For full reference, see bibliography).

The modes and methods employed by Dickinson to express her experience of spirituality and relation to orthodox religion will be analysed in light of her response to the symbolic nature of the hymn. The book will trace two dominant modes in Dickinson's poetry concerning religion. Firstly, the ways in which the poems challenge the portrayal of a direct and linear movement towards, and communication between, God and speaker in religious orthodoxy as exemplified in the hymns of Isaac Watts. Secondly, the ways in which Dickinson's poems emphasise, instead, the God-in-process and God-in-practice view of spirituality as asserted by twentieth-century feminist theologians.[16] The duality and contradictions which are inherent in Dickinson's relation to the divine have led inevitably to the application of different theoretical approaches in this book. The frequent paradoxes found in the work of Watts and other hymnists also belie the ultimate paradoxes within Puritan and traditionally dominant conceptions of the divine as well as within more radical ones. Theoretical approaches to Dickinson are necessarily dialectical, the intersections between different approaches being more sympathetic to the expansiveness of Dickinson's work, as Roland Hagenbuchle has argued.[17] Whilst there are points of contact with Post-Structuralist theories, some of which are used in this study in reference to feminism and mysticism, the aim of this book is to suggest that the method of Dickinson's poetic production can be seen within the context of the hymn genre and communal subjectivity as supporting the active way-of-being in the divine, which Dickinson's poems reconstruct and endlessly enact. The alternative metaphors for the divine in feminist theology, and Certeau's notion of 'heterologies' are both useful for describing this active mode of being-in-the divine.

In order to trace Dickinson's engagement with and experience of hymn culture, the early influence of the hymns of eighteenth-century hymnographer Isaac Watts will first be examined in Section Two. The motifs of eyes and wings which signal in Watts's hymns the experience of sight and flight, that is, of knowledge of the divine and of spiritual transcendence, will be analysed in relation to Dickinson's use of them. This will be followed by a comparative analysis of Evangelical and Unitarian women hymn writers who were contemporary with Dickinson through her mother's generation of Praying Circles. This chapter assesses the shape of female spiritual community and the ways in which common hymnic motifs are used in their hymns to connote spiritual transport. Section Three serves as the exemplificative section of the book and provides analysis of Dickinson's use of bee imagery. The bee imagery is examined as a 'long-term pattern' which most

---

[16]   Both terms 'God-in-process' and 'God-in-practice' used in this book allude to Mary Daly's notion of 'God the Verb.' See Mary Daly, *Beyond God the Father: Toward a Philosophy of Women's Liberation* (1973, London: The Women's Press, 1995) p. xvii. Daly describes the trajectory of her book's 'task:' 'of changing the conception/perception of god from 'the supreme being' to Be-ing. The naming of Be-ing as Verb'.

[17]   Roland Hagenbuchle, 'Dickinson and Literary Theory' in *The Emily Dickinson Handbook*, pp. 356–84 (p. 381).

closely signals her engagement with hymn culture, bees being both singers and poets, both workers and revellers, both solitary and communal at different stages in her poetics. Bee imagery is examined as an alternative liturgical symbolism and further explored as part of a theoretical examination of 'community'. Debates about articulating the spiritual in both feminist literary theory and feminist theology are used in order to forge a connection between Dickinson's use of hymn culture and the powerful transformation of 'liturgical' emblems in her work, and what can be seen as a systematic critical engagement with orthodox religion which is hierarchically constructed. In doing so, the arguments in this book serve to provide new debate within Dickinson studies which brings together feminist theology and theories about space in discourse to uncover new ways in which to approach the shape and shaping of Dickinson's spirituality in poetry.

Dickinson and Belief

We know from Dickinson's letters that she saw herself as being at odds with Evangelical Protestant Christianity. The extent of her 'atheism' has provided a constant source of discussion within Dickinson criticism. Much of Dickinson's poetry does seem to express a reaction against orthodox Christian modes of thinking and practices, and yet the extent and meaning of this reaction is difficult to assess because it also bears affinities with nonProtestant groups prevalent in the mid nineteenth century such as Catholicism and also with the most liberal of the Dissenting Protestant sects, Unitarianism.[18]

However, it was early on in her life that Dickinson dispensed with the comfort of religious orthodoxy and the apparent certainties it brought many of her contemporaries. In a letter to her friend Abiah Root, the sixteen year old Dickinson recalls an earlier time when she had momentarily felt the 'perfect happiness' of religious conviction:

> I think of the perfect happiness I experienced while I felt I was an heir of heaven as of a delightful dream, out of which the Evil one bid me wake & again return to the world & its pleasures. [...] The few short moments in which I loved my Saviour I would not now exchange for a thousand worlds like this. It was then my greatest pleasure to commune alone with the great God & to feel that he would listen to my prayers. [...] But the world allured me & in an unguarded moment I listened to her syren voice. From that moment I seemed to lose my interest in heavenly things by degrees. (28 March 1846, L: I, pp. 30–31)[19]

---

[18]   For discussion of religious plurality in nineteenth-century America, see Catherine A. Brekus, 'Interpreting American Religion' in *A Companion to Nineteenth-Century America*, (ed.), William L. Barney (Oxford: Blackwell, 2001) pp. 317–33.

[19]   *The Letters of Emily Dickinson*, 3 vols, (ed.), T.H. Johnson (Cambridge, MA: The Belknap Press of Harvard University Press, 1958) vol 1, pp. 30–31. Hereafter 'L' followed by volume number and page.

In this letter she describes the 'syren voice' of worldly life which tempted her away from religion. However, for the rest of her life, and from the huge corpus of poetry that she left behind, we can discern an unflinching dedication to the 'syren voice' or poetic muse. As I shall argue this poetic 'syren voice' cannot be divorced from her own spiritual conviction, or the ongoing evaluation of 'heavenly things' which most of her poems convey. For Dickinson, experience of the world and spiritual experience were necessarily concomitant, and her letters and poetry chart equally, a spirituality which developed to collapse the distinction between 'heavenly things' and the 'syren voice' of worldly experience which inspired her writing. The 'heavenly things' in the letter above is conspicuously dismissive, characterising a rehearsal of Calvinist Election rhetoric ('heir of heaven') and Evangelical fervour ('Evil one' and 'great God') as an immature aberration, as opposed to a lamentable lost state of grace.

Connecting the shaping of Dickinson's spirituality with hymn culture serves both to re-contextualise her position within nineteenth-century American society and also within recent criticism which sees her work as having no 'frame of reference'[20] or specific social context. In uncovering the ways in which Dickinson interrogates the hierarchical structures implied by organised religion, we can also highlight her critique of a society that is founded on those structures. Although space and time do not allow for a definitive account of each religious group, effort has been made throughout to distinguish between the various modes of Christianity in mid-nineteenth-century New England. The literary form of the hymn provides a focus through which to see Dickinson's relation to such a culture and her defiance against, as she writes, being 'shut up in prose' (Fr 445)[21] and restricted from speaking against the Church's desire to regulate experience of spirituality. If we view Dickinson's engagement with Isaac Watts and the popular hymn form as a model for dissent and for an articulation of protest, then her apparently heretical stance can be redefined as a desire to be connected to the world in a more solid way. Such a connection with the world also implied for Dickinson a closer experience of heaven.

In a letter written to a friend in 1850 Dickinson denounced the revival and religious fervour engulfing her home town of Amherst. She says:

---

[20] Lynn Shakinovsky, *No Frame of Reference: The Absence of Context in Emily Dickinson's Poetry*, in *Emily Dickinson: Critical Assessments*, vol 4, (ed.), Graham Clarke (Mountfield: Helm Information Ltd, 2002) pp. 703–16 (p. 714).

[21] *The Poems of Emily Dickinson: Reading Edition* (ed.), R.W. Franklin (Cambridge MA: Harvard University Press, 2005) poem number 445. Franklin's reading edition of Dickinson's poems will be referred to throughout. Poems will hereafter appear with the abbreviation 'Fr' followed by the poem number in this edition. As they do not have titles, poems are sometimes referred to by their initial lines, as well as the poem number. Reasons for using this edition are that Franklin uses the final fair copy of Dickinson's manuscript and also retains all original spelling and punctuation.

> Christ is calling everyone here, all my companions have answered, even my darling Vinnie believes she loves and trusts him, and I am standing alone in my rebellion, and growing very careless. (3 April 1850, to Jane Humphrey, L: I, p. 94)[22]

Her 'rebellion' I want to argue is not against the God she redefines and articulates in her poems but, rather, against the need to organise spirituality and society in a hierarchical way. The fact that organised religion played such a big part in Dickinson's community means that any critique of it, including her own, implied also a critique of that particular society, and its effects upon the individual as well. Paradoxically, it is through her interaction with the popular but restrictive nature of hymnody that Dickinson's sense of spirituality, or, in her own words, her 'carelessness' can be most recognised and registered.

In a letter to Mrs Joseph Haven in 1859, when discussing a recent sermon given by Mr Seelye, she clearly states her mistrust of 'doctrines:'

> Mr S preached in our church last Sabbath upon "Predestination," but I do not respect "doctrines," and did not listen to him, so I can neither praise, nor blame. (13 February 1859, L: II, p. 346)

Whilst stating that she could 'neither praise, nor blame' the preacher and his doctrinal assertions, Dickinson's stance against orthodox religion was rather more critical and pro-active than this comment suggests. The excerpt below, from a letter written in 1856 to Dr and Mrs J.G. Holland, is particularly interesting because it is typical of the critical nature of her response to religious ideals, and echoes those set out in her poetry:

> Don't tell, dear Mrs. Holland, but wicked as I am, I read my Bible sometimes, [...] and I wished [...] that wonderful world had commenced, which makes such promises [...] If God had been here this summer, and seen the things that I have seen – I guess that He would think His Paradise superfluous. Don't tell Him, for the world, though, for after all He's said about it, I should like to see what He was building for us, with no hammer, and no stone, and no journeyman either. (L: II, pp. 140–41)

Her derisive distrust of the 'wonderful world' of Heaven anticipated and portrayed in the Bible verses she read is equally as vivid as her vision of the paradisal on earth. Her ability to perceive Godliness in nature, and, simultaneously, to be highly critical of traditional ideas about salvation and 'Heaven' is a perspective which she senses would be deemed as a form of heresy, or as an unwelcome challenge to her local community's religious culture if spoken aloud. 'Don't tell Him' is mocking and gossipy in tone, yet seems to characterise Dickinson's interest in revering that

---

[22]   Leder and Abbott discuss this letter briefly in *The Language of Exclusion: The Poetry of Emily Dickinson and Christina Rossetti* (New York: Greenwood Press, 1987) in order to highlight her increasingly independent stance (pp. 46–7).

which is not said, and her distrust of the process which translates the unsaid into dogma. Whilst appearing to reject the biblical utopian vision of a world beyond death and mortality which has been built by and upon 'His' words alone, she then presents her own version of paradise which, she implies, is less 'superfluous' to the one she reads about in the Bible. Therefore, it is the unsaid, the space in Dickinson's poems which is emphasised by contradictory states, in which such 'Paradise' can be articulated.

Reading Dickinson's Hymnic Space

> Most she touched me by her muteness -
> Most she won me by the way
> She presented her small figure -
> Plea itself - for Charity -
>
> Were a Crumb my whole possession -
> Were there famine in the land -
> Were it my resource from starving -
> Could I such a plea withstand -
>
> Not opon [*sic*] her knee to thank me
> Sank this Beggar from the Sky -
> But the Crumb partook - departed -
> And returned on High -
>
> I supposed - when sudden
> Such a Praise began
> 'Twas as Space sat singing
> To herself - and men -
>
> 'Twas the Winged Beggar -
> Afterward I learned
> To her Benefactor
> Making Gratitude. (Fr 483)

Dickinson describes in the final two stanzas of this poem the moment at which a bird's song is heard by the speaker/listener, and is then interpreted as a song of gratitude from the bird, for its being fed. The moment between hearing the birdsong and recognition of where it emanates from is the poem's climactic moment, temporarily delayed and stretched out ('I supposed' - 'Afterward I learned') as a dramatic ploy in which the reader is invited to consider the strangeness of listening to singing which erupts, apparently out of nowhere, out of 'Space.' For the moment, Dickinson compels us to contemplate an absence, to imagine a void which sings both 'to herself - and men - ;' a space which is both self-gratifying *and* which also extends such singing, such self-generative 'praise' outwards towards others/ 'men.' The poem is striking because its central proposition (to imagine such a 'Space') anticipates, not without irony, the perplexing space that Dickinson the poet has occupied within literary criticism ever since her poems became publicly available. Which spaces do Dickinson's poems inhabit? The many theoretical and cultural spaces, ranging from the various academic and critical perspectives her work has been read through, to the interpretations of her work in popular culture, such as music, film and theatre.[23] The challenge of positioning Dickinson within a particular literary tradition and/or framing her work within specific critical discourses persists because Dickinson's writing privileges this kind of 'space' which accommodates a decentred simultaneity and thus resists cognitive and imaginative boundaries.

However, in this poem, 'Space' is decidedly feminine. Dickinson's gendering of space ('herself') in this poem is striking as the information appears where it is not needed, space usually being perceived in terms of neutrality. Although Dickinson often disrupts expectations of gender assignment, in this case she provides it where it seems unnecessary. The brief moment when the poet contemplates such space, in between connecting the sound to the bird, is amplified to epiphanic proportions, and the fact that space is mirrored as female serves to connect contemplation of space with contemplation of the speaker-self. Re-cognition of the self and consciousness appears to have replaced God, and yet the poem itself replicates the surface features and concerns of traditional hymnody, such as the line of relation between a 'supplicant' speaker and a transcendent being. However, the deeper function of the hymn, to reinscribe or mirror the divine, is radically repositioned here as feminine.[24]

By expanding and dramatising this brief exchange between the speaker and the bird (which is not named but described only in relation to 'her' gender and lowly position as 'beggar') Dickinson invokes a connection or interchangeability between the poem's speaker and the bird/singer, and calls to attention culturally prescribed notions of the female poet. The speaker's view of the bird parodies the expectation of Christian humility and coy reticence often associated with socially prescribed femininity in patriarchal nineteenth-century culture. At the beginning of the poem, the bird is described as winning the speaker's attention and affection, initially, 'by her muteness' and the way in which she presents herself in supplication:

> Most she touched me by her muteness -
> Most she won me by the way
> She presented her small figure -
> Plea itself - for Charity - (Fr 483)

---

[23] For a survey of the critical reception of Dickinson, see Marietta Mesmer, 'Dickinson's Critical Reception', and for adaptations in the arts, see Jonnie Guerra, 'Dickinson Adaptations in the Arts and Theatre', both in *The Emily Dickinson Handbook*, pp. 299–322 and pp. 385–407.

[24] Definitions of hymns and particular qualities of a hymn, such as narrative including a climactic moment such as the one in this poem, and as representing an 'agreed' notion of the divine are explored in Chapter 2, p. 51 and Chapter 3, pp. 60–65.

Dickinson places herself as the masculine eye, the 'Benefactor'/God who judges such behaviour as worthy of essential 'Crumb' or not. And yet, simultaneously, the bird is heaven-bound whilst the speaker is decidedly earthly; the bird has to 'sink' in order to reach the speaker's lower position, take the food ('the Crumb partook' conveying the bird's eucharistic participation) and 'return[ed]on High.' As with most poems by Dickinson, hierarchical positions are interchangeable and ultimately destabilised. The hierarchy between speaker and God to be found in traditional hymnody is inverted in this poem; the speaker is positioned as 'Benefactor,' and the bird singing praise is decidedly anthropomorphic ('her small figure' and 'this Beggar'). Not only is the hierarchical distinction between God-human to be found in traditional hymnody destabilised in this poem, but the dramatised delay between hearing the birdsong and recognition performs as a visibly dramatic construction which only thinly veils (and thus invites) the conclusion that the speaker and 'singer' can be perceived as being one and the same.

The poem of course works on a simpler level, where the irrational expectation of gratitude from a bird is eclipsed by a greater and more perceptive gratitude on the part of the bird to God as the ultimate source of crumbs and nourishment. However, it also conveys that although the speaker's initial desire is for a display of the bird's 'gratitude,' the power of melody is arresting in itself, and enough to propel the speaker (and the reader) into contemplation of singing that isn't merely 'gratitude.' One of the associations with hymnody, of 'making gratitude' towards a Creator, together with notions of the woman poet are compared strikingly with an imagined but also momentarily potential alternative within the hymn-poem; the vastness of 'Space' which does not come with limitation, where singing is unrestricted and is also arresting enough to be heard by 'men.' When the birdsong is finally located, the speaker's 'explanation' of the bird's singing in the poem's final stanza describes the pattern of praise to be found in traditional hymnody, as the bird sings; 'To her Benefactor/Making gratitude.' The final stanza is however surplus to requirement; the 'gratitude' is expected in the poem's third stanza, where disappointingly, 'Not opon [*sic*] her knee to thank me/Sank this beggar from the Sky -' and provided in the fourth '-when sudden such Praise began-'. The explanation of the bird's singing, which comes in the final, fifth stanza, moves us towards the conclusion we would expect to reach if we were reading a traditional hymn; gratitude to a 'Benefactor'/God is the aim of 'Praise'/singing, not self-gratification or the gratification of 'men.' However, Dickinson relegates the function of 'praise,' the act of 'making gratitude' described within the scene/poem to a secondary position. The delayed conclusion the speaker in this poem reaches is secondary to the primary focus for consideration, which is the instance of 'space singing to herself - and men -'. What matters is not whether the bird is singing 'for' the speaker or not, but rather, the moment at which the speaker experiences the liberation of the 'sudden' birdsong. As a result of the birdsong, the speaker is allowed to contemplate an ideal, anarchic space in which the seemingly impossible can exist. Such space is anarchic because it allows for explosive articulation which is both self-generated and ungoverned by social conventions.

A new experience of 'praise' emerges out of the experience which the space (and therefore also interchangeability and interconnection) between 'Benefactor' and 'Beggar' has allowed. By destabilising the traditionally imposed divisions between God and speaker as modelled in conventional hymns, this poem highlights the way in which Dickinson's poems negotiate an ideal space in which the both/and position is achieved, where the poet sings both 'to herself - and men -', a space in which the divine is reimagined as relational, antihierarchical, and always open.

The suspension of the question of the bird's 'gratitude' in this poem is also a deliberate suspension of the divisions which are made between a hymn and a poem, suspending also in turn for the reader, the question of Dickinson's religious faith or doubt. If the bird's singing is a praise, or song of gratitude toward a 'benefactor,' then it is a hymn of sorts. Indeed, Rivkah Zim has argued that many of the images in Psalms come from nature, which 'contributes to their relevance and appeal beyond particular time or place.'[25] In the following Psalm, which is dedicated to a musician specifically, we can see the connection between nature as a natural enactment of devotion, and a human's devotion to God:

> My soul longeth, yea, even fainteth for the courts of the Lord: my heart and my flesh crieth out for the living God.
>
> Yea, the sparrow hath found an house, and the swallow a nest for herself, where she may lay a nest for her young, even thine altars, O Lord of hosts, my King, and my God.
>
> Blessed are they that dwell in thy house: they will be still praising thee. (Psalm 84:2–4, 'To the chief Musician upon Gittith, A Psalm for the Sons of Korah')[26]

The emphasis on music in this psalm, and the equation between the birds singing, whose nests are 'even thine altars,' and the practice of religious worship 'still praising thee' can also be seen in Dickinson's poem. Just as the speaker's observation of the 'praise' from 'space' in the poem confers its hymnic quality, so too can Dickinson's poem be seen as a form of (automatic, inadvert) praise. Dickinson's poems do not make any attempt to bridge the gap between poem and hymn, faith and doubt, but the status conferred upon a hymn as being a depiction of a speaker's relation to the divine is always presented for consideration. Wendy Martin (1984) argues that 'her poems and letters are not hymns to a transcendent God but a celebration of 'the moment immortal.'[27] However, Dickinson utilises the premises, structure and imagery of traditional hymnody in order to allow

---

[25]   Rivkah Zim, *English Metrical Psalms: Poetry as Praise and Prayer 1535–1601* (Cambridge: Cambridge University Press, 1987) p. 35. Aspects of psalmody are discussed further in the following chapter, pp. 38–40.

[26]   *King James Version of the Bible*, Psalm 84.2–4, p. 680.

[27]   Wendy Martin, *An American Triptych: Anne Bradstreet, Emily Dickinson, Adrienne Rich*, p. 164.

creative space to reaffirm itself, and to suggest that the 'celebration of the moment immortal' in *relation* is perhaps the best version of gratitude a poet can provide. By utilising and reading hymnic space in this way, Dickinson's poems connect ideas about the divine with the act of writing. Her writing privileges and elicits notions of relationality and process. As will be discussed in Chapter Three, these notions bear affinities with both mystical discourse and debates around a female version of/relation to the divine in feminist theology and feminist literary theory.

Beyond Doubleness

Women's poetry of the nineteenth century can be understood as both utilising and subverting the dominant modes of expression and assumptions of a religious culture which is essentially oppressive towards women. This process is described by Isobel Armstrong as follows:

> The doubleness of women's poetry comes from its ostensible adoption of an affective mode, often simple, often pious, often conventional. But those conventions are subjected to investigation, questioned, or used for unexpected purposes. The simpler the surface of the poem, the more likely it is that a second and more difficult poem will exist beneath it.[28]

Although the hymnic mode of Dickinson's poems does offer a simple 'cover' for complexity, equally it utilises and exploits the communicative aspect of hymns and religious worship and therefore presents a three dimensional version of the 'double' poem. Complexity which is derived from a dialogical relation to devotional hymns and poetic expression necessarily also takes upon itself a concern which goes beyond the expression of resistance and subversion. It becomes in and of itself a new and transformative mode of expression. We can see this process at work in Dickinson's poetry as it struggles to shape alternative values and beliefs to those, particularly with regard to religion, which she found did not resonate with her own experience and views. With this in mind, we can see the ways in which both a feminist theoretical framework and cultural context can inform readings of the work of women poets such as Dickinson and the ways in which their representations of spirituality have been shaped. Despite being both white and middle class (and so operating within the defining hierarchy) I will argue that Dickinson actively struggles to shape her relation to the dominant patriarchal and capitalistic implications of orthodox spirituality in her own society.

Although Dickinson was not aligned to any particular group, her engagement with the work of Watts also includes the modes of expression that were the result of his position as a Dissenter. As Chapter Four will explore, Watts was part of a visible group who engaged dialogically with the rituals of Anglicanism and Catholicism

---

[28]   Isobel Armstrong, *Victorian Poetry: Poetry, Poetics, and Politics* (London: Routledge, 1993) p. 324.

that the Puritans regarded as obscuring a person's direct relation to God. With this in mind, Dickinson's engagement with Watts can be seen in two ways. Firstly, Watts can be seen as representing the tradition of established orthodox religion and an 'obscurer' of her own spiritual experience. Although himself a Puritan and Dissenter, the popularity of Watts's hymns made him the 'father of the modern hymn'[29] whose work was championed during the Evangelical religious revivals in New England. In this way he is also a cultural touchstone, representing the repressive tradition of religion Dickinson derides (commenting upon her family's religion, she notes the 'eclipse they call their 'Father', SL, p. 173) and associates with the Evangelical fervour of her childhood. Fearing her brother's waywardness, Dickinson mocks; 'I will send you *Village Hymns* at earliest opportunity' (SL, p. 101), a volume in wide circulation during their childhood and which included the hymns of Isaac Watts.[30] Secondly, however, Watts's position as Dissenter and innovator of poetic and religious expression meant that he offered an example of someone who attempted to bridge the gap between religious and lyrical expression and produced such expression as a form of protest against a stifling dominant ideology and regime.[31] Such an examination of Watts in relation to Dickinson provides an important counterpoint to the minimal criticism that exists in this area, most of which has read Dickinson's memory and use of Watts as being ultimately and foremost as a critical subversion of religious faith.[32] Focusing on Dickinson's use of Watts's hymn form (always remembering that Watts is regarded as the 'Father of Hymnody') is a way of uncovering Dickinson's critique of society and methods of formulating her own ideas about spirituality and her relationship to orthodox religion in general. This in turn reveals how she uses one of the primary tools of that orthodoxy and effectively turns it back on itself, in order to criticise the hierarchical structures of an inherently conservative social order and to offer an impassioned and important overhaul of orthodox modes of thinking about spirituality.

In revivalist nineteenth-century New England, spiritual conversion provided a fundamental method of organising society, of keeping people in their allotted places, and of being 'saved' from the dangers of competing and 'ill' influences. Much emphasis was placed upon conversion in Dickinson's community; Edward Hitchcock, a well-known writer much respected in Amherst, describes the act of

---

[29]   David G. Fountain, *Isaac Watts Remembered* (Harpenden: Gospel Standard Baptist Trust Ltd, 1974) p. 102.

[30]   As will be discussed in Chapter 5, this popular hymnal also included the hymns of Phoebe Hinsdale Brown.

[31]   Chapter 4 provides discussion on Watts as poetic innovator and Dissenter.

[32]   As discussed in Chapter 4, critics such as Wendy Martin and Shira Wolosky tend towards such a view of Dickinson's use of Watts. See Wendy Martin, *An American Triptych: Anne Bradstreet, Emily Dickinson, Adrienne Rich*, pp. 138–9. and Shira Wolosky, 'Rhetoric or Not: Hymnal Tropes in Emily Dickinson and Isaac Watts' *The New England Quarterly* 61 (1988) 214–32.

conversion of a young man as being like the 'ring inserted through the young bullock's septum which allows the owner to lead the animal at will after it matures.'[33] With this in mind, we can see how it was necessary for Dickinson to forge a considered distance from such socially controlling forces. What is more, her work can thus be seen as a deliberate construction of resistance which is not, as Habegger argues, 'a silent, a non-act, a turning away' (Habegger, p. 386.) from such religious fervour, but a bold and loud protest in poetic form which was deliberately dissonant. Her mode of questioning dominant religious ideology is consistent; 'Why do they shut me out of Heaven? / Did I sing - too loud?' (Fr 268), and frequently related directly to the act of writing poetry ('singing') itself. The role of poet as a form of industry becomes a central concern in Dickinson and it is by foregrounding the roots of the Protestant work ethic that the extent of Dickinson's dissent can be illuminated. The important connection between ecstatic pleasure and 'industry' we find in Dickinson's bee imagery (explored in depth in Section Three) is a crucial explication of the relation between subjectivity and spirituality so prevalent in twentieth/twenty-first century feminist literary theory and feminist theology. The ecstatic community in Dickinson's bee imagery also leads us to a new metaphor for the divine.

There has been a shift in recent scholarship on Dickinson which has highlighted a desire to uncover the many ways in which Dickinson was engaged with and creatively stimulated by her own society and context of late nineteenth century New England. There is currently a need to recover Dickinson's work from decades of criticism which defined it as being absent of any frame of reference or social context and displaying evidence of a severe alienation from (and disinterest in) her own society. Part of this book's project is to highlight important connections between what has been the obfuscation of Dickinson's engagement with society, and, configurations of spirituality as a politically viable option. Betsy Erkkila skillfully employs Habermas's *The Structural Transformation of the Public Sphere* to describe the ways in which the public and private spheres have been falsely separated, and the private sphere depoliticised, to support criticism of Dickinson as a reclusive poet, ultimately uninterested in engaging with society or the political environment of her day.[34] Although Dickinson was not interested in publication, apart from the self-publication her fascicles and poems in letters provided her with, Dickinson's poems paradoxically demand the engagement of the reader, almost as if their existence was dependent upon reader's response, as the proliferation of Dickinson criticism since their publication has proved. As Erkkila's essay shows, Dickinson's most prolific period can be seen as being connected directly with the American Civil War (1861–1865) and her responses as a poet to it:

---

[33]   Alfred Habegger, 'Evangelicalism and its Discontents: Hannah Porter versus Emily Dickinson,' *The New England Quarterly* 70: 3 (1997) 386–414 (p. 389). Habegger discusses Edward Hitchcock's use of this metaphor in his *Reminiscences of Amherst College* (1863).

[34]   Betsy Erkkila, 'Dickinson and the Art of Politics' in *A Historical Guide to Emily Dickinson*, (ed.), Vivian R. Pollak, pp. 133–74.

in [...] poems composed during the war years, Dickinson enacts her artistic
dedication in language that uses biblical symbolism and Church ritual to
challenge the social, sexual and religious ideologies that eclipse and shroud
women's lives. (Erkkila, p. 157)

The shape of Dickinson's writing during the Civil War period which Erkkila
observes, and which this book also takes as its focus, demonstrates increasingly
outwards, externalised or 'centrifugal'[35] focus in her poetics. Apart from the fact
that Dickinson composed the majority of poems during the Civil War period, it is
also during this period that her concern with the motifs and practices associated
with hymnody comes most creatively to the fore. This can be seen namely in her
poetics of flight (utilised by other female hymnists as Chapter 5 shows) such as the
bee imagery examined closely in Chapter 6 (i) and (ii).

Overall, then, this book examines the representation of spirituality in Dickinson's
work by focusing on her relation to hymnody and by providing analysis of hymnic
space as heterologous. It revisits her relation to the work of Isaac Watts in light of
his position as a Dissenter, and analyses her use of the hymn form alongside that
of other contemporary women hymn writers. It also provides new research into
the ways in which Dickinson utilised particular images, such as in the example of
the bee, and in doing so, invokes culturally specific ideas about orthodox religion,
spirituality, community, and the intersection between them. In analysing such
representations of spirituality in relation to specific texts and cultural contexts, this
book provides a new foray into Dickinson criticism, and also fills the current gap
within criticism with regard to this particular aspect of her work. Moreover, it aims
to uncover the ways in which Dickinson's poetic adoption and adaptation of the
modes of religious orthodoxy and traditional devotional expression goes beyond
the characteristics of Armstrong's 'double poem.' As Armstrong argues, feminist
analysis of nineteenth-century poetry by women often 'retrieves the protest, but
not the poem.'(Armstrong, p. 319.) With this in mind, the book suggests ways in
which Dickinson's hymnic poems go beyond this doubleness to produce new ways
of thinking about and expressing spirituality. Dickinson's poetry is transformative.
Therefore, the book also aims to show how reading Dickinson in this way may
present new opportunities for reading representations of spirituality in nineteenth-
century poetry by women.

---

[35]   Jay Ladin's term for one of the forces in Dickinson's work, as discussed in the
following chapter, pp. 53–56. See Jay Ladin, "So Anthracite to Live:' Emily Dickinson and
American Literary History', *The Emily Dickinson Journal* 13:1 (2004) 19–50 (p. 28).

Chapter 2
The Hymn – A Form of Devotion?

This chapter outlines a brief history of hymn culture together with some of the features of the genre, and introduces the ways in which 'hymn' is discussed in this book, in relation to Dickinson's engagement with it. The term 'hymn culture' is used here with reference to the tradition of writing, editing and compiling hymns and also the practical experience of hymns; singing, sharing and using them as points of reference in every day life. It also refers to the various conventions hymns follow, such as hierarchical address, teleological narrative and particular imagery. 'Hymn culture' also encompasses the rationale and specific ideas about social cohesion that such conventions produce, and the various effects those ideas have upon the editorial choices made during the compiling of hymnals. Hymns are *ideally* relational because they invoke the individual's communion with God and also the congregation, that is, a *diverse relation in unity*. However, the hierarchical model of relation commonly found in hymn address ('I-Thou') reflects thinking on the divine which is inherently oppositional. The representation of spiritual experience to be found in the poems and hymns examined in this book present a negotiation of, and alternative to, such oppositional conceptions of the divine.

The aim of this and the following chapter is not to argue for a reclassification of Dickinson's poems as hymns, but rather, to outline the flexibility between lyric poetry and hymns which Dickinson's work exploits. Understanding hymnic space as heterologous can inform readings of Dickinson's representations of spirituality. Heterologous spaces are those which allow individuality and difference to exist within a contained connection to a larger body. The difficulties of framing Dickinson's work within a particular genre have been explored by Virginia Jackson. Her reading of Dickinson as a poet whose work often does not conform to the parameters of lyric poetry but has been affected by, and read through, various theories of lyrical expression is instructive. She identifies the 'posthumous transmission and reception of her writing as lyric.'[1] Whilst repositioning Dickinson as a hymnist is not the aim of this book, exploring the connections her work has with hymnody provides a fruitful alternative to confining her work to the genre of lyric poetry. It also uncovers new ways in which to explore Dickinson's engagement with the discourses that constructed a woman's relation to the divine through the role of the traditional female hymnist. In this way, the hymn can be seen not only as a form of religious devotion, but also as a site of political dissent which articulates an alternative version of devotion, both religious and/or secular. In order to understand the fluidity between lyric poetry and hymns and the gravity

---

[1]   Virginia Jackson, *Dickinson's Misery: A Theory of Lyric Reading* (Princeton: Princeton University Press, 2005) p. 212.

and effects of Dickinson's use of the hymn form, a brief outline of the development of hymnody up to the mid-nineteenth century will be useful.

A Brief History of Hymns

The journey of the hymn from its origins up to the mid-nineteenth century in America is a long and somewhat complicated one. The ways in which hymns have been used, and how they have served a public function of worship over the centuries inevitably tells us a lot about the different historical periods in which they are written (and written about), both culturally and politically. Cheslyn Jones's definition of hymns is pertinent here, as it applies as well to nineteenth-century as to twentieth-century hymns. Jones sees hymns as corresponding directly with 'those ritual situations when the congregation acts as a group, whether to reply to the word of God or to utter praise and entreaty. The hymn acts as a mirror in which the congregation can see itself.'[2] The history of the hymn, therefore, can be seen as a representation or mirror of the various versions of the divine that were agreed upon and expressed by a particular group, at a particular moment in history. The fact that other versions would be suppressed, edited or excluded is also part of that history.

Most hymns currently in existence date from after the seventeenth century; before then the act of writing hymns often relied upon the practice of paraphrasing Holy Scripture. When writing about hymns before this period, compilers and commentators refer largely to the tradition of paraphrasing liturgical sources. The tradition of setting sacred poetry to music has a long history, and the ways in which hymns were used to perform particular functions within society can be traced as far back as the fourth century, when hymns were used not only to perform public celebration of the Christian mysteries, but also to promote or refute heresy.[3] Hymns enabled a literal performance of social and political identity, foreshadowing the use of hymns in the cultivation of a woman's 'domestic' identity during the mid-nineteenth century.

The debate over what should and should not be included in hymns as part of devotional worship has fluctuated over time within different periods, inevitably reflecting shifting power relations between Church and State.[4] The shift in the usage of hymns is mainly attributed to the work of St. Ambrose, the fourth century Bishop of Milan, who championed their use as a simple and direct part of formal worship. Nearly one hundred hymns have been described as 'Ambrosian',

---

[2]　　Cheslyn Jones, (ed.), and others, *The Study of Liturgy* (London: SPCK, 1979) p. 452.

[3]　　*DCC*, p. 281.

[4]　　In the fifth-century Eastern Orthodox Church, hymns did not deviate from biblical text, giving rise to *troparia*, hymns of a single stanza in length, and *contakia* which were a series of stanzas. The later, Latin hymns signified an important shift as hymns gradually infiltrated the Western Churches and by the twelfth century were a fully recognised part of religious worship (*DCC*, p. 281).

but John Julian's *Dictionary of Hymnology* (1892) tells us that only three can be attributed to Ambrose with any certainty.[5] However, we do know that as a composer and writer of sacred poetry, Ambrose sought to systematize the form of musical worship within the liturgy and as a result served to promote the use of hymns in the Western Church.

A significant figure to emerge during the Middle Ages is twelfth-century German woman mystic and composer Hildegard Von Bingen (1098–1179). She was a notable figure in the development of the hymn form and it is useful to remember her in this book in particular, as one of the earliest women hymnists. Hildegard wrote liturgical plainchants and also a few hymns in Latin in honour of saints, virgins and the Virgin Mary.[6] John Julian dismisses her contribution to the hymnody of her day as 'neither numerous nor important' (Julian, p. 523). However, the distinction Julian imposes between Hildegard's 'mystical verse' and her more 'traditional' hymns ultimately affects his conservative estimation of her contribution to hymnody as he sees it. Regardless of how her works are categorized, Hildegard's compositions provide an example of a woman engaging with the form as early as the twelfth century, and despite Julian's record, her work is regarded highly today.

With the onset of the Reformation in the sixteenth century there were changes again to how hymns were regarded as part of formal worship. Martin Luther (and followers of Lutheran philosophy) wrote many hymns during the German Reformation period which are in use today and place emphasis on personal justification by faith (*DCC*, p. 281), a tenet that became part of the basis for the Protestant attack on Catholicism and which was also important for the Puritans in the seventeenth century. At much the same time Calvin worked to establish a theocratic regime and his influence led to a series of more rigid guidelines on the use of hymns and the insistence that they should be comprised of scriptural words only. So there came with Calvinism a need to place greater emphasis on the psalms, giving rise to the singing of metrical psalms instead of hymns, which were seen as being a deviation from scripture. Rivkah Zim explains how different versions of psalms embody 'contemporary views of what was thought to be proper to the nature of a psalm,' and how writers in the sixteenth century 'exploited the shared, contemporary resources of that kind.'[7] In the sixteenth century, poets 'inherited a devotional tradition in which the Psalms provided a nucleus for the private prayers of the laity and this tradition persisted among Catholics and Protestants alike.'(Zim, p. 3.) Thus, there was a desire to paraphrase the Psalms from all walks of literary life, including those who were not devout reformers.

The eighteenth century was pivotal in the received history of hymnody largely because of the minister and hymnographer Isaac Watts (1674–1748). Watts was

---

[5]   John Julian, *Dictionary of Hymnology* (London: John Murray, 1907) p. 56.

[6]   See Sabina Flanagan, *Secrets of God: Writings of Hildegard of Bingen* (Shambhala Publications: Boston and London, 1996).

[7]   Rivkah Zim, *English Metrical Psalms: Poetry as Praise and Prayer 1535–1601*, p. 2.

instrumental in changing the way people worship and in the move away from the singing of metrical psalms exclusively, as favoured by Calvinism, back towards the use of wider ranging forms and content that existed before the Reformation. The work of Watts was extremely popular and collections such as *Hymns and Spiritual Songs* (1707–9) were instrumental in effecting this change. Thus, hymns which drew from scripture but did not rely upon paraphrasing it became much more acceptable during the eighteenth century and set the precedent for the fluidity between lyrical expression and 'hymnody' thereafter.

Barton Levi St. Armand's labelling of Dickinson's poetry as a 'Christian Psalmody of questioning and protest' (St. Armand, p. 158.) is instructive. Reading Dickinson's poetry through the tradition of psalmody (encompassing here both hymn-singing and psalm-singing) highlights a process of dissent, questioning and reconfiguration of spirituality in her work. Thought to have been written by David, although its multiple viewpoints suggest otherwise to scholars today, the Bible's *Book of Psalms* expresses one particular human's experience of God. The personal tone of the 150 psalms, and the imitation of it, lends itself to the articulation of a personal and personalised relationship to God or the divine, and the often problematic nature of that relationship. Watts's extensive *The Psalms of David Imitated in the Language of the New Testament, and Applied to the Christian State and Worship* (1719) provide a good model for the reinterpretation of personal experience. Through this work we can trace an attitude of personal response which might inform Dickinson's mode of 'protest'. The residual influence of Calvinism in Dickinson's society remained strong. However, despite the element of personal response within orthodoxy that the metrical psalms encourage, the practice of hymn-singing in church worship, which is a less restrictive form of expression than the singing of metrical psalms, combines the personal mode with a more liberated and looser expression of spirituality. It was congregational hymns, more than the singing of psalms, which held sway in the period of religious revivals during the early to mid nineteenth century. They were used as a method and display of conversion, much as psalms were used in early Christian church history, as explained above. Therefore, the personal mode associated with the composition and practice of singing psalms is pertinent to this study as much as the assumptions about social cohesion which are implicit in the hymn. The containing structure of hymn metre found in congregational hymnody and the act of singing reinforces the representation of an agreed or communal version of the divine. The ways in which this communal version is represented, together with the personal mode associated with the psalm, bear equally upon the readings of Dickinson that make up this study. Importantly, St. Armand's comment sets a precedent for reading structure and method in Dickinson's corpus where other critics have been less inclined to do so.

As this brief history of hymnody demonstrates, gradual shifts in the political and social climates which affected western church history can be identified and demonstrated by the differing levels on restriction placed upon hymn usage in public worship. Therefore, particular uses of the hymn (or psalm) can tell us a lot about the kinds of expectations from readers at the time they were written and their cultural contexts. Like the psalm, the space of the hymn carries with it a set of expectations, but a gradual shift can be identified from the use of strictly paraphrastic verse, to a more lyrical expression in congregational hymnody from the eighteenth century onwards. This shift occurs partly through imitation which at times is akin to parody.

Writing about Dickinson's use of the hymn form, Martha Winburn England underscores the fact that it is a form with specific associations and assumptions. She compares Dickinson's use of the hymn to T.S. Eliot's use of 'orthodox' forms:

> The method is parody in the usual sense: the imitation of an art form that handles any element of art so as to criticize the original form with more or less serious intent. [...] Mr T.S. Eliot['s] [...] frustrates the expectations raised by some familiar verse form, and turns the reader from lyric mood to critical evaluation of statements commonly associated with the original form. Emily Dickinson handled various elements of words and music so as to comment on statements commonly associated with the hymn form.[8]

Dickinson uses the hymn form to provide comment on 'statements commonly associated with the hymn form'. In other words, she questions the premises about spiritual experience which the hymn form gives structure to. This book traces her treatment of such 'statements' and the ways of articulating them, such as the metaphors for the divine and for one's relationship to the divine found in Watts's hymns. However, because Dickinson's treatment of the hymn form does not rely upon paraphrasing and reworking the psalms, the way in which to approach the extent of her 'comment' differs from those employed when examining traditional hymnody. Recurrent images such as the bee indicate Dickinson's 'comment' on the Puritan-Protestant work ethic conveyed in many hymns. Motifs of flight can be traced in relation to those in Watts and also in contemporary hymns by women of whose work Dickinson would almost certainly have been aware. As this book will explore, mobile and fluid metaphors for the divine emerge in Dickinson's work to create a new hymnic space. In this way, her method can be seen as much more than 'parody in the usual sense', and as a transformative practice which gives rise to new ways of expressing experience of the divine in language.

Hymns which do not follow the traditional paraphrastic structure of psalmody are by their nature slightly more difficult to define. At the end of the seventeenth century, hymns no longer relied exclusively upon paraphrase and poems which were simply religious verse were admitted into the Non-Conformist Church as hymns. However the considerable criticism that greeted Benjamin Keach's defence of hymns in his *The Breach Repaired* (1691) shows that the incorporation of such unscriptural songs into church services was controversial. It was only

---

[8]   Martha Winburn England, and John Sparrow, *Hymns Unbidden: Donne, Herbert, Blake, Emily Dickinson and the Hymnographers* (New York: New York Public Library, 1966) p. 121.

with Watts, who popularised the use of hymns via congregational singing in the eighteenth century, that the hymn finally became established as an accepted form of worship. Watts's hymns are an example of verse that does not rely entirely upon paraphrasing scripture. They are short and direct in their structure and approach, usually written in the Hymnic Common Metre with its 4-3, 4-3, formulation, and appeal to a more personalised experience of faith than the generalised expression associated with paraphrases of scripture.[9] Watts has since become known as the 'father of the modern hymn'[10] and his influence is recognised on a global scale as being someone who radically altered the mode of church practice with his support of congregational hymn singing. Watt's preference for this simple but taut structure that encourages plainness of language was perceived by some as evidence of a lack of poetic skill.[11] However, this unadorned style can be connected to Watts's politics and position as a Dissenter with Puritan roots.

An increased questioning of religious faith is reflected in the writings of the Victorian period both in Britain and America. The expanding critical awareness of the Bible and the proliferation of linguistic and historical studies of biblical texts, in the nineteenth century as a whole, gave rise to scepticism towards literalist interpretations of the Bible as the word of God. Krueger argues that such developments led to the 'empowerment of individual conscience as the final authority.'[12] With this increased biblical literacy there was also an increase in church personnel. The number of laity incorporated into the workings of church practices grew. These changes contributed to what Krueger terms as 'common cultural currency' and a 'widely shared typology by which to interpret history, politics, art, and individual experience'. (Krueger, p. 142).

During the nineteenth century the proliferation of hymn collections compiled for both public and private usage led to many alterations at the hands of editors.

---

[9]   Watts used three metres for all of his hymns; Common Metre (4-3 4-3), Short Metre (3-3 4-3) and Long Metre (4-4 4-4). Hymn Common Metre (also the same as the Ballad Stanza) is usually comprised of four-line verses with each line alternately comprising of three (trimeter) and four (tetrameter) iambic metrical feet. An iambic line begins with an unstressed syllable which then 'rises' to a stressed syllable or beat, and is often called 'rising' metre. Trochaic lines begin with a stressed syllable or beat, and then fall to an off-beat, and is thus often called a 'falling metre.' Dickinson uses both iambic and trochaic stresses/unstresses or 'feet' in her use of the Hymn Common Metre to achieve metrical emphasis. See Thomas Carper and Derek Attridge, *Meter and Meaning: An Introduction to Rhythm in Poetry* (London: Routledge, 2003) pp. 88–93 for fuller explanation of metre labels.

[10]   David G. Fountain, *Isaac Watts Remembered* (Harpenden: Gospel Standard Baptist Trust Ltd, 1974) p. 102.

[11]   As discussed in Chapter 4. See Rufus Griswold, (ed.), *Sacred Poets of England and America* (New York: D. Appleton and Company, 1848) p. 241, and Bernard L. Manning, *The Hymns of Wesley and Watts* (London: Epworth Press, 1942) pp. 88–9.

[12]   Christine Krueger, 'Clerical,' in *A Companion to Victorian Literature and Culture*, (ed.), H.F. Tucker (Oxford: Blackwell, 2004) pp. 141–54 (p. 142).

The nature of hymns as a tool for 'moulding' theology meant that hymns were altered frequently to accommodate the different theological leanings of religious groups. Hymns were also compiled for social hymn-books which had varying purposes and levels of formality associated with them. However, this also led to anxiety about the corruption of hymns which, as essentially sacred texts, should remain intact. An article from *Atlantic Monthly* (1882) entitled 'Hymns and Hymn-Tinkers,' conveys such anxieties:

> All these and many more have had their words passed under the harrow and mangled with needless and cruel wounds. It is the duty of all who have the interests of an authentic literature at heart to manifest their disapproval of such literary crimes.[13]

The nature or 'integrity' of a hymn therefore becomes a matter of literary taste, and is supported by dedication to a nonspecific claim to 'authenticity.' Dickinson's 'tinkering' or 'mangling' of the traditional hymn metre challenges claims to what constitutes a particular type of 'authenticity,' as demonstrated by the anonymous critic above whose focus is on the importance of preserving the linguistic idiosyncrasies in the hymns of canonical male hymnists, Watts and Wesley.

Tensions and difficulties are implicit when attempting to define differences and/or similarities between lyric poetry and hymns. Dickinson's work emphasises and exploits such problems. Definitions of lyric poetry include nondramatic and nonnarrative verse. The hymn, which both dramatises a speaker's relation to the divine and presents a clear narrative in which speaker and God are defined, can be distinguished from lyric poetry on this basis. Dickinson's work ruptures the expectation of narrative and resolution associated with the hymn and in this sense can be seen as lyric poetry. Thus the two main qualities of hymnody relevant for this book are the assumption of their articulation of an agreed 'common bond' of a Christian community, and what Baynes described in 1867 as their desired effect of being able to 'mould our theology':

> Next to the bible itself, hymns have done more to influence our views, and mould our theology, than any other instrumentality whatever. There is a power in hymns which never dies. Easily learned in the days of childhood and of youth; often repeated; seldom, if ever forgotten; they abide with us, a most precious heritage amid all the changes of our earthly life.[14]

Dickinson's challenges to theology and to notions of community as defined by religious culture can therefore be seen through her engagement with hymn culture, which directly underpins and reflects both theology and community. In the same

---

[13] A.P. Hitchcock, 'Hymns and Hymn-Tinkers,' in *Atlantic Monthly* 46:3 (1882) 336–46 (p. 345).

[14] Rev. Robert Baynes, (ed.), *Lyra Anglicana: Hymns and Sacred Songs* (London: Houlston and Wright, 1867) p. 6.

way that the Puritan's conscience might be seen as being powerfully effective because each person becomes, with an internalised self-censure, to use Foucault's phrase, a 'judge of normality,'[15] so too does the hymn reflect such versions of 'normality.'

Defining the Hymn: 'Acid Test Questions' and Naming the Divine

The division between lyric poetry and hymns is somewhat debatable. Dickinson's work frustrates the attempt to impose boundaries by offering allusions to hymn culture within contexts which seem alien, absurd even. It allows us to question whether lyric poetry is essentially secular, produced in inspired isolation or whether hymns really do represent a cohesive community (as Baynes describes 'Christ's mystical body'). Most engagingly, by including references to hymn culture in her spiritually probing poems, she confronts the power of hymns to shape theology. By using a form of traditional Christian devotion as a form of dissent, Dickinson's relation to hymns can be seen as producing an alternative form of devotion. That is, an alternative mystical spirituality which is produced dialogically alongside Christian theology and negotiates alternatives to the 'I-Thou' model of relation in traditional hymn address.[16] An alternative mode of relation is signalled in Dickinson's poems through imagery connected with flight. As Chapter Six will demonstrate with reference to bee imagery, her poems convey an alternative version of community through tropes of diverse and multiple relation and interconnectedness. Moreover, her use of language is relational:

> The Drop that wrestles in the Sea -
> Forgets her own locality
> As I, in Thee - (Fr 255)

The speaker in this poem voices concern over the potential loss of individuality and freedom, of losing a sense of self and being absorbed by an other. Be it a lover, friend or God, one is tempted to place 'Thee' in a position of comparative supremacy to 'I' when reading such lines. However, rather than simply deconstructing the mechanism of relation which connects 'drop' and 'ocean', the poem reproduces relation and interconnectedness, and ultimately an alternative vision of community, by the consideration of 'locality' the poem promotes. The urge to redefine self through myths of difference and hierarchies subsumes in the poem into an ultimate reconsideration of 'locality' and how that locality ('Drop')

---

[15]   Michel Foucault, *Discipline and Punish: The Birth of the Prison* (1975) (London: Penguin, 1986) p. 304.

[16]   As discussed in detail in the following chapter, this hierarchical model for prayer, also a central feature of hymns, is considered in Daphne Hampson's book in terms of its inadequacy for feminist relations to/versions of the divine. See *Theology and Feminism*, p. 169.

might operate in relation to vastness ('Ocean'). In this way, the poem considers the hierarchical model of address ('As I, in Thee'), from the speaker to God, common in hymns. The poem exemplifies the possibilities of heterologous space, where difference might not be lost, but exist productively within, and be necessary to, a wider body. Such relational language not only accommodates a fluidity between poetry and hymns but also necessarily enacts it.

A good example of the fluidity between poetry and hymns is given in the introduction to Tom Ingram and Douglas Newton's anthology *Hymns as Poetry* (1956). The editors begin by asking themselves the two 'acid test' questions when considering a poem or hymn for inclusion in their collection: 'Does this express any kind of relationship between the worshipper and God?' and 'Was this hymn ever sung, or was it at least written for singing?'[17] The first question appears to be rather straightforward, and the editors do not feel it necessary to give examples. However, as in the case of many women hymn writers, the ways in which 'God,' or the relationship between 'God' and the speaker, is depicted or encoded often differs radically from, or is at least more complex than, the model of ideal reciprocity projected in more 'traditional' hymns. The depiction of the relationship between speaker and God in hymns is crucial to Dickinson's use of the form to articulate dissent. As will be discussed in Chapter 5, hymns were often modified by compilers, or the authors were asked to modify them themselves, in order to make them more suitable for the 'rationale' of the collection.[18]

Ingram and Douglas explain that answers to the second 'acid test' question are less easy to provide, conceding that there are so many cases where hymns were written but never sung. Equally, poems which were not written with the hymn-book in mind were adapted and permanently enshrined within the hymn genre. They concede, moreover, that the apparent 'intention' of the writer (whether the work was intended as a hymn or not) becomes the somewhat haphazard ruling principle for classification.[19] Dickinson's poems hold culturally received or known ('sacred') and unknown ('heretical') versions of God in tension with each other. As will be illustrated further on, the verse form tugs thoughts about the

---

[17]   Tom Ingram, and Douglas Newton, (eds), *Hymns as Poetry* (London: Constable, 1956) p. 1.

[18]   John Julian's *Dictionary of Hymnology* cites many examples of hymns written by women that were altered, usually by the hymnist, in order to be included in particular hymnals. As in the case of Phoebe Hinsdale Brown (p. 185). As will be discussed in chapter 5, although male hymnists were also altered, the practice of editing women's hymns proves interesting because of the differing social roles ascribed to women in the nineteenth-century period, as Van Zanten Gallagher describes in 'Domesticity in American Hymns, 1820–1870' in *'Sing Them Over To Me Again: Hymns and Hymnbooks in America* (Alabama: The University of Alabama Press, 2006) (ed.), Mark E. Knoll and Edith L. Blumhofer, pp. 235–52.

[19]   Ingram and Newton, p. 2. Examples of prolific writers whose complete volume of work was never sung include Mrs Alexander and Fanny Crosby as well as Watts and Wesley. John Keble's *The Christian Year* (1827) is given as a key example of poetry being sung and functioning as hymns.

divine generated within the poem in opposite directions and works to destabilise received notions of Protestant, Christian faith while elevating the experiential and 'heretical'. By favouring a decentred simultaneity over linearity, her poetics deflate the apparatus of the traditionally sacred and transcendent. Each of these has the effect of creating a mystical aspect to her verse. In this way, and if what we mean by 'hymns' is re-examined and challenged, then Dickinson's verse can be read as hymns, not because they are poems intended for singing (traditional hymns), but because they enact what hymns are supposed to do; that is, express a relation to the divine. Moreover, the metaphors of relation which give shape to Dickinson's poetics invoke the symbolic values of the hymn, such as community and relation, more so than other devotional verse. Indeed, the dialogism at work in Dickinson's scrutiny of religious culture as exemplified by her use of the hymn genre, has led to a number of varying interpretations of her relation to Christian faith. Although not used as hymns, many of Dickinson's poems have been put to music and are sung.[20] Roger Lundin's recently revised biography, which takes Dickinson's experience of faith as its focus, maintains that Dickinson did in fact create 'her own body of hymns.' The fact that these hymns ranged in tone from what Lundin sees as 'devastating irony and sincere devotion' does not affect his classification.[21] The inclusion of Dickinson's poems in collections such as Donald Davie's *New Oxford Book of Christian Verse* (1981)[22] indicates both the narrow gap between Dickinson's poems and more traditional Christian verse, and also the wider definition applied by 'modern' editors. It is clear that such editors perceive Christian faith as incorporating not only moments of doubt, but also explicit challenges to institutionalised and specified versions of the divine, and regard such challenges and dissent as being an integral part of the religious experience.

In contrast, feminist critics such as Adrienne Rich and Camille Paglia view Dickinson as a solitary woman and a decadent late Romantic. Rich and Paglia wish to counter the marketable image of Dickinson as the benign nature-poet with ruffles and curls, as the doctored version of the original daguerreotype aims to portray. This version became the public image of the poet in 1924.[23] Paglia's essay 'Amherst's Madame de Sade' (1990) pictures Dickinson's work as the 'womb

---

[20]   A major collection and early example of Dickinson's poetry set to music is Aaron Copland's *Twelve Poems of Emily Dickinson, Set to Music, Voice and Piano.* (New York: Boosey and Hawkes, 1951). In addition many individual poems have been put to music, such as Wim de Ruiter's 1983 setting of poem Fr1742, which became known as 'In Winter, In My Room.' See Jonnie Guerra, 'Dickinson Adaptations in the Arts and the Theatre,' in Gudrun Grabher, and others, (eds), *The Emily Dickinson Handbook*, pp. 385–407.

[21]   Roger Lundin, *Emily Dickinson and the Art of Belief*, p. 146.

[22]   Donald Davie, (ed.), *New Oxford Book of Christian Verse* (Oxford: Oxford University Press, 1981). This collection includes 18 poems by Dickinson and 11 hymns by Isaac Watts.

[23]   The only daguerreotype of Dickinson dating from 1847 (as appears on the cover of this book) was used in 1924 to create a more sentimental image with a ruffle and curls, and included in Martha Dickinson Bianchi's *The Life and Letters*. See Judith Farr, *The Gardens of Emily Dickinson* (Cambridge, MA: Harvard University Press, 2004) p. 75.

tomb of decadent closure,' arguing that 'Blake and Spenser are her allies in helping pagan Coleridge defeat Protestant Wordsworth.'[24] Rich's 'vesuvian' view of Dickinson is one which observes a similarly explosive power. However, Rich positions Dickinson's depictions of violence upon the self as a dominating poetic force, often depicted as masculine in her poetry because culturally poetic power is ascribed to men.[25] It may be surprising, then, to want to align Dickinson, the energetic, anarchic and 'heretical' poet, with a traditionally sacred (and therefore also implicitly patriarchally determined) genre, whose structures and formulations she does indeed go at length to bend and parody. Nevertheless, hymn culture provides a lens through which to contextualise the tensions implicit in issues of identity and spirituality which organised religion exploits. Such tensions, as those which exist between concepts of individuality and community or pleasure and industry, are continually brought to the fore in Dickinson's work.

Categorising Dickinson's poems as hymns should not in theory relegate them to a decidedly lower order of poetry. The pressures placed upon poetic expression from the legacy of Romanticism perhaps contributed to the division between hymnody and lyrical expression in the nineteenth century.[26] The masculinist criteria and precedent which was set for individualised lyrical expression during the Romantic period, and which gendered nature as feminine, perhaps also fuelled a desire to move away from the communal aspect of the hymn. The 'communal' aspect of hymns became synonymous with 'commonplace,' and the tendency to position them as a lesser form of poetry can be seen in Tennyson's remark upon the 'difficulty' of hymn writing:

> A good hymn is the most difficult thing in the world to write – you have to be both commonplace and poetical.[27]

However, 'commonplace' also implies the idea of communal orthodoxy which is implicit in group hymn-singing. Increasingly, then, the realm of hymnody became an 'acceptable' arena of expression for women in the eyes of society in general.

---

[24] Camille Paglia, *Sexual Personae: Art and Decadence from Nerfertiti to Emily Dickinson* (New Haven: Yale University Press, 1990) p. 624. Adrienne Rich's essay, 'Vesuvius at Home,' provides a similarly explosive view of Dickinson, see Adrienne Rich, 'Vesuvius at Home: The Power of Emily Dickinson,' (1975) in *Adrienne Rich's Poetry and Prose,* 2nd edn, (eds), Barbara Charlesworth Gelpi and Albert Gelpi (New York: Norton, 1993) pp. 177–95.

[25] Adrienne Rich, 'Vesuvius at Home', p. 187.

[26] See Margaret Homans, *Women Writers and their Poetic Identity: Dorothy Wordsworth, Emily Bronte and Emily Dickinson* (Princeton: Princeton University Press, 1980). Homans argues that the legacy of Romanticism, which gendered nature as feminine and perceived poetic creativity through masculinist criteria created obstacles for women writers of the nineteenth century. Wordsworth's 'feminization of nature' (p. 13.) is given much consideration in this context.

[27] Mark Bryant, (ed.), *Literary Hymns: An Anthology* (London: Hodder and Stoughton, 1999) p. 16. Bryant quotes Tennyson in the Preface to the anthology.

The role of the hymnist, together with that of educationalist, became one which women frequently adopted to enable their writing.[28] As will be discussed further in Chapter 5 in relation to the work of hymnists Brown and Follen, the 'cult of domesticity' which served to idealise women's position (and status as 'moral centre') within the home leant itself to this acceptability of hymn writing by women. It is because the acceptability of the hymn rests on this domestic basis that Dickinson's use of it is, in the first instance, ironic. It is also why her poems offer a direct challenge to the central premises of hymn culture.

Separate Spheres: Women's Hymns/Warring Hymns

Despite the concept of congregational hymns being an ideal discourse space in which a person's relation to the divine can be articulated without an intermediary, or intervening formal restrictions (hence the notion of their 'levelling effect') the pressures of gender division are perhaps made most visible in the hymn. In her 1892 anthology, *Lady Hymn Writers*, Mrs E.R. Pitman claims that:

> [...] God's singers have come from all ranks and conditions of life, as well as from all branches of the Church militant. Some have worn queenly crowns, others have toiled for a daily living [...]. Yet in one and all we can trace a family likeness. A congregation may sing at one and the same service hymns from Mrs Adams, Charlotte Elliott, Frances Ridley Havergal and Adelaide Anne Procter, and never find anything in one hymn to clash with another, so true is it that in the region of hymns all doctrinal differences are forgotten.[29]

And:

> Somebody has well said "there is no heresy in hymns;" and we verily believe that there is more true Christian unity to be found in hymns than anywhere else. Matthew Arnold says: "The strongest part of our religion today is its unconscious poetry." (Pitman, *Lady Hymn Writers*, p. 64)

The level of 'unity' in women's hymns can be seen as asserting a communal understanding of subjectivity based upon a connectedness and less masculinised version of the divine. However, Pitman's insistence upon their sameness elides class difference. She uses Arnold's views on religion and poetry to support her relegation of hymns to the 'unconscious' level. This stance also reaffirms the association of women's hymns with the cult of domesticity ('Hymns have soothed the pulse of sorrow, have brightened darkest days', Pitman, *Lady Hymn Writers*, p. 15.) and emphasises their functional, rather than expressive, aspect.

---

[28] See J.R. Watson, *The English Hymn: A Critical and Historical Study* (Oxford: Clarendon Press, 1997) p. 430.

[29] E.R. Pitman, *Lady Hymn Writers* (London: T. Nelson and Sons, 1892) p. 19.

Such a view of the hymn undermines the possibility for fluidity and self-reflexivity within the form. Pitman ignores the possibility whereby women speakers may both adopt but also reflect upon the version of self experienced within the cult of domesticity. Such self-narratives were popular in Puritan culture.[30] Versions of self (and therefore also of the divine) which are counter to the dominant socially prescribed ones are vividly present in women's hymns of the period. Dickinson's use of the hymn form both radically contests the 'redemptive' power of hymns, and simultaneously, invokes a reconfigured notion of spiritual community and connectedness which accommodates the troublesome 'I'. In this way, hymnic space operates as heterologous within Dickinson's poems.

Dickinson's use of the hymn as a form of 'heresy' and dissent can be contextualised as being both a response to and also operating within the cult of domesticity, born from a 'separate spheres' ideology which posited home as an earthly heaven for women. Critics point out the ways in which Dickinson utilised the domestic space of the home to create her own 'workshop' of literary production.[31] Her evocations of 'home' in poetry, such as 'Some keep the Sabbath going to Church - / I keep it, staying at Home' (Fr 236) and 'I learned - at least - what Home could be - ' (Fr 891) are both ironical reflections upon the cult of domesticity and depictions of 'heavenly home' which appeared in domestic literature of the period. They are also, at the same time, a defiant refusal of the practices and nature of church worship available to her. The separate spheres ideology which served to promote the 'cult of domesticity' can be seen clearly in Alexis de Tocqueville's observations in *Democracy in America* (1835–1840).[32] His views on the division between public and private spheres which involved also division between the sexes in nineteenth-century American society are perplexing because of their assurance:

> In America […] care has been taken constantly to trace clearly distinct spheres of action for the two sexes […]. You will never find American women in charge of the external relations of the family, managing a business, or interfering in politics; but they are also never obliged to undertake rough labourer's work or any task requiring hard physical exertion. No family is so poor that it makes an exception to this rule. (Tocqueville, vol 2., p. 601)

Tocqueville's observations seem to take account of all classes, as the final statement about women not having to undertake 'hard physical exertion' above suggests,

---

[30] For discussion of self-narratives within a Puritan redemptive framework, See C. Steedman, 'Enforced Narratives: Stories of Another Self,' in *Feminism and Autobiography: Texts, Theories, Methods* (London: Routledge, 2000) (eds) T. Cosslett, C. Lury and P. Summerfield, pp. 25–39.

[31] Fr, p. 2. Franklin refers to Dickinson's method of self-publishing and dividing her poems into individual packets or fascicles as being akin to a 'workshop'.

[32] Alexis de Tocqueville, *Democracy in America* (1835–40), 2 vols, (ed.) by J.P. Mayer (London: Fontana Press, 1994).

although in fact such comments simply deny the existence of the woman labourer. What is clear, however, is that the 'cult of domesticity' which is a production of the separate spheres ideology Tocqueville here espouses, is well established as a much debated social paradigm for women's experiences. Not everyone agreed with such versions of domestic bliss: Susan Van Zanten Gallagher argues that many hymns written by women during the mid 1800s did much to challenge this 'cult of domesticity'. The increasing opportunity in the nineteenth-century for women to engage in hymn writing gave them a way of being critical of the assumptions implicit in the 'cult of domesticity'. Such assumptions elide issues of class by taking it for granted that men enter the workforce whilst women remain in the 'heavenly' home. The many non-idealised descriptions of 'home' to be found in their hymns question the perception of women as the moral centre of the home, as prescribed in domestic literature and novels of the period.[33]

As will be discussed in Chapter 5, Protestant Evangelical hymnody supported, and was supported by, nineteenth-century gender ideology which stressed the division between public and private spheres. Such division served to ensconce middle-class women such as Dickinson within the domestic arena, as the moral centre of family life. Although still outnumbered within the 'tradition' of male hymnists, women's hymn writing during the nineteenth century witnesses an increased participation in religious practices. During this time Britain continued to be a source of inspiration for American women who wished to participate in religious life. The influence of British women hymn writers was clear from the outset; the first important American hymnbook, Asahel Nettleton's *Village Hymns* (1824), significantly retained British writers such as Anne Steele alongside American counterparts, such as Phoebe Brown.[34] The devotional mode of the hymn thus became a socially acceptable form of writing that women could actively pursue, without attracting the stigma that was frequently attached to women who desired publication of secular verse. Edward Dickinson's anxieties about his daughter's desire to learn no doubt contributed to her ambivalence about publication. 'He buys me many Books – but begs me not to read them – because he fears they joggle the Mind. (to T.W. Higginson, 25 April 1862, SL, p. 267.) Despite her assertion that 'publication is the auction of the mind' (Fr 788) Dickinson's preparation of poems into packets or 'fascicles' was a form of self-publication. As we shall see, women hymn writers develop ways to negotiate and harness the

---

[33]   Susan Van Zanten Gallagher cites images of toil in the home in hymns by Phoebe Hinsdale Brown and Charlotte Elliott as examples of such challenges, and provides examples in domestic literature, such as *Godey's Lady's Book, Lady's Home Journal, Good Housekeeping* and books such as Catherine Beecher's *A Treatise on Domestic Economy* (1841) and Lydia Maria Child's *The Frugal Housewife* (1830). See 'Domesticity in American Hymns, 1820–1850,' in *'Sing them Over Again to Me:' Hymns and Hymnbooks in America* (Alabama: The University of Alabama Press, 2006) (eds) Mark. A. Knoll and Edith L. Blumhoffer. pp. 235–52 (p. 237).

[34]   See J.R. Watson, *The English Hymn: A Critical and Historical Study* (Oxford: Clarendon Press, 1997) p. 462.

performative power of the hymn. In this they challenge the traditional emphasis on linearity and phallogocentric movement upwards/towards a centre of God as a simple reflection of the speaker's (usually masculine) desires.

Dickinson and Hymns: How and Why?

When Dickinson uses metre it is often only to disrupt it; presenting to the ear the idea of regularity which has gone askew. The metres she uses mainly to this end are the Common Hymnic Metre and the Common Particular Metre. The Common Hymnic Metre has alternating lines of 8/6 syllables and the Common Particular Metre has syllable lines of 8/8/6 (so 4/3 metrical feet alternating in the Common Hymnic Metre or 4/4/3 metrical feet in the Common Particular Metre). Although Dickinson is clearly guided by these forms, her metrics are rarely strictly regular. A good example is:

> A transport one cannot contain
> May yet, a transport be -
> Though God forbid it lift the lid,
> Unto it's Extasy!
>
> A Diagram - of Rapture!
> A sixpence at a show -
> With Holy Ghosts in Cages!
> The universe would go! (Fr 212, with ED's spelling and punctuation)

The first stanza of this poem, which conveys scepticism on the ability to 'contain' the divine, follows the common hymnic metre exactly with its alternating 4/3 metrical feet. However, in the second stanza the number of syllables per line differs to become 7/6. The irregularity of the metre encourages us to read the dash as a syllable, as we expect eight syllables until line three to this stanza confirms the seven syllable line. This achieves the dramatic effect of the reader having to linger longer over words such as 'diagram'. The effect posits an incredulity about connecting 'diagram' with 'transport', the initial consideration in the poem. One cannot produce nor purchase a 'diagram' of the divine, though many preachers may try. The poem argues that the divine ('transport') cannot be contained or described, but does so within what is recognisably a hymn; a form which traditionally 'contains' expressions of one's relation to the divine with a simple, formal, and regular structure. Dickinson's poem, however, disrupts that regularity and simplicity in order to illustrate the impossibility of holding or containing the 'transport' which links the poet to the divine. Paradoxically, then, the effect of Dickinson's conceptual and metrical deviations rely upon the structure they explode outwards from. Yet while they depend upon the genre's association with regularity and simplicity, they also re-shape the 'hymn' for the reader in order to accommodate variation and experimentation. In other words, Dickinson's 'atheisms' and 'irregularities' become part of a reformulated hymn, a version of praise which is her own. Dickinson reclaims the hymn as an ideal and heterologous space which accommodates difference. Her use of the hymn form can therefore be read as utopian, as presenting to the reader an example of the possibilities for what praise can look like.

Ingram and Newton have argued that hymns invoke the power of many in agreement about the shape and experience of God (usually in the form of the congregation or worshipping community). They assert that it is this power which symbolically defines the hymn as a hymn: '[...] it has been the proof of long practice which has become decisive: the congregational voice has transmuted poem into hymn.' (Ingram and Newton, p. 2.) Their explanation of the process as 'decisive practice' is telling of the power of congregation and affirmation. Therefore, the poem becomes a hymn through the power of agreement on who or what God is, on what is 'Christian,' or a proper mode of expression of 'a speaker's relation to God.' Dickinson's poems interrogate this process by undoing the oppositional thinking which has allowed such inherently exclusionary versions of the divine to be proliferated. As will be illustrated in Chapter Five, hymns by women contemporary with Dickinson similarly express the 'shades' and 'holes', the moments of escape, which cannot fit with such formal structures.

Dickinson's use of hymn metre thus always implies a challenge to the notion that religious faith is 'agreed,' simple and known. The hymn common metre works in her poems to undermine such definitions on matters spiritual by enhancing it out of all proportion, much in the same way as Dickinson conveys her observation of a preacher's sermon in the following poem:

> He preached upon "Breadth" till it argued him narrow -
> The Broad are too broad to define
> And of "Truth" until it proclaimed him a Liar -
> The Truth never flaunted a Sign -
>
> Simplicity fled from his counterfeit presence
> As Gold the Pyrites would shun -
> What confusion would cover the innocent Jesus
> To meet so enabled a Man! (Fr 1266)

There are more syllables in this poem, both stressed and unstressed, than in the previous example above (here alternating lines of 12 and eight syllables). However the 4-3/4-3 metre of this poem enhances the preacher's inability to convey 'simplicity' by drawing out the repetitive hollowness of 'broad' and 'truth,' highlighting also the inability of language to capture the essence of such an all-encompassing knowledge of the divine. In contrast, the poem also reaffirms the need for a relative 'simplicity' when approaching the divine, going so far as to reproduce linguistic as well as cognitive absences; spaces where the divine can't be expressed or known. The parallel formation of the first two lines of the second stanza convey that simplicity is paradoxically also the essence of authenticity which eludes the most confident preacher. It is itself the 'gold' which does not belong with 'counterfeit' goods. The rare qualities which make gold more desirable than the 'pyrite' (the yellow mineral also known as 'fools' gold') are overlooked and 'shun[ned]'. Like gold overlooked, the preacher here shuns the imaginative space to contemplate the divine, which simplicity allows. The invited pun on pyrite/pirate further conveys the absurdity that pirates would never shun gold and therefore the preacher shunning simplicity is equally as misplaced. The imaginative space that the preacher shuns in this poem is echoed frequently in poems such as 'I'm Nobody! Who are you?' (Fr 260) which assert not so much self-abnegation or denial of physical pleasure, as a denial of the societal status which such 'counterfeit' knowledge of the divine promotes. As will be shown throughout this book, Dickinson's style and thematics invoke so many elements of hymns, such as the experience of divine 'revery,' and the concern with the individual's position within a congregation/church/community, that her use of hymns goes beyond an interest in the formal effects of using metre to register deviation and conflict.

Dickinson's use of the hymn is multi-faceted and therefore highlights the tensions within such a genre associated with spirituality. Her use of the hymn functions as an implicit critique of the domestic ideology which posits a sentimentalised/idealised version of the home, with woman as the moral centre and close to the paternal God. Equally, it offers critique on the public/political rhetoric which promotes a masculinised, militaristic version of God. Furthermore, at the same time as it connotes a space in which particular versions of the divine inscribed and enclosed within can be challenged, it also signals an alternative mystical space in which the divine cannot be enclosed or defined.

> Over and over, like a Tune -
> The Recollection plays -
> Drums off the Phantom Battlements
> Coronets of Paradise -
>
> Snatches, from Baptized Generations -
> Cadences too grand
> But for the Justified Processions
> At the Lord's Right hand. (Fr 406)

In the above poem Dickinson describes the enduring power of the tune. Rendered in the hymnic common metre, each line alternating between tetrameter and trimeter, the poem enacts the highly-effective connection between meaning and form. Reading the poem out aloud confirms that the hymn form being utilised serves to both display and perform the experience of recollection in hand and is itself the 'tune' which beats 'over and over.' Written in 1862 during the second period of the American Civil War, Dickinson's 'tune' calls into question the role of music in religion and war, but also queries the militaristic aspect of hymns which extol explicitly masculinised versions of the divine. The fragmentary 'snatches' and 'cadences' of the 'tune' are likened to and connected with the accoutrements of war and kingdoms ('drums,' 'coronets'). This conveys the importance of music as an integral supportive, cohesive mechanism for both the 'Baptized Generations' and the 'Phantom Battlements' described in each stanza. Dickinson invokes the 'Grand' hymns often sung during battle or afterwards to honour the war dead. They were sung to boost morale among troops and as a way of 'justifying' the sacrifice of their lives in war for the greater, higher cause of God's divine purpose.[35] Her use of the trimeter in the initial and alternating lines exploits these associations by reproducing an elegiac echo of those who fell in battle. Thus the poem plausibly reproduces the mode of a battle hymn honouring the war dead and the lives of those who have achieved their rightful and final resting place at the Lord's right hand as reward for dying in the line of duty.

However, the speaker's sense of separation is not measured against personal or envisaged human loss, but by her loss of (or impaired) hearing. The poem begins with the word 'Over' which echoes the speaker's despondency while also conveying a sense of distance and reverberation of sound. The repetition of 'over' with 'and' in between serves to slow the line down and stretch it out so that the lingering and trailing quality of the tune/recollection is performed audibly. The 'Recollection' that the speaker in the poem describes but does not go far to explain might as easily be from early childhood as from an idealised pre-birth or resurrected, post-death, heavenly state. As a whole, the rhythm of the poem conveys a sense of the speaker's separation from the source of sound, and therefore also from the idealised state of either Christian resurrection or political, princely victory. Dickinson's 'loss of hearing' in this poem conveys a lack of identification with the idea of Christian redemption. It also displays a critical awareness about the hymn being a powerful mode of public devotion frequently employed for the purpose of social cohesion.

As with other Dickinson poems where the idea of Christian redemption or paradise is invoked, there is a palpable sense of separation and distance between poem and speaker because the version of the redemption offered is inadequate. Echoing the Calvinist doctrine of Election and Predestination, the 'tune' of Christian redemption is obscured from the speaker due to Calvinism's creed of the selection of the few and concomitant exclusion of the many. The poem touches uneasily on this as the sacred tune indicative of heaven is relegated to the 'Baptized,' 'justified' few who are also at the 'Lord's Right hand.' Dickinson accentuates this separation by the sudden turn from the preceding trimeter of 'cadences too grand' to the tetrameter in the third line of the second stanza. In it the word 'for' is emphasised and signals a shift between the speaker's access to the sacred 'tune' and the 'justified processions' of those who are already redeemed. Furthermore, the coherence of the tune identified in the first stanza is broken into lesser 'snatches', and then more formally into 'cadences too grand' in the second. It is finally subsumed into the dominant rhythm of the poem itself, further accentuating the broken quality of the tune which has reached the speaker's world.

---

[35] For example, Julia Ward Howe's 'Battle Hymn of the Republic' (1862) became an anthem for Union troops during the Civil War, see Janet Gray, (ed.), *She Wields a Pen: American Women Poets of the Nineteenth Century* (London: J.M. Dent, 1997) p. 67.

This poem was written at the peak of Dickinson's poetic career, during her most prolific period. In it she displays an acute awareness of the power of its traditional form, normally reserved for Christian devotion. She manages to convey both an original poetic voice and resistance against the forces of separation and exclusion perpetuated by religious orthodoxy. Dickinson's subtle and powerful manipulation of the hymn form is not derived solely from an understanding of the effects which metrical emphasis or de-emphasis has on meaning. Although the compactness of the genre lends itself to being a structural platform for Dickinson's metrical variations, it is the associations of the hymn as a sacred form which promotes social cohesion that makes Dickinson's use of it so striking. By invoking the purposes and meanings implicit in the hymn as a devotional genre, as against her own experience of spirituality, Dickinson levels a series of challenges to the cohesive core of Protestant hymnody.

Much can be gained from analysing Dickinson's prosody in terms of the pressure it places on the hymn's parameters, as other critics have done.[36] However, focusing on the symbolic value of the hymn allows for a more expansive view of Dickinson's poetic vision. The hymn is an ideologically loaded genre and a traditionally sacred devotional space in which a woman's alternative/jarring experiences in relation to the divine can be interpreted as competing ideologies or theologies. Dickinson's association of traditional hymns with an oppressive Christian dogma is conveyed strongly in another poem which makes the use of 'tunes' explicit. This time a winter afternoon is compared with 'Cathedral Tunes':

> There's a certain Slant of light,
> Winter Afternoons -
> That oppresses, like the Heft
> Of Cathedral Tunes -
>
> Heavenly Hurt, it gives us -
> We can find no scar,
> But internal difference,
> Where the meanings, are -
>
> None may teach it - Any -
> 'Tis the Seal Despair -
> An imperial affliction
> Sent us of the Air -
>
> When it comes, the Landscape listens -
> Shadows - hold their breath -
> When it goes, 'tis like the Distance
> On the look of Death - (Fr 320)

---

[36] See for example, Christanne Miller, *Emily Dickinson: A Poet's Grammar* (Cambridge, MA: Harvard University Press, 1987) and Wendy Martin, *An American Triptych: Anne Bradstreet, Emily Dickinson, Adrienne Rich.*

Primarily the poem attempts to trace the origin of feelings of despair which appear to arrive almost as a seasonal change, 'from the air', like the change in light in winter. However, in likening winter light to a cathedral tune, the poem captures the oppressive weight ('heft') of religious dogma in Church practices. As a New England Congregationalist Dickinson would not have attended cathedrals as a child, but the scale of a cathedral organ rather than a country church organ or piano lends weight to the metaphor of oppressive religious orthodoxy. It also invokes a Puritan's dissenting relation to an Episcopal mode of worship. The 'listening' landscape, like a church congregation, is altered ('internal difference') by the change in tone which winter brings. Such a change as perhaps from the optimism of spring and birth to the reminder of death and possible salvation or damnation that might be exacted thereafter. Although in reality the seasonal change is a natural, cyclical process, the transition from birth to death in Dickinson's portrayal of winter is conveyed with deliberate and horrifying linearity. Once death has arrived, the message the 'tune' appears to bring is that there can be no turning back; 'tis like the Distance/ On the look of Death.' The poem produces a dialogical tension between the finite, linear journey of mortality, the transition from this world to the next implied in the weight of 'Cathedral tunes', against the cyclical, endlessly regenerative reality of the changing seasons. One is mapped onto the other with momentarily horrifying consequences. The congregation, or nature, is temporarily stunned by the prospect of stasis instead of the natural, flowing energy. The 'slant' of light, like a blade that wounds, not only recalls Christ's suffering and crucifixion but also induces suffering in the speaker that is in turn produced by the scene before her. However, unlike the wound in Christ's side which provided material evidence of his resurrection to the disciples, the congregational 'we' whom the speaker speaks on behalf of, cannot find a corresponding wound. There is no evidence ('we can find no scar') to trace the damage or 'hurt' which the reminder of death in the 'tune' of the dying season has inflicted.

Although the speaker maintains that 'none may teach' this apprehension of 'despair,' the fact that it is conveyed in terms of a Church ritual (it is the hymn tune which arrives through the 'air') implies a connection between religious dogma and the pain of human suffering. The light which arrives from above effects a change, and symbolises the moment of heavenly judgement upon which salvation or damnation rests. However, the poem concludes by returning to the cyclicality of the seasons, over what has been a temporary disruption. When the particular light-effect brought on by winter finally recedes, there is perhaps an opportunity for hope. The passing despair brought on by the light is, after all, only 'like' the distance on the look of death, not actually death itself. In this way, the poem illustrates how 'despair' becomes an effect of particular uses of religious dogma, such as Calvinist fear of judgement or damnation, as expressed in popular hymns like those of Watts. It also conveys Dickinson's poetic counter to this dogma. The poem makes evident the temporary and subordinate position Christian dogma and its 'tunes' occupies in relation to nature's ultimate indefatigability. By implication that dogma is also subordinate to human feeling, which in this poem is intimately connected to nature's cycles.

Where 'Cathedral Tunes' in poem Fr 320 are associated with the weight of internalised despair, in Fr 891 the hymn is invoked as a part of the heavenly 'new fireside', the new 'Home' of relation and friendship:

> I learned - at least - what Home could be -
> How ignorant I had been
> Of pretty ways of Covenant -
> How awkward at the Hymn
>
> Round our new Fireside - but for this -
> This pattern - of the way -
> Whose Memory drowns me, like the Dip
> Of a Celestial Sea -
>
> What Mornings in our Garden - guessed -
> What Bees - for us - to hum -
> With only Birds to interrupt
> The Ripple of our Theme - (Fr 891)

The speaker associates the new rituals of friendship and love with those of traditional worship ('How awkward at the hymn') and describes a new mode of being ('This pattern - of the way -') in which experience is unfettered and 'rippling'. Such freedom is reflected and enacted (again, invoking hymn singing) in nature ('What Bees - for us - to hum -'). In contrast with poem Fr 320, the hymn is invoked in this poem to convey an alternative mode of relation which is, for the speaker, divine.

Dickinson's work challenges the parameters of the hymn, not only for demarcating social cohesion, but also the limits and boundaries within patriarchally conceived notions of the divine and of praise. Traditional distinctions between hymns and poetry are also predicated upon assumptions about the nature and form of religious worship. They focus on defining features of such worship, such as the articulation of faith in and praise towards God. However, the distinction between hymns and poetry is less clear than the proliferation and amount of study devoted to the study of hymns suggests. Since the eighteenth century, the distinction between hymns and the poetic and lyrical expression of religious lyrics has been increasingly less clear. Poetry, if it is executed in the hymn style with similar metre and themes, and is concerned with the negotiation and expression spirituality, cannot be entirely divorced from the realm of hymnody.

When Dickinson uses hymn metre it is almost always merely a cursory allusion to regularity, being in the main, highly irregular in its execution. There are some poems in the Dickinson corpus which are in the hymn common metre and are also strictly regular. Equally, there are also early experiments with longer verse lines, such as Dickinson's 'Valentine' poem (40 lines in rhyming couplets), and later poems which tend towards the economic aphorism such as Fr1720 and 1727, which are only two lines long. Such poems show that Dickinson was clearly capable of writing in a variety of verse formations. Her decision to use form in a way that alludes to hymns at all, whether that be to highlight her own 'deviations' and irregularities or not, suggests a level of engagement with that genre which inevitably includes, but also goes beyond, formal concerns such as metre. As established earlier with reference to a woman's place in the domestic sphere, hymns were associated with feminine submission to the (patriarchal and patriarchally conceived) divine. Such an association makes it a particularly attractive genre for Dickinson, whose poetry describes, recapitulates and re-inscribes versions of the divine through her own experience of it. By alluding to the hymn, a genre of worship, as she does in Fr 891 and also in Fr 320 with her reference to 'Cathedral Tunes', Dickinson is able to both interrogate and critique religious culture. Personal rebellion is thus enclosed and disguised at the same time as being pointedly highlighted. Such a dialogic approach provides trajectories for alternatives to the dominant ideologies at work in traditional hymns. A *heterologous space* of relation to religious tradition is forged within the poems to allow escapes and to generate new metaphors for personal experience of the divine.

Hymns and Performativity

A key aspect of Dickinson's engagement with hymns is their power to generate questions about unity and social cohesion. It is the association with communal participation which makes hymnody, and Dickinson's use of it, highly performative. The act of writing a hymn invokes the participation of a shared community, with shared ideas about God, and anticipates listeners and those who would engage in singing together despite whether or not the hymn is actually put to music and sung. The ways in which a hymnic text asserts or elides conclusive statements about God means that it also takes a position on hierarchical structures and the associated values upon which orthodox religion resides. Such values are encoded within the schema of the hymn form in various ways. Francis O'Gorman includes four Victorian hymns in his anthology of poetry and outlines in his annotation the 'qualities of a good hymn' which he argues should be:

> Consistent in theme, but not repetitive; progressive in the development of ideas
> (and moving towards a climax) but not confusingly rapid or overweighted with
> thought, and with a clear meaning to each line, even if enjambment is used (and,
> of course, absolutely metrical). [37]

In this sense hymns in general, and Dickinson's critical use of hymn structures and motifs, is performative. Not in the standard usage of 'performative', for example in relation to performing an oath, but in the way that they engage with the assumed stylistic expectations of a hymn, as outlined above. Dickinson's poems are performative in the way they rupture such expectations, linguistically

---

[37] Francis O'Gorman, (ed.), *Victorian Poetry: An Annotated Anthology* (Oxford: Blackwell, 2004) p. 566.

and conceptually. They perform a disruption and renegotiation of a hymn's symbolic values. The extent to which hymns meet with expectations of what a 'good hymn' should be, as those outlined above, correlates with the degree of satisfaction both the writer and the listener/singer feel with the mode of devotion being expressed. A crucial aspect of Dickinson's use of the hymn is its ability, like the praxis of mystical discourse, to make visible the moments of disagreement which the speaker in her poems often articulates. Dickinson's poems represent relation to the divine against that which Protestant hymnody asserts through the 'development of ideas' 'moving towards a climax' and with the 'clear meaning' that they seek to convey. Thus Protestant hymnody can be described as 'linear,' and as possessing a unilateral movement from the speaker towards the divine, which is necessarily free from rupture, 'confusion,' or 'overweighted thought.' The performative aspect of hymns is also important in connection with Dickinson because it replicates how the hymn writer regards their position, and worthiness of their hymn writing, as good work. As Chapter 4 will discuss, Isaac Watts's regard for himself as a producer of praise, as a writer of hymns, also enables him to take lyrical and sublime 'flight'. This 'flight' cannot be divorced, at times, from a dedication to poetic autonomy which is essentially counter to the Calvinist and Puritan requirement for simplicity and piety in art. The 'good work' of the hymn also feeds, playfully, into Dickinson's view of herself as industrious artist.

An aspect of hymn culture which is related to the performativity of hymns is that they are often perceived by their writers as a suitable form of labour. The ultimate goal of the Evangelical hymnist is to spread the 'good news' of the gospels, of Christ's resurrection and the possibility of immortality through faith in and duty towards God. The hymn more than any other genre posits a self-reflexivity on the nature of articulation through writing, because of the work ethic that Protestant Christianity in particular emphasises. As the detailed discussion in Section Three of this book will show, the notion of industry is a central concern for Puritans. Watts's popular verse for children 'How doth the busy bee' epitomises this, and Dickinson's engagement with orthodox religion explores and frequently parodies this aspect of Puritan culture. A hymn writer's relation to the work she/he creates differs somewhat from that of secular poetry because of the moral expectations that the particular branch of religion the writer chooses to follow places upon the genre. For example, Unitarian hymnody seeks to emphasise the unified nature or essence of God, as opposed to the Trinitarian concept of three distinct but essentially linked aspects of Father, Son and Holy Ghost. The Unitarian hymn writer seeks to convey a sense of unity in both the scene she/he describes and the attitude towards the self that they adopt. The hymn form simultaneously has expectations placed upon it through its usage within established Conformist or Anglican practice. The relative simplicity of the hymn common metre conveys the assumption of praise to a clearly defined Christian God, but Dickinson's use of it invokes these expectations only to rupture and radically reconfigure them.

Recent scholarship in Dickinson studies which aims to locate Dickinson's work within and in relation to nineteenth-century literary and popular culture inevitably attends to the forms of Protestant hymnody that are present in her work. It also takes into account the modes which make it performative. Critics such as Jay Ladin and Christine Ross see the hymn form as one of many, but not the primary influence on Dickinson's poetic style.[38] In order to connect Dickinson's mode with that of American twentieth-century modernist writers, Jay Ladin utilises Bakhtin's terms 'centripetal' and 'centrifugal' to describe her dialogic voice. Ladin observes Dickinson's dialogic voice in the ways her poems use and fuse both modes of discourse which either recapitulate or resist socially formulated hierarchies. He argues that in this way her dialogic voice produces a 'centrifugally weighted balance of centripetal and centrifugal forces' within the poems.

Bakhtin's terms are useful here as they describe a movement away from the centre outwards (centrifugal) and a driving force towards the centre (centripetal) that can be applied to the 'I-Thou' model of address in traditional hymnody. Bakhtin writes:

> Every utterance participates in the 'unitary language' (in its centripetal forces and tendencies) and at the same time partakes of social and historical heteroglossia (the centrifugal, stratifying forces).[39]

He then goes on to describe the 'contradiction-ridden, tension-filled unity of two embattled tendencies in the life of language' (Bakhtin, p. 272). The dual and competing forces of Dickinson's poetics can be seen, as Ladin has shown, in relation to the structure of hymnody. Ladin agrees with David Reynolds that the pattern and structure of English hymnody provides Dickinson (as it did other women poets) with a method to contain disparate elements of her many literary influences.[40] Ladin argues that Dickinson's poems incorporate centripetal aspects derived from the prosody of Protestant hymnody, because of the association of them with thought and feeling moving towards a reachable, and easily accessible 'centre' of God. Movement towards reaching the centre of God and of defining the divine can be seen as a centripetal or 'unitary' force. However, the drive to see and reach the divine and achieve spiritual transcendence in the act of singing hymns

---

[38]   Christine Ross, 'Uncommon Measures: Emily Dickinson's Subversive Prosody', *The Emily Dickinson Journal* 10:1 (2001) 70–98. Jay Ladin, "So Anthracite to Live:' Emily Dickinson and American Literary History', *The Emily Dickinson Journal* 13:1 (2004) 19–50 (p. 28). Ladin cites Bakhtin's terms which are related to the discourse of the novel in *The Dialogic Imagination: Four Essays by M.M. Bakhtin* (ed.), Michael Holquist (Austin: University of Texas Press, 1981) pp. 272–3.

[39]   *The Dialogic Imagination: Four Essays by M.M. Bakhtin*, p. 272.

[40]   David S. Reynolds, 'Emily Dickinson and Popular Culture,' p. 189. Reynolds concludes his analysis of the influence of popular culture evident in Dickinson's poems, such as temperance literature, by writing; 'She appropriated the iambic rhythms and simple verse patterns of English hymnody, which had been famously utilized in the Isaac Watts hymns she knew from childhood, as controlling devices to lend structure and resonance to these disparate themes.'

can be described as a centrifugal movement extending away from the self towards the divine. This version of the divine is usually described as being 'above' the self. Dickinson's poems animate both forces, and collapse the traditional 'I-Thou' distinction by using the hymn as a mode of expression which articulates the divine in the self as much as in relation. This allows the possibility for space and dialogic movement between centripetal and centrifugal modes. Instead of replicating the linear movement upwards to a fixed God-head, Dickinson's poems restore the centrifugal aspect of hymn address and forge a multiple and diverse relation which is connoted by flight imagery and non-static metaphors. In this way, they illuminate further the absence or space which is left when the centripetal impulses of patriarchal hymnody and orthodox religion's relation to God the Father fail. The desire to reach a fixed centre of God often leads to a u-turn, a turning outwards and away from the self that produces a quality of incompleteness or rupture which is often found in traditional church hymns.

Even Isaac Watts's boldly devotional hymns include instances where such a movement is problematised by the speaker's limiting, human and temporal position in relation to God's timelessness. This is evident in hymns such as 'Sight through a glass, and face to face,' where Watts employs Pauline imagery to describe his separation from God. Watts dislikes the 'interposing days' which mean that he has to tolerate 'a glass between' him and God. (*HSS*, II, 145: 458–9)[41] Even Watts's hymns depict the speaker as travelling along a path that is primarily only *ideally* centripetal, held in place by the speaker's faith in a centrifugal movement from the self towards God. Crucially, perceiving God as a fixed point to get to, rather than as present and dispersed within and without each tangential dimension, including those of the self, is a central concern in representations of the divine and theological interpretation. Such models describe the way in which Dickinson's poems negotiate hymn space to perform the movement of diverse and multiple relation which moves simultaneously both outwards towards the divine and inwards towards the divine, thus dissolving the 'I-Thou' model of address. Her admission that 'when I try to organize - my little Force explodes - and leaves me bare and charred -' (To T.W. Higginson, August 1862, SL, p. 178) suggests that her poetic force fed upon the destruction of such methods of organisation.

The structure and premise of hymns, in that they articulate the speaker's relation to the divine, the voice of the created towards the Creator, serves only to collapse both categories. The speaker's relation to the 'centre' is always suspended, always in process, as opposed one movement either away from it or towards it. Bakhtin's terms are useful for describing movement in Dickinson's linguistic modes and

---

[41] Isaac Watts, *The Psalms, Hymns and Spiritual Songs of the Rev. Isaac Watts, D.D. To which are added Select Hymns from other Authors; and Directions for Musical Expression* (Boston: Samuel T. Armstrong and Crocker and Brewster, 1832) p. 458. From *Hymns and Spiritual Songs* (1707–1709), Book II, Hymn 145. Hereafter abbreviated to '*HSS*' followed by hymn and page number as appears in the cited 1832 collection of Watts, '*PHSS*'.

assimilation of cultural influences. However, another model needs to be invoked in order to describe the mode of the hymn, which is, contrary to Ladin's claim, both centripetal and centrifugal, and therefore also is Dickinson's relation to it. The following chapter assesses alternatives to the 'I-Thou' model of relation in hymnody and considers Certeau's notion of heterologies as one such alternative.

Dickinson's interpretation of the imagery and form of hymnody does not present itself as being an easy option. Moreover, Dickinson makes a difficult choice to connect expression of spiritual experience with the modes of religious orthodoxy. It is more difficult for her than for established male poets such as Bryant or Longfellow. The separate-spheres ideology would not influence interpretation of their hymns as being the product of ideal domesticity and Christian morality. As nineteenth-century commentators on hymns such as Mrs Pitman illustrate, the hymn is often associated with ideas of social cohesion, allowing for the articulation of spiritual praise across social division.[42] Dickinson's engagement with the popular form of hymnody articulates a voice which is not only or merely 'heretical' in the context of its response to evangelical Protestantism. Watts offers a precedent for creative autonomy and for heterodoxy within the terms of conventional Dissent as well as being a barometer for orthodoxy. Dickinson's responses to Protestantism are stimulated by hope as much as by religious doubt. The heterologous, performative space of the hymn form paradoxically allows hope to be enacted, repeated and perpetuated. That is to say, in Dickinson's critical engagement with orthodox religion we can see the expression of a struggle for a sense of 'unity' and community that could not be ascertained without a series of problematic collisions.

Dickinson famously remarked that her 'business' was 'circumference'; 'Perhaps you smile at me. I could not stop for that - My Business is Circumference - ' (To T.W. Higginson, July 1862, SL, p. 176). This comment is instructive because it describes a process which privileges circumnavigation over linearity. This can be compared with the modes of writing or speaking about the divine to be found in mystical discourse (which will be discussed in the following chapter). The effort to describe a pattern as opposed to defining what that pattern might contain or explain to the reader is paramount in mystical discourse. Similarly, a dedication to 'circumference' can be seen in Dickinson's engagement with hymn culture, where narratives of linearity and definitions of the divine are persistently destabilised. Dickinson's poetry shares with mystical discourse a reluctance to define or rely upon a locus or centre when articulating spiritual experience. Moreover, although a subversion of and challenge to the modes and assumptions of evangelical Protestantism is produced in Dickinson's hymn-like poems, so also is a new form of devotion. A devotion ('Business') to describing the relation between self and world ('Circumference') through the medium of poetry. For Dickinson, poetic expression and spiritual experience are symbiotic and her poetry articulates the tension this produces. In her dialogic response to Protestant hymnody, by exposing

---

[42]   See E.R. Pitman, *The Lady Hymn Writers*, p. 19.

the gaps in its assumed ontology, Dickinson is bound to an unconventional poetics where community, individuality and space are always in tension.

The ability to inscribe the divine in language is a topic which occupies a large area in feminist theology, philosophy and literary criticism. Feminist critics Luce Irigaray, Hélène Cixous and Julia Kristeva each draw upon Lacanian psychoanalytic theories of subject formation in order to identify a feminine 'jouissance' or Other or 'abject' (linguistic ruptures) which the patriarchal symbolic order cannot accommodate.[43] In the following chapter the work of Luce Irigaray and Michel de Certeau will be discussed alongside the idea of spirituality as community and relation, as expressed in feminist theology. Although Certeau's work is not explicitly 'feminist',[44] the works of both Irigaray and Certeau under scrutiny here share a concern with mysticism that is rooted in issues of specificity and practicality. This provides one theoretical framework through which to read Dickinson's performative hymns. Here the hymn form as a dominant structure can be likened to a mirror which is fractured, and also re-envisioned by Dickinson. It is re-envisioned not as a single, unified reflection, but as a mosaic with multiple refractions all held in relation to each by a frame. The theoretical writings of Irigaray and Certeau, which draw on psychoanalytic models of subject formation and of 'the other' in different ways, present an alternative to the mirror of false representation that is the symbolic. The alternatives to representation within the symbolic order that their writing demonstrates can be compared with Dickinson's re-visioning of the hymn and assertion of spiritual experience.

---

[43] See Luce Irigaray, 'Divine Women,' in *Sexes and Genealogies*, pp. 57–88, Hélène Cixous, 'Sorties: Out and Out: Attacks/Ways Out/ Forays', and Julia Kristeva, 'Women's Time', both in Catherine Belsey and Jane Moore, (eds), *The Feminist Reader: Essays in Gender and the Politics of Literary Criticism*, 2nd edn (London: Macmillan, 1997) pp. 91–103 and pp. 201–16.

[44] Certeau associates 'feminine discourse' with the mystical in his concept of 'heterologies', the practice of voicing the other; 'it is still a theology (a discourse of the male, of the unique, of the same: a henology) that excludes the mystical (an altered feminine discourse: a heterology).' *Heterologies: Discourse on the Other*, p. 165.

Chapter 3
Theorising Hymnic Space:
Language, Subjectivity and
Re-Visioning the Divine

Why - do they shut me out of Heaven?
Did I sing - too loud?
But - I can say a little "minor"
Timid as a Bird! (Fr 268)

The previous chapter provided an outline of the tradition of hymnody and illustrated how the frequent 'protests' in Dickinson's work can be identified as being in defiant opposition to such a tradition. Traditional hymnody has been appropriated to privilege and recapitulate patriarchal and hierarchical versions of the divine and to promote ideas of 'social cohesion' that reflect such structuring. The explicit challenge and protest in the stanza above is pointedly positioned by Dickinson within the context of singing. Exiled from 'Heaven', the speaker reminds us of the hierarchical power exerted by a congregation of others ('they') who define 'correct' spirituality and how it should be expressed. The speaker's comparatively 'minor' voice and role, as one 'shut out' from both the dominant discourses and social organisation of spirituality can be registered and described with technical precision. Dickinson's technical disruption of traditional hymn metrics is undoubtedly a marker of her engagement with such a tradition. This will be considered fully in the following chapter in relation to critical reception of Dickinson's use of Wattsian hymnody. However, the level of Dickinson's engagement with hymn culture can be seen as extending beyond this in important ways. Understanding the ways in which Dickinson uses the hymn as a dynamic space, in a manner that offers comparisons with a mystic's relation to language and form, allows further insight into the gravity and complexity of her engagement with hymn culture. Using theoretical discourse on the divine in language and theology provides us with critical tools to describe what is generated by this engagement, other than parody. Whilst her use of hymnic space alludes to the modes of traditional hymnody it also generates space in which the divine can be re-imagined.

This chapter works towards a consideration of Michel de Certeau's writing on 'Mystic Speech', via feminist conceptions of the divine in theology and Luce Irigaray's writing on belief and the female divine. It formulates a theoretical basis for *hymnic space*, which will be referred to and used throughout this book in relation to the expression of spirituality, and connection between spirituality and writing, in Dickinson's work. Certeau and Irigaray are employed in this theoretical basis because of their relationship with absence, or space. The qualities that their writings share with mystical discourse are primarily connected to such absence, to gaps and spaces.[1] This chapter traces Irigaray's ideas of the female divine (viewing Irigaray's writing itself to a certain extent as a mystical discourse) through to Certeau's writing on mystical discourse. It explores the mystic's ability to use language in a way which both conveys experience of the divine and yet avoids defining it. In this way the mystic's writing generates space. The work of Irigaray and Certeau is helpful at this point because it describes the production of space in ways which can be applied to readings of poetic language. The various methods of expression used to achieve this production of space, which is both outlined and demonstrated in their work, is instructive when reading Dickinson's use of hymnic space. Mystical discourse is used in this chapter and referred to throughout with a particular emphasis on its ability to make absences and spaces visible. However, before describing the linguistic and literary aspects of expressing the divine in these two writers, this chapter will first examine the defining 'problem'; the hierarchical nature of hymn address. It will then consider the ideas of community in feminist theology in order to establish the alternatives to patriarchally conceived notions of the divine in theology. Points of contact will then be identified between ideas of community in feminist theology, features of mystical discourse, and the ideas of relation to be found in Dickinson's work. Thus a theoretical basis will be established for analysing the use of hymnic space in Dickinson' vast performative body of 'alternative hymns.'

The Act of Naming: Hierarchies in Hymn Address

Graham Ward (2005) describes the hymn as being 'a response to the reception of what is given'. He identifies this process, which he sees as being at work in the hymn, as being ultimately an 'act of naming:'

> One of the main shifts within the hymn is from the language of form (morphe and schema) to the act of naming. The act of naming is made to participate in the form of revelation – for the name revealed, and then confessed, is God's own name, Lord. [2]

The notion of the hymn as being both an 'act of naming' God, and also as a response to what 'is given' has crucial implications when accounting for the different versions of the speaker-God relation depicted in hymns, especially those

---

[1]   Both writers have origins in philosophy and psychoanalysis and frequently display a mystical style of writing which lends itself to inter-disciplinarity. Ward describes Certeau's 'oeuvre' as 'a continual [...] journeying from one [...] academic discipline to another, crossing, recrossing and confusing disciplinary boundaries.' *The Certeau Reader* (ed.), Graham Ward (Oxford: Blackwell, 2000) p. 2.

[2]   Graham Ward, *Christ and Culture* (Oxford: Blackwell, 2005) p. 185.

written by women. If experience of the divine is not conceived of in terms of a fundamental difference or separation ('I-Thou') or a teleological trajectory (Earth-Heaven) then the forms and imagery of a hymn will be an expression of this. By Ward's definition, a hymn is characterised by a 'self-reflexive meditation,' which supposes that the version of self being reflexive is traceable and known, just as God must be traceable and known within the traditional hymn. The performative aspect of the genre thus goes beyond church singing. The 'poetic performance' that the hymn allows provides a space for particular versions of the divine to come into being and to be 'enacted':

> In other words, the hymn re-presents. It is not separated as an act from the action it tells. It is a poetic enactment reflecting upon three enfolded forms of representation [...] and the act of naming and speaking as a response to the reception of what is given. The hymn is characterised by a self-reflexive meditation upon the theological, ethical and linguistic imitation - salvation, the appropriate behaviour of those being saved and language. The kenotic economy turns, then, upon [...] words associated with mimesis [...].[3]

However, if the hymn is a reflection, a 'poetic performance', then there is also, to a certain extent, always a sublimation or masking of experience of the divine at work in the hymn as well. A palatable version of experience of the divine is reproduced within the hymn with the point of being (and in terms to be) understood by others. If a recognisable term such as 'Lord' or 'God' is reproduced by the 'act of naming,' then by Ward's definition, the point of the hymn has been achieved. Indeed, the act of naming God appears to be the point of the expression of the hymn. The self-reflexivity, the process by which such a conclusion, such a version of God, is reproduced within it, is often subsumed by this act of naming in traditional hymnody. Therefore if the point of the hymn is not for the comprehension and vicarious experience of others to reaffirm a shared faith (i.e. a congregation or community of worshippers) then the hymn, by this definition, would be unintelligible and ultimately pointless. The fact that the hymn is perceived as being mimetic, and mirror-like, and as a traditionally sacred genre with an implied revelatory authorial intention which cannot be challenged is inextricably bound to the power of language and 'act of naming' which it preserves.

The 'I-Thou' model of address in traditional hymnody connotes a relation that is linear and teleological, invoking vertical (and it is hoped reciprocal) movement between the speaker and God. As in this example from Watts:

> My God, my life, my love,
> To thee, to thee I call;
> I cannot live, if thou remove,
> For thou art all in all. (*HSS*, II, 93:431)

---

3   Ibid, p. 185.

Although the sentiment is that God is everywhere and is 'all in all', the relation of 'I-Thou' which the speaker repeats serves not to demonstrate the 'all in all' but only the nature of the relation being described. With Ward's notion of the hymn involving mimesis in mind, the hymn therefore acts as the mirror of representation that reflects both particular versions of the divine and assertions of subjectivity which are both inherently exclusionary. Traditional hymns are inherently exclusionary not merely in ways relating to gender because a vast majority utilise androcentric pronouns and imagery, but because of the fundamental premise of separation which the 'I-Thou' relation in hymn address endlessly re-enacts. The implications this premise of separation has are wide-reaching. If separation, opposition and teleological narratives lie at the core of a vision of the divine then these values are inevitably recapitulated through our sense of ourselves (subjectivities) and in turn, through social ordering. The mimetic, performative quality of the hymn, by Ward's definition, means that it is also has an immensely transformative power. One cited definition of the hymn is that it displays 'clear meaning' that should be both 'progressive', 'consistent' and result in a 'climax'. (O'Gorman, p. 51) Although Dickinson was not aligned to a particular religious group and we would therefore not expect her poems to divulge 'clear meaning' about the divine, her use of the hymn form and of flight imagery common in hymnody suggests an attachment to the communal aspect of the devotional mode. Moreover, her poetics reinscribe an alternative version of the divine which goes against the teleological elements of the hymn as the ones cited above.

The 'I-Thou' address in traditional hymnody is only one version of relation. Dickinson's poetics of flight, and particularly her use of bee imagery, serve to carve out an alternative, multiple and multivalent *relationality*. Her use of form and imagery is conducive to poetics which are anti-teleological and open. While some traditional hymns are relational in the sense that they invoke community and communal 'I', or 'we', the emphasis on diverse relationality as opposed to a linear, teleological relation negotiates the dual 'I-Thou' and shifts emphasis away from phallocentric versions of the divine. In this way, Dickinson's use of hymn metre signals identification with a particular group and traditional forms of worship and also establishes her separation from them. She refuses to offer a 'legitimate' self and uses the style of the hymn and associated imagery to highlight her deviation from Non-Conformist and Evangelical churches. It also highlights the extent to which her re-visioned metaphors of transcendence differ from that of traditional hymnody. Dickinson draws on notions of childhood correction, morality and development to register her comparative 'disobedience' and also her own separation from depictions of the recuperative self. She refuses to 'tell' her own devotion directly ('Tell all the truth but tell it slant' Fr 1263) because the terms which are on offer muzzle and constrain. Instead, she produces the unexpected, appropriating the forms/terms which aim to legitimise her, thus evading genuine opportunity for such legitimisation to occur. Perhaps one of the reasons Dickinson's work perplexes many critics who aim to classify it is because her resistance to such classification was and is political. The speaker in Dickinson's hymnic poems plays with the pointers of a legitimised self whilst using them at the same time to register defiance and deviance. The use of hymn metre is one such pointer. It constructs a 'legitimate' frame around her poetics and signals a 'traditional' devotional mode whilst also highlighting the deviations from what would be expected in a traditional hymn. Another is the use of particular imagery traditionally associated with religious devotion and spiritual transcendence (and especially 'angelic', pious females) such as wings and associated imagery of flight ('Some keep the Sabbath in Surplice -/ I, just wear my Wings -' Fr 236). The use of bee imagery (also signalling non-static flight) is another pointer of legitimacy which conveys the notion of 'justification' for work/writing which the hymn requires, as it invokes the model for the Protestant work ethic ('His labour is a Chant-/ His Idleness - a Tune - ' Fr 979). The bee also serves, simultaneously, as a trope for the radical alternative spiritual flight of her own 'erring' poetics ('Fame is a Bee' Fr 1788).[4] Her poetics constantly remind us of the orthodoxy of her religious, literary and political culture and in doing so also pose the question of whether her writing is a 'legitimate' practice or not. She reminds us, therefore, that her alternative 'hymns' enact a worship and praise that is born out of the rebellion they articulate.

As established in Chapter 2, the label of 'traditional hymns' is used in this book to refer largely to the work of 'canonical' hymnists, such as Isaac Watts and Charles Wesley. Traditional hymns have been both conceived of and appropriated by their various authors and hymnal editors to mould theology and to colonise the devotional space of the hymn. Assumptions about linearity and fixity with regard to the speaker-God relation have been imposed upon this space. This has affected the ways in which many hymns, including those written by women, have been read as reasserting ideas of a specific type of social cohesion that supports a God-Man-Woman hierarchical model. As will be discussed in the following chapter, most critical examinations of the influence of Watts's hymns on Dickinson's verse focus upon the extent to which Watts's metre presents a 'regularity' to be subverted.[5] Such a 'regularity' of metre correlates also with the apparent transparency and clarity of the depiction of spiritual 'truths' in Watts's hymns. This 'regularity' implies also a linearity of argument and a degree of fixity in a perception of the divine. For example, Shira Wolosky's 1988 study on rhetoric and biblical tropes in Dickinson presents the argument that she 'makes explicit' the problematic relation between figuration and Christian truth in Watts's hymns. In other words, the supposed clarity in Watts's depiction of biblical events and figures to convey

---

[4]   'Erring' is Mark C. Taylor's term for discourse which navigates linearity and opposition in language, thus producing an alternative discourse akin to mystical writing which voices the 'other.' See Mark C. Taylor, *Erring: A Postmodern A/Theology* (Chicago: The University of Chicago Press, 1987) (pp. 8–9).

[5]   For example, Wendy Martin identifies a 'rigid regularity' and 'pious certainty' in Watts's hymns. *An American Triptych: Anne Bradstreet, Emily Dickinson, Adrienne Rich*, pp. 138–9.

spiritual truth is undermined by Dickinson's use of similar conventions, phrases and idioms which do not convey a similar effect.[6]

Graham Ward's definition of the hymn as a genre that involves 'poetic performance' and the notion of mimesis (Ward, *Christ and Culture*, p. 185) is crucial in understanding the ideological disruption Dickinson's engagement with hymnody produces. The writings of Certeau and Irigaray highlight the performative aspect of mystical discourse and of writing the 'other', which can be usefully compared with Dickinson's invocation of community and multiple relation through non-static metaphors of flight. The communicable and received knowledge apparent in traditional hymnody (or the 'response to the reception of what is given' as Ward describes in *Christ and Culture*, p. 185.), as the following chapter explores in Watts's hymns, provides Dickinson with a structure against which to juxtapose her own experiences. Dickinson's poetic meditations on the divine are frequently connected with gaps and absences ('Can the Dumb - define the Divine? / The definition of Melody - is - / That definition is none -' Fr 849) and in this sense her poetic strategies are akin to the 'non-saying' of the divine in mystical discourse. However, despite the non-saying and 'gaps' the poetry reproduces, it also produces challenges to religious orthodoxy. It performs resistance within language via an engagement with hymn culture and the versions of the divine which it generates. In challenging the vertical linearity of hymns, Dickinson's poems make a significant 'act' within language, performing subjectivity, and thus inscribing her own version of the divine. Reading Dickinson as a subversive hymn writer brings into sharp focus the importance of writing as an act which is performative. The assumption of addressing and communicating with the divine that the hymn form contains, and which Ward's definition describes, presents a particularly strong case for its performativity and for viewing it as 'poetic performance' (Ward, *Christ and Culture*, p. 185). By using the hymn form Dickinson 'act[s] in language'[7] and both engages with a past discourse and registers the effects of the present upon it, producing a site for an immanence of her own, and for the expression of her own version of the divine in poetry.

Feminist Theology: Re-visioning the Divine through Relation

The implications of the hierarchical model of relation of 'I-Thou', which is common in prayer and a central feature of traditional hymnody, is also a focus in

------

[6]   Wolosky lists several examples of phrases from Watts alongside similar formulations used by Dickinson, which have the effect of undermining the cognitive ease and depiction of 'truth' in Watts's use of particular images. See Shira Wolosky, 'Rhetoric or Not: Hymnal Tropes in Emily Dickinson and Isaac Watts,' pp. 214–32 in *The New England Quarterly* Vol. 61, June, 1998. p. 216.

[7]   As will be discussed further in this chapter, Sabine Sielke's term for the 'intertextual networking' she identifies in Dickinson, Moore and Rich. See Sabine Sielke, *Fashioning the Female Subject: The Intertextual Networking of Dickinson, Moore and Rich* (Michigan: The University of Michigan Press, 1997) (p. 228).

much feminist theology. Re-visioning the definition of a hymn inevitably involves a radical reconsideration of its central defining quality, that is, the depiction of the speaker's relation to God through the 'I-Thou' address. Hymns by women are of particular interest in this respect, as depictions of God are negotiated around the associations of gender and the limiting binaries proliferated by orthodox religion. There are many limiting binaries which serve to reinscribe hierarchical structuring, such as God/Human, Man/Woman, Mind/Body, Good/Evil and so on. Much of recent feminist theology's search for an alternative to a patriarchal, phallogocentric version of the divine has led to discussions of alternative metaphors and symbols for the divine which invoke the qualities of relation and community. Some feminist theologians rely upon theological symbolism, whilst others attempt to develop their own metaphors. Such developments in feminist theology provide an important example of an engagement with religious forms and symbolism, and the need for an alternative to those of an established religious tradition, whether theologically based or otherwise. 'Liberation theologian' Sharon Welch, argues for:

> [...] a search for alternative symbols and structures of religious life that might effectively challenge oppressive manifestations of faith (symbols, rituals, polity, doctrines) and that might meet, in less oppressive ways, some of the needs being met by the problematic religious discourse. The truth of such theological construction is not measured by its 'coherence' or 'adequacy' but by its efficacy in enhancing a particular process of liberation.[8]

Welch finds her own appropriate metaphor in 'beloved community', that site of relational inter-subjective power which does not depend upon an externalised 'God':

> An appropriate symbol for the process of celebrating life, enduring limits, and resisting injustice is not the kingdom of God; it is the beloved community. The kingdom of God implies conquest, control, and final victory over the elements of nature as well as over the structures of injustice. The 'beloved community' names the matrix within which life is celebrated, love is worshipped, and partial victories over injustice lay the groundwork for further acts of criticism and courageous defiance. (Welch, pp. 160–61)

Welch's symbol, or metaphor of the beloved community, is problematic in that it stands for both the dissolution of, and transcendence of, social boundaries including those constructed around gender and class. It also prescribes resting with the 'conflicts of social life and the limitations of nature' that 'cannot be controlled or transcended' (Welch, p. 159). Such a model seems to reconstruct conflict as much as it attempts to renegotiate it.[9] Mary Daly and Daphne Hampson similarly set

---

8   Sharon D. Welch, *A Feminist Ethics of Risk* (Minneapolis: Fortress Press, 2000) p. 158.

9   For further discussion on Welch, see Grace Janzen, *Becoming Divine: Towards a Feminist Philosophy of Religion* (Manchester: Manchester University Press, 1998) pp. 218–26. Janzen's main criticism of Welch is her concern with 'truth' and the problematic notion of 'relative truth' as opposed to the effects of a religious symbolic (p. 223).

out to describe possible alternatives to a patriarchally conceived God that are not based upon the 'transcendent monotheism of an all-powerful God' as promulgated within the western Christian tradition.[10] Hampson argues that this version of God is incompatible with feminism and feminist theology because it reinscribes 'a certain social paradigm and a particular understanding of the human being' (Hampson, p. 151) which is inherently hierarchical and patriarchal. Although the Christian God can be perceived in ways other than all-powerful and transcendent, such as within the imagery of the Trinity and the Incarnation, she argues that these are also incompatible with feminism. They generate hierarchical models (Father-Son) of social ordering and also ideas of self-abnegation, or *kenosis*, which she argues:

> [...] does not build what might be said to be specifically feminist values into our understanding of God. Such feminist themes as that for example of mutual empowerment of persons would seem to be absent from the Symbolism of Christian theology. (Hampson, p. 155)

The notion of a post-Christian 'mutual empowerment of persons' which is compatible to feminist theology is compelling. Hampson's writing makes this idea conceivable toward the end of the book by moving through two subheadings, 'The Shape of God,' and 'Perceptivity'. This is the part of the book where she considers the importance of prayer and the referential quality of the word 'God'. Hampson argues the potential of and possibilities for reconceptualising the anthropomorphic/ dialogic 'I-Thou' model for prayer. She explains that this model, which is dominant in the West, could be reconceptualised to the point where God and self become indistinguishable:

> Nor should one limit the possibility of prayer to a situation conceived as dialogue between an I and a thou. As one's intellectual understanding of what the word God connotes changes, so too may one's practice. It may well become more natural (perhaps building on sensibilities which were earlier present in one's prayer but not dominant) to speak of resting in God. One may think of oneself as being open and present to what one conceives to be a greater reality than one's self, knowing oneself as loved and upheld. I should not now want to speak of worship of God, which has hierarchical connotations. I tend not to think of God as 'thou.' But I should have no difficulty in saying, with Julian of Norwich, of God, that God is one 'in whom my soul standeth.' Furthermore I am - as a feminist interested in coming into my own – excited by the possibility of taking up the daring words which Catherine of Sienna is reputed to have uttered: 'My real me is God.' (Hampson, p. 169)

The 'I-thou' model invoked in prayer which Hampson refers to is also the central feature of the hymn. It is this linear dialogue which can be seen as re-shaped in Dickinson's poems which make use of the hymn form as a genre which is

---

[10]   Daphne Hampson, *Theology and Feminism* (Oxford: Blackwell, 1990) p. 155. See also Mary Daly, *Beyond God the Father: Toward a Philosophy of Women's Liberation*.

traditionally designated as a space for worship. Crucially, it is the absences and gaps created by the 'I-thou' model[11] which mystical discourse makes visible. Furthermore, the collapsing of the 'I-thou' model in prayer which Hampson conveys, ('My real me is God') bears affinities with the ideal 'herself-God,' and achievement of subjectivity that Luce Irigaray has described. Hampson shows how it may be possible to think about the divine in ways which are not hierarchical. She describes herself as 'religious, but not a Christian' (Hampson, p. 172). Such feminist 'religiosity' takes the form of being perceptive of God through experience, which is not thought through patriarchal models or Christian 'myths':

> Women have thought their thoughts within the context of a patriarchal society, dominated by patriarchal religion. What I think we can say is that some of the thought forms which have developed, not least within feminism, in recent years, may be peculiarly suited to expressing what we mean by God. Thus a realisation of relationality and of connectedness may well allow us the better to conceive how it is that prayer for another is effective. (Hampson, p. 173)

Hampson projects 'relationality,' 'connectedness' and the effectiveness of prayer as qualities of her own version of spirituality which is 'religion,' but not Christianity. Arguably her version of spirituality bears affinities with Christ's action within the world ('connectedness' and 'prayer for another') rather than its transmutation into language which cannot accommodate it.

Further alternatives to the 'I-Thou' model have been put forward by other feminist theologians such as Elisabeth Johnson, who builds upon theological symbolism. Johnson explores 'female metaphors' for describing the divine by utilising a triune model (composed of not two but three elements) which is based ultimately upon Christian Trinitarian doctrine. She uses this model to underscore a vision of the divine which is rooted in relation and mutuality. She writes:

> When language about the triune God in female metaphor is spoken from an explicitly feminist theological stance, it becomes clear that central aspects of classical Trinitarian doctrine are strongly compatible with insights prized by this perspective. As the sustaining ground and ultimate reference point for the human and natural world, the Trinitarian symbol for God may function in at least three beneficial ways. The God who is thrice personal signifies that the very essence

---

[11]   Hampson draws upon the 'I-Thou' model considered in Martin Buber's (1878–1965) *I and Thou* (*Ich Und Du*) (1937). Buber's notion of the 'I-Thou' relation as 'I' relating to others as another 'I', that subjectivity is relational, is compelling but also problematic for feminist theoretical approaches to language and the negotiation of binaries. Buber's terms for encounters with the divine reinscribe the 'I-Thou' model which Hampson views as unhelpful: 'There is no I as such but only the I of the basic word I-You and the I of the basic word I-It.' *I and Thou*, trans. by Walter Kaufmann, 3rd edn (Edinburgh: T and T Clark, 1970) p. 54. Although Buber's notion of the divine as experienced through relation and reciprocal address is important, this study focuses on the hierarchies generated by the 'I-Thou' model in hymns and its effects on Dickinson's poetry.

of God is to be in relation, and thus relatedness rather than the solitary ego is the heart of all reality. Furthermore, this symbol indicates that the particular kind of relatedness than which nothing greater can be conceived is not one of hierarchy involving domination/subordination, but rather one of genuine mutuality in which there is radical equality while distinctions are respected.[12]

Such emphasis on relationality and a triune model of the divine serves to counter the teleological narratives of the Protestant view of God and Christianity which have been used to promote the 'solitary ego' of individualism and capitalist notions of industry.[13] Although Dickinson cannot be aligned with a particular traditional theology and practice, her poetics frequently build upon a principle of indivisibility that Johnson's triune female metaphor of the divine demonstrates. Johnson's notion of triune relation allows for space within relation which is not dualistic and not oppositional in its structure. Dickinson's poetics generate space through their similar resistance towards oppositions, by privileging instead a decentred simultaneity.

Grace Janzen's investigation of Christian theology and concern with 'natality'[14] is another example of the desire in feminist criticism and feminist theology to develop an alternative imaginary. That is, a form and mode of expression for the female divine which is practically applicable and resonant within the symbolic order. She refers to this as an 'embodied situatedness' (Janzen, p. 218). As Dickinson's poetry exemplifies, it is necessary to develop alternatives within the symbolic order, to work creatively with language, if such an 'embodied situatedness' is to be exacted. The various models of community and relationality to come out of recent feminist theology's critique of the religious symbolic are important and instructive for establishing an alternative view of the divine that has theological grounding. The 'mystical' writing of Irigaray and Certeau offer insights into the linguistic and literary construction of subjectivity, and its connection with the divine 'other'. And it is the connection between subjectivity, language and the divine that Dickinson's hymnic poems highlight and perform. In this way they also project an 'embodied situatedness' within writing. Rather than thinking about 'perceptivity' or 'experience' in an abstract way, writing such as that of Irigaray and Certeau describes/performs ways in which language can potentially negotiate space for the other within the symbolic. Moreover, mysticism is understood in this chapter and throughout this book as being connected with and necessarily dependent upon an 'embodied situatedness', and as inextricably connected with language and subjectivity.

---

[12]   Elizabeth Johnson, *She Who Is: The Mystery of God in Feminist Discourse*, tenth anniversary edition (1992; New York: Herder and Herder, 2003) p. 216.

[13]   See Max Weber, *The Protestant Ethic and the Spirit of Capitalism* (1930; London: Routledge, 2004).

[14]   Janzen names the feminist symbolic 'natality' (birth) which is also a form of action, and argues that a 'feminist symbolic whose source and criteria are found in women's lives starts from the ethical, indeed from acting for love of the world'. Grace M. Janzen, *Becoming Divine: Towards a Feminist Philosophy of Religion*, p. 236.

Mystical Discourse as Praxis

Janzen is keen to clarify the usefulness of mystical discourse in relation to social justice:

> Feminists have every reason, both historical and current, to be suspicious of an understanding of mysticism which allows that women may be mystics, but which makes mysticism a private and ineffable psychological occurrence and which detaches it from the considerations of social justice.[15]

The shape that mystical discourse takes cannot be separated from issues surrounding the development of subjectivity. As will be discussed further on, Certeau's notion of 'heterologies' describes a place for the 'embodied situatedness' appealed for by feminist critics such as Janzen. Daphne Hampson admits that theology predicated upon experience is difficult to convey to others, and that 'experience at second hand is easy to dismiss' (Hampson, p. 170). However Dickinson's poems do not simply re-present experience or perceptivity. Like Certeau's notion of heterologies, they reproduce a space in which thought on the 'other' is made possible and in which the 'other' can be endlessly animated. Dickinson's hymn-poems enact a 'relationality' and 'connectedness' through invoking the participation of the reader and also the experience of relation. In this way they produce a reconfiguration of the hymn-as-prayer. Her hymn-poems negotiate the 'I-thou' model of worship in religion which is patriarchally conceived and asks to be 'named.' In other words, the 'the act of naming and speaking as a response to the reception of what is given' which Ward's definition of the hymn invokes (*Christ and Culture*, p. 185) is avoided in Dickinson's alternative 'schema' for the divine ('And make much blunder, if at last/ I take the clue divine - ' Fr 1107).

Definitions of mysticism often emphasise the practice of going beyond what is 'normally' perceived in an understanding of the world and reality, suggesting an individualised and exclusive mode of aspiration or spirituality. Yet, for many mystics, Dickinson among them, the world is itself a source of divine immanence. In many of her poems the speaker's relation to the natural world is evocative of divine immanence described in mystical writings. Evelyn Underhill (1875–1941), a British novelist, poet and writer on mysticism, provides examples of poems which are explicit about mysticism and the speaker's immanent relation to the world. Her poem 'Immanence' (1912) describes the mystical significance of the natural world, in which attention is paid to 'the little things,' the practice of everyday life. The divine is perceived in the fleeting moment, 'on the glancing wings/Of eager birds', rather than in the 'morning wings of majesty' and the hierarchical grandeur which that image connotes.[16] In Underhill's poem the ways and nature of God are

---

[15] Grace Janzen, *Power, Gender and Christian Mysticism* (Cambridge: Cambridge University Press, 1995) p. 326.

[16] 'Immanence' an excerpt quoted in; Brenda Blanch, (ed.), *Heaven A Dance: An Evelyn Underhill Anthology* (London: SPCK, 1992) pp. 7–8. Taken from the complete poem 'Immanence' in Underhill, Evelyn, *Immanence: A Book of Verses* (London: J. M. Dent, 1912).

described in a series of repetitions ('I come in the little things'). Repetition is a key technique of mystical writing and can be seen in a broad range of writers whose work shares some or all of the features of mystical discourse, from Teresa de Avila, to Kathleen Raine.[17] Such a technique or 'system' seems to be at odds with the diffusive nature of the 'Godhead' in mystical writing as described in this poem. It suggests a method or structure towards reaching that which ultimately eludes definitive definitions. Rather than focusing on the 'essence' of the divine as a specific entity, as in the 'I-Thou' model of prayer, the emphasis on the 'little things' in this poem rests upon multiplicity. The 'little things' depict the mystical and immanent as being multiple and multivalent, and yet paradoxically, remaining 'not broken or divided.' Essence in this poem is in the very multiplicity and timelessness it conveys. All action is rendered as being-in-action, in the moment ('glancing'), and it is not defined through reaching an ultimate telos. The 'appointed hour' for love is always the present. Linguistic depictions of the divine in mystical discourse merely convey paths and trajectories for the divine, and avoid descriptions which privilege essence, fixity or linearity with implied 'goals.'

Dickinson's use of repetition (such as her repeated use of bee imagery), and the multivalency of her language and uses of metre, bears affinities with the methods employed in mystical writing such as those explicated in Underhill's poem. There is in this poem, as in Dickinson's poems, an emphasis upon partial sight ('glancing wings') as opposed to a clearly visible, singular and fixed vision and version of the divine. The partial sight and avoidance of full disclosure of the divine in Dickinson's poems (to be discussed in the following chapter) is akin to the non-fixity and instability of authenticity within language which the writings of Irigaray and Certeau both display.

In not privileging fixity, essence or linearity when describing the mystical trajectory of the 'other'/God, mystical discourse is inherently anti-hierarchical. This anti-hierarchical aspect is reinforced by another feature of mystical discourse, that is, the tendency for self-abnegation and naturally assuming the lowest position. In Underhill's poem, the speaker's dedication to self-abnegation and the lowest place ('The furrowed sod' and 'My starry wings I do forsake') echoes Christ's teachings about self-sacrifice in the New Testament. And yet the tendency towards a personalised version of God, or the dualistic, hierarchical relation between speaker and 'other' found in traditional protestant hymns is circumnavigated. This aspect of mystical discourse and the implied individualistic approach opens up a dichotomy between the individual and the extension outwards of self to perceive the divine in relation. As described in feminist theology, this version of the divine is inherent within the reality of the world including other human beings. Mystical discourse is both derived from, and centred upon, the individual

---

[17]   Although not categorised as a mystical writer, Kathleen Raine's poems often display the qualities of repetition and articulation of a mystical immanence through relation to the world. See, for example the poems 'Amo Ergo Sum' and 'Night Sky' pp. 62–9 in Couzyn, Jeni, (ed.), *The Bloodaxe Book of Contemporary Women Poets: Eleven British Writers* (Newcastle: Bloodaxe, 1998).

but it is also connected to the rest of the world through immanent relation and the production of absences and an open space. The spaces in mystical discourse are directly related to the various 'wordly' or 'known' discourses which produce them. Mystical discourse allows the space between the self and the other to rest, suspended, creating a dynamic dialogism between what is sayable and unsayable, between shared, communicable experience and individual experience. The relation between self and the other that mystical discourse exploits is also analogous to the relation between structure and agency which is evident in the hymn form. In a similar way, Dickinson's structure of repeated imagery within the traditionally devotional space of the hymn can be seen as *heterologous*. Her voice endlessly enacts alternative versions and experiences of the divine within poetics.

The history and nature of mystical discourse is a large area which cannot be presented in detail here.[18] Connections between Dickinson's mode of writing and that described by Michel de Certeau and the mode of writing the female divine 'other' in the work of Luce Irigaray are both to be discussed in this chapter. However, the focus here is not to prove Dickinson as a mystic, but to demonstrate parallels between her mode of expression as against the assumptions surrounding the expression of spiritual experience in traditional hymnody. Some aspects of her life, namely, the reclusive discipline with which she adopted the role of poet, have been likened to those of women mystics.[19] However, her writing does not follow the clearly delineated, identifiable set of 'stages' or elements of those associated with mystical discourse, so much as it bears affinities with the style and *praxis* of mystical discourse.

Divining the Other: Luce Irigaray

Luce Irigaray writes through (but also within) the tradition of psychoanalytic theory which analyses subject formation in terms of gender and opposition. Thus although voicing feminine negotiations and subversions of the symbolic, those negotiations are defined in relation to terms which are oppositional. However, her writing on belief and on the female divine provide useful examples of how the 'I-Thou' model of relation might be alternatively envisioned. She writes:

> Religion marks the place of the absolute *for us*, its path, the hope of its fulfilment. All too often that fulfilment has been postponed or transferred to some transcendental time and place. It has not been interpreted as the infinite

---

[18] For further discussion on mystics and mystical discourse, see Evelyn Underhill, *Mystics of the Church* (1925) (London: James Clarke, 1975) and *Practical Mysticism* (1914) (London: Eagle, 1991).

[19] See for example; Gerda Lerna, *The Creation of Feminist Consciousness: From the Middle Ages to Eighteen-Seventy* (Oxford: Oxford University Press, 1993) pp. 181–2. Lerna links Dickinson's rejection of 'normal life' with women mystics such as Hildegard Von Bingen, Mechthilld of Magdeburg, Christine Ebner, Julian of Norwich and most directly with Isotta Nogarola, who chose to live only with her mother.

that resides within us and among us, the god in us, the Other for us, becoming with and in us – as yet manifest only through his creation (the Father), present in his form (the son), mediator between the two (spirit). Here the capital letter designates the horizon of fulfilment of a gender, not a transcendent entity that exists outside becoming.[20]

Postmodernist and Post-Structuralist accounts of language serve to highlight its ultimate instability in relating definitive meaning. The implications this has for religion has generated much debate within feminist theology and feminist literary criticism, and also within literary criticism more generally.[21] The work of Michel de Certeau and Luce Irigaray connects them in some ways with the Post-Structuralist view of language and therefore also the Postmodernist tradition. However their consideration of the ways in which the 'other' may be accommodated within society, and within language respectively, conveys ways of thinking which are rooted in specific practices. Dickinson's engagement with the imagery and form of hymnody is one such practice which allows the 'other' to come to the fore in a similar way to the methods described by Irigaray and Certeau. Psychoanalytic and feminist theories of language highlight the relation between subjectivity and the divine and their use of Freudian subject-formation models is instructive. Such models explain female subjectivity as ultimately predicated upon lack, absence, and exclusion from the defining power of the phallus. By extension also, they 'explain' culturally dominant versions of the divine. The hymn is a traditionally sacred form of writing on the divine, concerning both language and subjectivity within a traditionally phallogocentric discourse, and so any discussion of it shares ground with Lacanian school theorists such as Luce Irigaray and Helene Cixous. In 'The Laugh of the Medusa,' Cixous uses the term 'phallogocentrism' in her discussion of the type of language that promotes binary oppositions. This type of language, in her view, confines women and men through its repression of multiplicity, indefiniteness and feminine 'jouissance.'[22]

Psychoanalytic and feminist theories of language have been utilised by a few Dickinson critics in order to account for the ways in which her work negotiates symbolic ordering to achieve subjectivity.[23] Sabine Sielke utilises the work of

---

[20]   Luce Irigaray, 'Divine Women,' in *Sexes and Genealogies*, trans. by Gillian C. Gill (New York: Columbia University Press, 1993) pp. 57–88 (p. 63).

[21]   See Philippa Berry and Andrew Wernick, (eds), *Shadow of Spirit: Postmodernism and Religion* (London: Routledge, 1992).

[22]   See Helene Cixous, 'The Laugh of the Medusa', in *New French Feminisms: An Anthology* (eds) Elaine Marks and Isabelle de Courtivron (Brighton: Harvester Wheatsheaf, 1981) pp. 245–64.

[23]   For example, Helen Shoobridge, '"Reverence for each Other being Sweet Aim:" Dickinson Face to face with the Masculine', *The Emily Dickinson Journal* 9:1 (2000) 87–111. Shoobridge uses Irigaray's *Ethics of Sexual Difference* to highlight the repositioning of the subject/ 'other' relation in Dickinson's 'Master' letters, thus renegotiating the sexual binaries associated with Lacanian psychoanalytic theory.

Kristeva, Irigaray and Cixous in her study of female subjectivity which discusses the 'intertextual networking' of Dickinson alongside the poetry of both Marianne Moore and Adrienne Rich. Sielke argues that such 'networking' can be seen in the act of writing, which includes techniques such as mimicry and camouflage, which negotiate female space through past and present discourses, and 'perform' female subjectivity:

> [...] I want to conclude by redefining (female) subjectivity with Dickinson, Moore, Rich, Kristeva, Irigaray, and Cixous as a process that is never coherent and historically continuous but, rather, negotiates between deconstructive and (re) constructive modes as well as between past and present discourses. [...] Female subjectivity thus is a matter of intertextual networking, in and across time, performed not by language itself but by those who - both consciously and unconsciously - act in language and keep doing so in the future.[24]

Sielke reads Dickinson alongside other women writers who 'act in language', and as a poet who 'recognises subjectivity and history as constructs and rhetorical strategies' and 'appropriates dominant cultural rhetoric to invest it with new meaning' (Sielke, p. 17). Although Sielke ultimately underestimates the call to inter-subjectivity in Dickinson's work by declaring that she 'dismissed history and transcendence for the temporality of writing,' (Sielke, p. 217.) such a position places emphasis on the specific cultures in which such subjectivities are constructed. Therefore it can be used to support an understanding of Dickinson's engagement with hymn culture. By using the hymn form and imagery associated with religion and moral correctness during the Civil War period (such as the bee) Dickinson pointedly engages with the use of theology for political ends. Her poems demarcate a space between past and present discourse in the subject of the divine or 'other.' They also generate activity within this space by producing a new kind of voice. For example, in poem Fr 979 (as discussed in detail in Chapter 6). Dickinson draws upon imagery associated with the Book of Revelations to confer onto the image of the bee an association with the Puritan, wearing a 'helmet' and a breastplate, defending faith in battle. By doing this she utilises past discourses on the divine (biblical text and also Puritan interpretations of scripture to defend war) whilst also connecting with it her own, present thoughts on the example of the divine in nature. The bee connotes to some the idea of perfect community. Her voice also draws upon the relevance of the bee image within 'current', nineteenth-century uses of rhetoric on the Protestant work ethic, as the poem considers the bee's experience of producing in both states of 'labour' *and* during 'idleness':

His Labour is a Chant -
His Idleness - a Tune -
Oh, for a Bee's experience
Of Clovers, and of Noon! (Fr 979)

---

[24]   Sabine Sielke, *Fashioning the Female Subject: The Intertextual Networking of Dickinson, Moore and Rich* (Michigan: The University of Michigan Press, 1997) p. 228.

Rather than simply representing discourse on the divine, Dickinson 'acts within language' (Sielke, p. 228) to reposition it. The poetic language created is itself endlessly active. The reader is left to consider the bee's 'experience' as described in the poem, the state of being-in-relation (such as that of the bee within its community) where pleasure and industry are both equally productive and equally valued. This alternative mode of relation to the world that Dickinson's poems trace remains a possibility to be considered. It offers an inkling of the divine-in-action and the divine through multiple relation that bee imagery implies without the dogmatic proclamation of presenting a version of the divine. Dickinson's poetics convey a mysticism as praxis which can also be seen in Irigaray's project of producing metaphors to describe the female divine which enact 'becoming space'.[25]

However, Sielke's use of Irigaray in this instance does not extend beyond the notions of mimicry and camouflage as female subversion within symbolic order. Moreover, her reading of Dickinson alongside the work of Adrienne Rich serves to highlight what she calls a 'blind-spot' in feminist literary theory, that is, 'a sense of the position of the female subject as an agent of history' (Sielke, p. 16). Sielke argues for a new kind of investigation which might uncover the 'practice' of the poetry of Dickinson and Rich, the 'shape and temporality' of a female tradition, as opposed to their rhetorical refusals of patriarchal heritage.

Jan Montefiore's reading of Dickinson in view of Irigaray's notion of a female discourse is instructive, as she highlights the problem of locating the many guises she adopts in her poems within a theory of female identity:

> Dickinson's poems, then, are remarkably difficult to assimilate into a theory of female identity articulating itself through the writing of an Imaginary relationship between an 'I' and 'Thou', which could constitute a textual 'space' for specifically female meaning. They are too ambiguous and contradictory to be read as purely woman-centred texts. Dickinson uses such a variety of voices and positions to speak from that though she excels in poems which create an identity through reflection and opposition to a beloved, these seem characterized less by transcendence of gender than by irony, evasion and ambiguity. They are unsatisfactory if considered as poetic rendering of an Irigarayan female Imaginary: the only way in which Dickinson obviously conforms to Irigaray's account of female discourse being her indeterminable meanings and her contradictoriness.[26]

The 'contradictory' and 'ambiguous' nature of Dickinson's poetics are difficult to reconcile with a version of female identity, such as Irigaray's, which is predicated

---

[25]   Irigaray uses the term 'becoming space' to describe the formation of female subjectivity and the simultaneous realisation of the female divine in action. See Luce Irigaray, 'Divine Women,' in *Sexes and Genealogies*, trans. by Gillian C. Gill (New York: Columbia University Press, 1993) pp. 57–88 (p. 65).

[26]   Jan Montefiore, *Feminism and Poetry: Language, Experience, Identity in Women's Writing*, 3rd edn (1987; London: Pandora, 2004) pp. 177–8.

upon an 'I-Thou' model (which is also in this case the split between the female self and mother) because the poetics do not adhere to fixed and oppositional notions of gender. Moreover, as will be demonstrated in Chapter 6, Dickinson's bee imagery is a trope for the suspension of multiple possibilities and therefore also the ultimate collapse of the 'I-Thou' model of relation which is constructed as oppositional in traditional hymn address. Whilst the commitment to 'contradictoriness' we find in Dickinson's poems allows for recognition of Irigarayan female discourse as Montefiore observes, the dissent against (patriarchal) orthodox religion through engagement with hymn culture in her work makes it possible to move beyond Irigaray's terms for an understanding of Dickinson's poetics as a 'practice.' As will be discussed in a moment, in relation to Certeau's notion of heterologies, Dickinson's radical use of tropes associated with traditional hymnody (for example bird imagery for spiritual flight, or bees for industry and community) serves to delimit an ideal (heterologous) space in which the other is articulated. Her poems highlight the absences and experiences which traditional religious narratives and the implied hierarchical version of the divine can not accommodate. The persistent wrestling with contradictions that Dickinson's poetics inscribe bears affinities with alternative models for oppositional patriarchal versions of the divine as considered by feminist theologians, such as 'relation' and 'community' as described above.

However, Irigaray's positive and mystical turn on the notion of female lack or 'absence' as constructed through Freudian models of gender opposition, and the metaphors she uses to convey this in her writing about writing are useful. Her metaphors bear similarities with the motifs which evidence Dickinson's engagement with hymn culture and therefore assist our understanding of the shape of the 'practice' and 'temporality'[27] of Dickinson's writing.

Much of Luce Irigaray's work argues that female subjectivity is dependent upon articulating *jouissance*, the effusive response to connection with the 'other'. She sees *jouissance* as being connected with the divine, and its expression as the key to women's 'becoming'. Utilising Lacanian psychoanalytic theory (itself derived from Freudian models) she forges a positive model by associating *jouissance* (that which the symbolic order cannot contain and which is associated with the feminine) with various descriptions with the divine. In *Speculum of the Other Woman* (1985) she argues that the ideal state for woman is to be 'herself-God,' that is, the ideal where woman is;

> [...] no longer cut in two opposing directions of sheer elevation to the sky and sheer fall into the depths. I know, now, that both height and depth spawn - and split - each other in(de)finitely. And that the one is in the other, and the other in me, matters little since it is in me that they are created in rapture. [28]

---

[27]   Sabine Sielke, *Fashioning the Female Subject: The Intertextual Networking of Dickinson, Moore and Rich*, p. 16.

[28]   Luce Irigaray, *Speculum of the Other Woman*, trans. by Gillian C. Gill (New York: Cornell University Press, 1985) pp. 200–201.

The description of the 'two opposing directions' between 'sky' and 'depths' is evocative of the linearity of 'traditional' hymns, where the speaker-God relation as a vertical movement is clearly defined and made visible. This is done through metaphors of sight, transcendence and vision, within the hymn. Rather than utilising metaphors of transcendence which repeat the vertical reciprocity of 'I-Thou' and reconstruct exclusion and hierarchy, the metaphors of spiritual flight used by Dickinson and also other contemporary women hymnists (as discussed in Chapters Five and Six) connote instead a more diverse and inclusive relationality and signal the transcendence of hierarchical models of the divine.

Despite utilising what is ultimately another version of the 'I-Thou' model in which separation and lack are presupposed as a starting point for the expression of the female divine other, the metaphors Irigaray uses to connote spiritual flight are useful for reading alongside Dickinson's flight imagery. They demonstrate how divine space might be articulated. Such imagery, which Irigaray employs in the essays 'Belief Itself,' and 'Divine Women' will now be explored briefly in relation to her projection of an alternative 'horizon' for the female divine. In 'Divine Women' Irigaray describes the importance for women to have their own 'becoming space' (p. 65). In this she argues, a non-phallocentric version of a divine could exist and provide women with a horizon, a mode of being, of their own. She describes ways in which the connection between subjectivity and the divine might manifest itself purposefully, asserting that;

> [...] as long as woman lacks a divine made in her own image she cannot establish her subjectivity or achieve a goal of her own. (Irigaray, 'Divine Women', p. 63)

She utilises the framework of psychoanalytic theory, of a woman's problematic relation to the symbolic order, and describes woman's situation of being both of the womb and also defined culturally as emptiness or relatively 'empty' space in relation to the subject, the phallus that she lacks. Irigaray seeks to promote an alternative to the 'horizon of fulfilment of a gender' ('Divine Women', p. 63) in traditional (male-centered) religious discourse. She imagines woman's gestational process in terms of a transformation from water to air; the watery origin of the womb where woman was once like a fish, and the space where woman outside of the womb can be like a bird, where the 'womb' of the air envelopes woman. She thus describes this divine becoming as occurring within an 'airy space,' where the 'mirror' of representation[29] can be countered:

> Though it may at times help us to emerge, to move out of the water, the mirror blocks our energies, freezes us in our tracks, clips our wings. [...] Once we have left the *waters* of the womb, we have to construct a space for ourselves in the *air*

---

[29]   Although not made explicit, Irigaray's use of the 'mirror' echoes Lacanian psychoanalytic theory of subject-formation, where the mirror (real mirror or the 'mirror' of the patriarchal gaze upon the self) acts to reinforce socially prescribed notions of the female/male self.

[...]. Once we were fishes. It seems that we are destined to become birds. None of this is possible unless the air opens up freely to our movements.

To construct and inhabit our airy space is essential. It is the space of bodily autonomy, of free breath, free speech and song, of performing on the stage of life. (Irigaray, 'Divine Women', p. 66)

Irigaray's notion of 'airy space' is crucial for this study's understanding of Dickinson's use of hymnic space as it demonstrates the possibility for utilising, or reclaiming, the notion of 'emptiness'. This space has been negatively associated with gender, through the psychoanalytic womb-as-lack model. Dickinson's use of the hymn as a space in which to articulate her version of divine relation can be seen as a radical transformation of the hymn/'mirror' which reflects traditionally prescribed notions of the female supplicatory self in relation to a patriarchal/hierarchical God. Her use of hymnic space can be seen as that of a fluid, processual, 'becoming space' in which the female divine (and therefore also subjectivity) can exist. The use of imagery associated with flight and nonstatic movement in Dickinson's poems, through which her own intimations of the divine can be expressed in a nondirective way, recreates the ideal (poetic) space[s] which Irigaray argues is necessary for avoiding the 'mirror' of (false) representation. It also, as Irigaray suggests, fosters a space in which opportunities for contact with the other can swim freely. In Irigarayan terms, the hymn which represents/ reflects back a version of the divine which is inherently hierarchical, patriarchal and exclusionary can be seen as deflected and revisioned by Dickinson through her radical approach to hymnic space.

Irigaray uses the metaphor of a bird for woman's fulfilling inhabitation and negotiation of 'becoming space' and 'airy space'. It suggests ultimate freedom from the fixity of social roles and symbolic language which define woman and the divine. Earlier incarnations of the female divine 'horizon' or 'bird' can be seen in Irigaray's essay 'Belief Itself', where the angel, the figure associated also with nineteenth-century conceptions of ideal womanhood, is re-visioned. Here an alternative angelic 'flight' is conveyed, which does not seek to 'demonstrate', 'prove' or 'argue' the fact of its existence:

Thus, seeking to capture the angel in the home [...] to cage up within the domestic setting something that has always flowed uncontained is like turning free soaring, rapture, flight into parchments, skeletons, death masks.

If we do not rethink and rebuild the whole scene of representation, the angels will never find a home, never stay anywhere. [...] They can light up our sight and all our senses but only if we note the moment when they pass by, hear their word and fulfil it, without seeking to show, demonstrate, prove, argue about their coming, their speaking, or appearance.[30]

---

[30] Luce Irigaray, 'Belief Itself', in *Sexes and Genealogies*, trans. by Gillian C. Gill (New York: Columbia University Press, 1993) pp. 25–53 (pp. 42–3).

Irigaray's equation of the oppression of the 'angel at the hearth' with the angelic divine is explicit. The angel whose word must be heard and fulfilled is also undoubtedly another version of Irigaray's 'horizon of fulfilment of a gender' ('Divine Women', p. 63.) for women that the bird and its 'airy space' later symbolises. Rather than demand representation ('demonstrate, prove, argue') the practice of the angel is to guard and negotiate the 'free passage' which both delineates and enacts the divine. Drawing directly from biblical symbolism (Exodus 26: 17–22) Irigaray transforms the image of the angel, traditionally a patriarchally-biased metaphor for divine grace (as in the example of the messenger Gabriel), into one that 'guards' and suitably delineates the ideal space of the divine. Such a reading of scripture which places emphasis upon the space between two angels that face each other serves to reinforce the mystical non-saying about the 'airy space' and 'absence' of the divine:

> So here, two angels face one another to guard the presence of God, who may perhaps be turning away in his anger or absence. The angels face one another over the ark of the covenant. Beneath them, the tablets of the law, and between them, between their wings, the divine presence that cannot be sensed or seen. [...] It seems to be setting up the future presence of God in the more airy element: he can come and go freely, the word that has already been offered and inscribed in stone is loosed, and a new covenant is prepared. (Irigaray, 'Belief Itself', p. 44)

The 'free passage' of the divine is necessarily open and not constricted by the demands of signification and language. Irigaray's angelic imagery represents unbounded flight, signaled by birds and angels, within 'airy space'. Her use of angelic imagery supports a connection between the non-saying space of the other which language leaves out, and which the symbolic order cannot accommodate, and a version of a female divine which needs to be represented as a 'horizon' for women, for the achievement of female subjectivity.

Although the figure of the angel is perhaps more common in hymnody as a traditional 'messenger' of the divine, the bird is also commonly used to connote the divine and spiritual flight in hymnody. Moreover, the bird and cognate words for flight are particularly evident in women's hymnody and Dickinson's bee imagery draws upon this. The representation of 'flight' in Dickinson's work, which both connotes physical but also spiritual flight (as evidenced by her use of bee imagery in Chapter 6), conveys an unbounded antilinearity which goes against the linear ascending/descending movement and speaker-God relation in traditional masculine hymnody. As will be described in the following chapter, the speaker in Isaac Watts's hymns desires 'wings of faith' to 'rise' – to become like God, like the ideal of God he presents. Rather than describing praise as the invocation of an interaction between two forces of consciousness emanating from inherently oppositional directions, hymns can be observed in terms of a circular, and encircling, regenerative mode of expression. Hymn-praise could be refigured as that which explodes categories of opposition, neither pulling away from a centre or towards one. The mode which Dickinson and other hymn writers use can be seen as describing a trajectory which is never reached, portraying an endlessly regenerative cycle. Both Irigaray's metaphors of the bird/angel and Certeau's notion of 'mystic speech' are instructive with respect to the notion of hymnic space in this book as they both work to move away from the oppositional model of representation which 'I-Thou' epitomises.

Irigaray's suggestions for representing the female divine in 'Belief Itself' provide useful metaphors for this study of the negotiation of traditional religious discourse and representation of the divine in Dickinson's poems. However they also display an inability to support oppositions, where Dickinson's poems allow for expansion. For example, in order to 'imagine' God, Irigaray declares that 'the feeling or experience of a positive, objective, glorious existence, the feeling of subjectivity, is essential for us,'('Divine Women', p. 66.) and that 'no one has really taught us love of God. Only love of neighbour.' ('Divine Women', p. 68.) The tautological connection between a functioning community and the 'God in the feminine gender' that it depends upon in order to define and maintain itself is made explicit. Writing of the 'empirical parameters' in society that restrain women, Irigaray argues:

> Fenced in by these functions, how can a woman maintain a margin of singleness for herself, a nondeterminism that would allow her to become and remain herself? This margin [...] that gives us the authority yet to grow, to affirm and fulfil ourselves as individuals and members of a community, can be ours only if a God in the feminine gender can define it and keep it for us. As an other that we have yet to make actual, as a region of life, strength, imagination, creation, which exists for us both within and beyond, as our possibility of a present and a future.
>
> Is not God the name and the place that holds the promise of a new chapter in history and that also denies this can happen? Still invisible? Still to be discovered? To be incarnated? Archi-ancient and forever future. (Irigaray, 'Divine Women', p. 72)

However, Dickinson's radical transformation and reclaiming of hymnic space allows for the full resonance of the hymn with implied connection with community, and the individual's relation to the community, to come into being and exist also, within the poem. Dickinson therefore, allows the imagined space of God that Irigaray describes, the 'glorious existence'('Divine Women', p. 66), to be connected, irrevocably, with community and 'love of neighbour;' the connection that Irigaray's essay 'Divine Women' does not accommodate. The hymnic mode of Dickinson's poems allows for Irigaray's notion of divine 'jouissance' to be suspended *in relation* to an invocation and constant reminder of community which is also, for Dickinson, a form of labour. Bond-Stockton's reading of Irigaray's strategy to 'bend' psychoanalytic theories of female lack or absence 'back toward 'material opacity' and to cast lacking as a form of labour productive of pleasure' is useful as it underscores both the practice and performativity of

Irigaray's writing.[31] As Section Three of this book will demonstrate, writing the divine is a 'form of labour productive of pleasure' in Dickinson as much as it is in Irigaray. The importance Irigaray places upon achieving the divine in order to achieve subjectivity is put into practice in Dickinson's use of the hymn form because it both traces and articulates the divine and subjectivity. The ideas of a 'becoming space' and an 'airy space' in which women can move, bird-like, escaping the negative cycle of mimesis and representation in 'Divine Women' is useful for examining Dickinson's use of hymnic space and bee imagery. Dickinson's use of hymn space and bee imagery ultimately conveys her radical engagement with traditional religious discourse. Irigaray's notion of divine being is mystical in its emphasis on absence and space, and the circumnavigation of the divine as opposed to a linear, phallogocentric ideal. Her work on women's relation to the divine can be seen as mysticism as praxis, as it both describes and also enacts the ways in which a female divine can be articulated in language (which is akin to Dickinson's use of language and hymnic space). Michel de Certeau's 'Mystic Speech' provides a further understanding of the connection between mysticism and the act of writing and an instructive description of the practice of 'heterologies'.

Michel de Certeau and Heterologies

> Mystical would also be the relation of the poem to the religious tradition whose statements it presupposes, but uses in order to make them say the absence of what they designate.[32]

Michel de Certeau's essay on mystical discourse ('Mystic Speech') is useful to this study due to its depiction of individual and mystic spirituality which is defined through engagement with orthodox spirituality. Dickinson's relation to the assumptions surrounding Protestant hymn culture can be seen in a similar way. The connection between mystical discourse and poetry, which the essay and the excerpt above each describe, bears a striking affinity with Dickinson's use of language, orthodox religion and the hymn genre. Certeau sees a poem's relation to religious tradition as 'mystical', whereby it highlights absences in the dominant discourse. Dickinson's poems are 'mystical' in this specified way. For example, poem Fr 655, which depicts the life cycle of a butterfly or moth, simultaneously invokes a typical hymn subject in the life of Jesus. It then also considers the reception of the life of Jesus within orthodox religion. The final stanza suggests

---

31 Katherine Bond-Stockton, *God Between Their Lips: Desire Between Women in Irigaray, Bronte and Eliot* (Stanford: Stanford University Press, 1994) pp. xvi–xvii. Stockton's reading of Irigaray emphasises her insistence that 'escapes' exist for women within dominant constructions.

32 Michel de Certeau, 'Mystic Speech' in *The Certeau Reader* (ed.), Graham Ward (Oxford: Blackwell, 2000) pp. 188–201 (p. 205).

that the butterfly/moth, as analogous to the divine in orthodox Christianity, becomes housed in 'cabinets' and finally pinned down and on display - 'Abbey' and 'cocoon' being synonymous with this final resting place. However, the focus on the continual flight and evasiveness of the butterfly/moth in the poem's first three stanzas serves to establish and confer a non-saying and an absence of fixity and definition upon the divine:

> He parts Himself - like Leaves -
> And then - He closes up -
> Then stands opon the Bonnet
> Of Any Buttercup -
>
> And then He runs against
> And oversets a Rose -
> And then does Nothing -
> Then away opon a Jib - He goes -
>
> And dangles like a Mote
> Suspended in the Noon -
> Uncertain - to return Below -
> Or settle in the Moon -

The personified insect which 'dangles like a Mote' connotes the omniscient Holy Spirit and is finally connected with the life of Jesus in the fourth stanza with the Crucifixion which 'That Day' (with the poignant capitalisation of 'That') implies. In this way, the poem reverses the chronology of what we know of the life of Jesus. The poem 'ends' with the cocoon-state of the butterfly/moth, which invokes the 'sepulchre' of the 'That Day':

> What come of Him at Night -
> The privilege to say
> Be limited by Ignorance -
> What come of Him - That Day -
>
> The Frost - possess the World -
> In Cabinets - be shown -
> A Sepulchre of quaintest Floss -
> An Abbey - a Cocoon - (Fr 655)

The poem's first and final stanzas echo each other in the deferral of both 'beginning' and 'ending', and convey instead a cycle that could be endlessly repeated. The sacrificial 'parting' and opening out of the butterfly/moth's wings in the first stanza ('He parts Himself - like Leaves/ And then - He closes up -) is evocative of both the last supper and the Crucifixion. Similarly, the deathly stasis of 'That Day' which 'frost' and 'sepulchre' invoke in the final stanza simultaneously refer back to the beginning. This is because the cocoon state (like the Crucifixion) also symbolises the moment before rebirth and renewal. From the cocoon state, the emergent butterfly/moth is released into being, as is the Holy Spirit through the resurrection of Christ, beyond the Crucifixion. 'Evidence' of the existence of the divine in orthodox religion is readily available in churches ('abbey') through stories of the Crucifixion and yet Dickinson's description of the movements of the butterfly/moth 'at Night' is 'limited by Ignorance.' In other words, knowledge of the divine cannot be pinned down or known completely and the evidence of orthodox religion (like the Victorian taxonomical urge to name, pin and display an insect) is ultimately unreliable.

By looking at the way biblical imagery is employed in poems like the one above, we can see that Dickinson's hymn-poems co-opt the assumptions of the Protestant tradition. At the same time, they convey a strategy of mystical 'openness' in their refusal to 'say' or describe the divine. They draw attention to the absences or gaps in traditional religious discourse and orthodox ways of thinking about the divine are. The privileging of absence and non-saying in Dickinson's work and the aspect of leaving an open space for the reader is akin to the method of 'mystic speech' that Certeau describes. Certeau's perspective on mystical discourse highlights its anarchic power to make visible the absences and contradictions apparent in religious tradition by refusing definitions of the divine which constrict and attempt to shape it.

Certeau's background is Jesuit and Christian and this fact has been seen as shaping his mysticism.[33] His prose is itself dense and 'mystical' in preferring repetition and frequent allusion to absences and spaces within types of mystical discourses, to attempts to describe the divine, or the 'object' of mystical discourse. Certeau's position, to an extent, reasserts the view within early Christian mystical writing of an ultimately unknowable God.[34] In this sense the ideas he describes cannot be seen as being wholly divorced from a hitherto established religious tradition. However the effects of destabilising a 'knowable' God, as the ones his writing describes, are ultimately radical:

> It is by taking words seriously, a life and death game in the body of language, that the secret of what they give is torn from them - and, as St. John of the Cross says in relation to the "holy *doctors*," to do that is to make them confess the secret of their "impotence," of what they cannot "give." (Certeau, p. 205)

Certeau's recommendation against 'taking words seriously' would become a Postmodern polemic on aimless multiplicity, if it were not for the fact that the essay ends with a final suggestion as to the nature of the mystical. He encourages us to

---

[33] See Frederick Christian Bauerschmidt, 'Introduction: Michel de Certeau, Theologian' in *The Certeau Reader* (ed.), Graham Ward (Oxford: Blackwell, 2000) pp. 209–13.

[34] See for example: *The Cloud of Unknowing and Other Works* trans., Clifton Wolters (London: Penguin, 1978) p. 142. God is expressed as being ultimately unknowable, and to be 'nothing' and 'nowhere' is expressed as a path towards such a God.

consider in the mystical not to what leaves us bereft and directionless, but, more hopefully, with what it can provide:

> One more thing, perhaps, is mystical: the establishment of a space where change serves as a foundation and saying loss is another beginning. Because it is always *less* than what *comes* through it and allows a genesis, the mystic poem is connected to the *nothing* that opens the future, the time *to come*, and, more precisely, to that single work, "Yahweh," which forever makes possible the self-naming of that which induces departure. (Certeau, p. 205)

This description of the 'mystic poem' could easily be applied Dickinson's most powerful poetic strategy that allows for such openness. However, as demonstrated earlier in poem Fr 655, Dickinson's commitment to openness is itself, like Certeau's, polemical. Rather than producing an impotent silence, Dickinson's non-saying on the divine is charged with transformation. Her versions of hymnic imagery and engagement with hymn culture assert challenges to the representations of the divine in orthodox religion, creating a new dynamic space within the poem. In this, Dickinson's poems go beyond the Post-modernism that sees all manner of openness as lack of direction. To 'induce departure' is to let go of all certainties, the ultimate sacrifice which re-inscribes itself, paradoxically, as faith. As the following chapters will demonstrate, by systematically denying the urge to describe and define spiritual experience, Dickinson's poetics forge a pattern of relation which mimics the 'cohesive' power of the hymn. Simultaneously, this pattern of relation offers a radical, mystical openness which is itself the space of relation, the 'clue divine'(Fr 1107).

The connection Certeau makes explicit between mystical discourse and poetry in 'Mystic Speech' is illuminating because Dickinson's engagement with the hymn as a traditionally sacred form both underscores and masks the mystical aspect of her own poetics. Examining Dickinson's 'mystical' poems alongside examples of the hymn genre allows for a reconsideration of the genre and its implicit assumptions about writings (and one's licence to write) on the divine. It also allows for a re-envisioning of what a devotional form can do. Certeau's ideas about what poetry can do as a 'liberating space' is analogous to what a devotional form like the hymn could also do, and to what Dickinson's poems do:

> The poem - a cadenced repetition ... - does not stop at deconstructing meaning and making it music: it is what allows the very production of meaning. The 'taste for echoes' awakened by the poem leads one 'to seek a semantic connection between elements nothing binds together semantically;' it makes possible the indefinite prolongation of this semantical research as an echo effect. It says nothing. It permits saying. For that reason, it is a true 'beginning.' It is a liberating space, where yesterday's readers - but 'we' also - can find speech. The 'canciones' did not lay down a meaning once and for all; they created a place of origin for 'love effects.' (Certeau, p. 204)

The 'mystic poem' in Certeau's view allows for the production of meaning through what it does not say, and in this way produces an ideal, 'liberating' space of origins and beginnings which 'permits saying.' In a strikingly similar way, Dickinson's poems also have this mystical effect upon the reader. They produce many beginnings by avoiding endings, allowing for much thought to flow through and from them. This quality to Dickinson's poetics places pressure upon the hymn form in which it is presented, urging the reader to compare the experience of reading such openness with what they know of the hymn. Dickinson's form challenges the hymn genre but it also allows for a re-envisioning of what a hymn could be. As the following chapters will demonstrate, and particularly in relation to her use of bee imagery in Chapter Six, Dickinson's readers re-experience the hymn genre not as constrictive and descriptive, but as a heterologous, liberating space.

Dickinson's use of the hymn form bears affinities with Certeau's notion of poetry as a heterologous space which accommodates for difference within a scheme, for the individual's diversity within a community. The hymnic metre of Dickinson's poems serves to register grammatical, formal breaks and also semantic dissent, within the context of the individual's desire for autonomy and choice within religious orthodoxy. It also serves to remind us of the *ideal* of an individual's relation within community that Certeau's notion of a heterologous space describes.

Although the writing and use of the 'other' as a site of resistance in the works of Irigaray and Certeau discussed here does bear significant similarities, the emphasis placed upon the relation between discoursal spaces and history separates them. Irigaray's notion of a female divine does not seem to go too far beyond the terms and categories connected with the symbolic and representation which she describes as confining it. Although the concept of 'horizon' is useful and important to feminist affirmation of positive consciousness and the formation of subjectivity, it reproduces another (if radically altered and re-visioned) version of Lacan's 'mirror stage.' In this way, the practice recommended in 'Divine Women' does not go far enough to eschew the frameworks that are patriarchally defined. Although Certeau's concern with the 'other' has its roots in Lacanian psychoanalytic theory, his take on mystical discourse as 'heterologous' provides an alternative framework that places significant emphasis upon an individual's (i.e., a woman's) active role in historical processes. For Certeau, all discourses (even the 'broken' and 'fragmented' utterances of the mystic) are perceived in relation to their historicity. Therefore, although Certeau's writing on mystical discourse conveys similar elements of Irigaray's notion of the female divine in its appropriation of the 'other' as an ideal and potentially liberating position outside of the symbolic order, it is not 'siteless' and is firmly situated in relation to a specific discoursal space. Action which occurs within language, within this discoursal space, has an affect on historical processes. Certeau's emphasis on the connections between discoursal spaces and historical processes allows for the positioning of 'heterologies' in relation to the discourses which produced them. As Godzich explains:

This other, which forces discourses to take the meandering appearance that they have, is not a magical or transcendental entity; it is the discourse's mode of relation to its own historicity in the moment of its utterance.[35]

Connecting Certeau's notion of heterologous space to the hymn as a particular discourse takes an understanding of Dickinson's engagement with the hymn further than a matter of style. The incongruities and echoes from hymn culture we hear in Dickinson's work are evidence of her direct engagement with the discourses which produced hymnody its tradition. In other words, by viewing Dickinson's engagement with the hymn form as a site of discourses about spirituality and also about a woman's relation to the divine we can view her engagement with, and challenge to, those discourses. The power of Dickinson's mysticism comes in the ability of her poems to relate what is presented within them implicitly to what has gone before – in the representation of the divine in the tradition of hymnody she grew up with, but also within the context of her own position as a poet whose work seemingly arises out of 'nowhere.' The tension between the seemingly 'contextless' Dickinson, the 'siteless' mystic, and the woman poet, engaging with a specific tradition of sacred writing is brought to the fore in her radical engagement with hymn culture.

So when she asks:

> Why - do they shut me out of Heaven?
> Did I sing - too loud?
> But - I can say a little "minor"
> Timid as a bird!
>
> Wouldn't the Angels try me -
> Just - once - more -
> Just - see - if I troubled them -
> But don't - shut the door!
>
> Oh, if I - were the Gentleman
> In the "White Robe" -
> And they - were the little Hand - that knocked -
> Could - I - forbid? (Fr 268)

we can see that the full force of her confrontation rests not simply in the immediate questions of the first two lines. The alternating rhythm of the first stanza is unbroken and strong (nine then five syllable stresses), there are no deviations to register dissent, the initial questioning lines are enough to do this. The 'Gentleman' in the 'White Robe' represents the supposed focus or mediator for religious devotion, where God and the male preacher are depicted as interchangeable

---

[35] Godzich, Wlad, 'Foreword: The Further Possibility of Change,' in Michel de Certeau, *Heterologies: Discourse on the Other* trans. by Brian Massumi, 6th edn (Minneapolis: The University of Minnesota Press, 2000) pp. vii–xxii.

and representative of the figure of authority responsible for the speaker-poet's exclusion. The phrase is deliberately genteel, highlighting the 'civilized' but also infinitely inadequate nature of the devotion and path to the divine practiced in orthodox rituals of worship. It points to the inadequacy of those paths and rituals that seek to be inclusive and encompass all in community. A rather flimsy 'door' which can easily be flung shut separates the speaker from the 'angels,' who, like a panel of judges will 'try' the speaker whose infantilised status adds proportion to the sense of inequality.

And yet, the interchange between speaker and supposed hierarchical structure of hymnody and religious culture is frustrated by inconsistencies in Dickinson's referents and cannot be either recapitulated *or* cast aside. Dickinson's protest in this poem is also an alternative hymn to the devotional mode of her own writing; although Dickinson derides the inadequacies of traditional worship by highlighting her own distance, being 'shut out' also enables further thought on the divine which isn't conceived of in terms of traditional religion and mediated by a 'gentleman'. In articulating distance from the divine to be found in traditional hymnody, Dickinson reinscribes her own desire to connect with the divine, and in this poem, by being able to 'sing too loud'. What the reader is left with is a re-visioned hymnic space, and an alternative hymnody in which the phallogocentric impetus of hierarchical structuring is broken and rendered impotent. Relationality and ways of reaching the divine through language are not sacrificed either. The uniquely heterologous quality of the hymn, which invokes community whilst giving voice to the individual, allows Dickinson to manipulate a position which not only allows for the 'doubleness' which Armstrong identifies in women's poetry of the period,[36] but also produces a *third dimension*. This *third dimension* rests in an openness which is akin to that achieved in mystical writing. It is this third aspect, facilitated by her engagement with the premises and practices of hymn culture, which separates Dickinson's work from that of other nineteenth-century women poets and serves to imbue her work with a resonant creative power.

This chapter has foregrounded debates on alternative and feminist versions of the divine and notions of the 'other' in the mystical writing of Irigaray and Certeau. It has done this to demonstrate ways in which Dickinson's hymnic poems can be read as performing an alternative mystical theology of their own by inscribing the other which is an alternative to patriarchally envisioned notions of God. We have seen why feminist theologians such as Hampson and Daly think it is important to overcome limited notions of the divine and to assert alternatives. Dickinson's engagement with the hymns of Isaac Watts as a model for dissent, autonomy and choice provides her with a relation to the hymn as a space in which dissent can be registered and used effectively. As will be demonstrated in Chapter 5, Dickinson's contemporary women hymn writers made a similar use of hymnic space as a site where expression on the divine 'other' could occur. Dickinson's mode of relation

---

[36]   Isobel Armstrong, *Victorian Poetry: Poetry, Poetics, and Politics* (London: Routledge, 1993) p. 324. As cited in the previous chapter.

to traditional hymnody is not therefore simply one of subversion, but, is one that repositions the hymn as a heterologous space in which articulation of the divine could be expressed.

It has been necessary in this chapter to clarify ways in which 'mystical' is used in this book. Certeau's notion of mystical writings is crucial to an understanding of Dickinson's use of hymnic space. Certeau sees mystical discourse as delineating absences and ruptures, whilst also operating within a heterologous space of relation to the historicity of discourses which produced them. With this theoretical basis for hymnic space in mind, we turn in the next Section to examine ways in which Dickinson's radical hymn-poems can be seen in relation to the tradition of hymnody she grew up with, firstly, by examining the hymns of Isaac Watts.

PART 2
Tradition and Experience: Refiguring Dickinson's Experience of Hymn Culture

Chapter 4
Making the Sublime Ridiculous: Emily Dickinson and Isaac Watts in Dissent

Dickinson's engagement with the work of Isaac Watts needs re-examining. Although a Calvinist, Watts's Non-Conformist position, and the context of Protestant Dissent rife within the religious culture of his day, has been overlooked when discussing Dickinson's use of the hymn form and her allusions to his work. Watts's background of Dissent and his position as an Independent Congregationalist in relation to the Established church are aspects reflected within his devotional poems and hymns, where there is an emphasis on autonomy, choice and accessibility. In a similar way, Dickinson's poems articulate dissent and autonomy in relation to representations of the divine within orthodox religion. Protestant Dissent articulated itself in opposition to the 'Divine Right' of Kings during Watts's time. Also with an attitude of defiance, Dickinson finds her autonomous voice in opposition to the prescribed paradigms for spirituality in revivalist New England. She draws attention to this most notably in poems such as 'Title divine, is mine' (Fr 194) and 'Mine - by the Right of the White Election!' (Fr 411) where orthodox rhetoric 'divine right' and the Calvinist notion of 'election' are reclaimed, not without irony, within the context of her personal experience. Accessibility and autonomy in Watts is expressed by the enlarged and 'sublime'[1] view of the world that is defended rigorously in his hymns. This is also counterbalanced with a lowered linguistic register and dependable metre. But Watts's influence on Dickinson goes beyond simple matters of style. Dickinson's dissent is registered equally in her reluctance to name the divine and in her vigilance in avoiding being mastered by intimations of sublimity, Romantic or otherwise.

Both sought to redefine God in ways that were more compatible with their own experience. In Dickinson's work this arrives as describing ways of 'seeing' the divine that were in opposition to the masculinised and reductive versions perpetuated by religious orthodoxy. For Watts, representing spirituality in a way closer to his own experience meant accentuating the 'broadness' of the

---

[1]   John Hoyles draws attention to Watts's tendency for aesthetics of the 'sublime' in *Horae Lyricae,* linking this with his enlightenment 'free philosophy' which desires to rise above the microcosm to view the world, and humanity, at a distance, and thus achieving 'true sublimity'. He cites Watts's poem 'Free Philosophy' as the finest example of his dedication to aesthetics of the sublime. See *The Waning of the Renaissance 1640–1740: Studies in the Thought and Poetry of Henry More, John Norris and Isaac Watts* (The Hague: Martinus Nijhoff, 1971) pp. 199–212 (p. 201).

'road to heaven,' through simple verse forms which could be easily understood by those less literate than the clergy. Watts had a commitment to accessibility when articulating praise through hymn singing, and his writing allows for a wider participation. Although Calvinist, the central tenets of Calvinist predestination and election can be seen in many ways as running counter to Watts's radical approach. Robert Southey writes in his 'Memoir of the Author,' an introduction to the 1834 version of Watts's *Horae Lyricae: Poems, chiefly of the lyric kind* (1706), that Watts had a 'spirit of charity' in which all (including 'heathens' and 'savages') shall be accepted, and given hope. He quotes Watts:

> I am persuaded there is a breadth in the narrow road to Heaven, and persons may travel more than seven abreast in it. (*PW*, p. 34)[2]

This statement appears to contradict the Calvinist notion of the 'elect' society who is specifically chosen by God, and Southey is careful to assert that Watts's comments were borne from a 'spirit of charity,' rather than a 'loose latitude of opinion' (*PW*, p. 34). Watts was committed to the idea that everyone should be able to practice religious worship and the form of this worship should be easily accessible particularly for those who lacked a formal education. The dominant and balanced rhyme schemes, plain lexis, and definite beginning, middle and end that characterises Watts's hymns makes them easy to remember and recite. However, the lower register of language Watts uses serves to make the 'sublime flight' of his lyrical expression appear somewhat 'ridiculous'[3] at times.

Utilising the hymn form as a model for dissent serves to undermine the traditional religious 'sublime'. It re-establishes the hymn as an *ideal* space which challenges the inaccessible stasis that the 'sublime' has the potential to proliferate. Ironically, despite Southey's championing of Watts, the transmission of the religious sublime showed itself through Romanticism, and the high poetic ideals of the (usually male) individual. This served to problematise subjectivity and therefore also spiritual as well as artistic expression for women writers of the period.[4] In utilising the power of the hymn to invoke collective subjectivity,

---

[2]   Isaac Watts, *The Poetical Works of Isaac Watts; With a Memoir* (Boston: Little, Brown and Company, 1866) hereafter abbreviated to '*PW*'. Quotation from Robert Southey's 'Memoir of the Author,' an introduction to the 1834 edition of *Horae Lyricae* (1706).

[3]   B.L. Manning, *The Hymns of Wesley and Watts* (London: Epworth Press, 1942) p. 88. As discussed further on, Manning states that Watts sometimes makes the 'sublime ridiculous'.

[4]   See Margaret Homans, *Women Writers and Poetic Identity: Dorothy Wordsworth, Emily Bronte and Emily Dickinson* (Princeton: Princeton University Press, 1980). Homans describes the 'gendering' of nature as the 'feminine other' and how women writers of the Romantic period had to negotiate this when writing as the Self-as-Other. 'Romantic tradition makes it difficult for any writer to separate sexual identity from writing' (p. 3).

Dickinson circumnavigates the Romantic ideal of individual expression in which nature/inspiration is fetishised as female.

In a collection which Dickinson's family owned, and which Emily almost certainly read, Rufus Griswold's introduction to Watts's verse considers him as an equal to Milton in his popularity. This is despite the fact that they are also in his view 'not very carefully finished':

> They are not very carefully finished; but there is a remarkable sweetness and purity of thought in them. Perhaps the most successful of his poems are his 'Hymns for the Young,' which are admirably adapted for their purpose. His psalms and hymns have, for half a century, been used in nearly all the churches in that worship in the English language; and if popularity were a test of merit, Watts should be ranked with Milton.[5]

It is perhaps the 'sweetness and purity' in Watts that Dickinson found an easy target for parody.[6] It is this 'purity' and simplicity though, which illustrates Watts's desire to bring spirituality to the masses, and to challenge hierarchical claims to 'divine right'. And it is this which provides Dickinson with a model for dissent. Despite the recapitulation of hierarchical models of relation to the divine in Watts, the relative simplicity of his hymns and devotional poetry offered Dickinson a point of reference for a new kind of poetry, and crucially, for an expression of spirituality conveyed in an innovatively 'simple' way. Dickinson and Watts were both poetic innovators. They have received similar criticism because of their willingness to appear 'not very carefully finished' or 'spasmodic'. Benjamin Lease (1990) observes the equally negative reception of Watts and Dickinson in their respective eras, and cites a nineteenth-century review (1891) of Dickinson's 'I taste a liquor never brewed,' in which the reviewer laments:

> There are no words that can say how bad poetry may be when it is divorced from meaning, from music, from grammar, from rhyme; in brief, from articulate and intelligible speech. (*Emily Dickinson's Readings of Men and Books*, p. 51)[7]

This review is an extreme case of Dickinson's originality and innovation being misread. The sometimes childlike or '[un]intelligible' rhythms and diction in Dickinson's poems convey only a superficial 'simplicity'. Moreover, they delimit

---

[5]   Rufus Griswold, (ed.), *Sacred Poets of England and America* (New York: D. Appleton and Company, 1848) p. 241.

[6]   As discussed further on in this chapter, critics such as Shira Wolosky have highlighted instances where Dickinson parodies Watts. See, Shira Wolosky, 'Rhetoric or Not: Hymnal Tropes in Emily Dickinson and Isaac Watts', *The New England Quarterly* 61 (1988) 214–32 (pp. 216–17).

[7]   See Benjamin Lease, *Emily Dickinson's Readings of Men and Books* (London: Macmillan, 1990) p. 64. Hereafter '*RMB*'. Lease cites article 'The Newest Poet,' *London Daily News*, 2 January 1891; in *The Recognition of Emily Dickinson*, (ed.), Caesar R. Blake and Carlton F. Wells (Ann Arbour: University of Michigan Press, 1968) p. 27.

a use which is rigorously sophisticated. The surface 'simplicity' appeals by association for a 'simplification' of the divine in religious discourse. The notion of simplicity is problematic as one has a particularised view of what is deemed simple and what is over-complicated. (The Puritan desire for 'simplicity' in sixteenth century religious worship led to arguments about their narrow, literalised view of Scripture).[8] However, Watts was perceived during his time as being radical in his adoption of self-consciously simplistic language and attitude of autonomy with regard to worship. Manning argues, albeit somewhat dismissively, in his discussion of Watts that:

> Watts out-Wordsworths Wordsworth in his love of simple, everyday language; and as Wordsworth at times made the sublime ridiculous by his kindergarten expressions, so also did Watts. (Manning, p. 88)

It is this element of 'ridiculousness' or perceived childish simplicity that Dickinson perhaps found appealing in Watts. Watts often uses simple language and images in order to convey his message, and it is significant that criticisms of 'disordered' or 'defective' rhythms and 'bad rhymes' were leveled at both Dickinson and Watts in their respective lifetimes. (*RMB*, pp. 50–51.) Manning goes on to say that Watts's language is 'at best ... pure and transparent' and as 'Anglo-Saxon as Bunyan's own ... but at its worst banal beyond belief.' (Manning, pp. 88–9.) Dickinson's use of sometimes blunt, 'Anglo-Saxon' language frequently counterbalances any precious seriousness or morbidity, and places emphasis on worldly existence. Where Watts's hymns include references to bowels and worms, Dickinson's poems are filled with attacks on the body; eyes being put out and brains splitting. The speaker is frequently tortured, stunned or dealt a blow (not to mention the thought of being 'mangled' by pianos).

In contrast to this view, critics such as Gordon Jackson and James Sutherland both describe Watts as an innovator. Jackson remarks:

> In his strictly poetical pieces Watts enjoys his experiments with blank verse, couplets, Pindaric odes, and even Sapphics, but always seems most at home in quatrains.[9]

Sutherland sees Watts's 'imaginative energy' as that which marks him out as a 'Dissenter in poetry as well as in religion.'[10] Although Sutherland's comments refer to Watts's use of the Pindaric form and not to his hymns, Watts's innovation in the area of hymns is also widely accepted, as he made the break from paraphrasing psalms to more lyrical expression in congregational hymnody.

---

[8]   Kai, T. Erikson, *Wayward Puritans: A Study in the Sociology of Deviance* (New York: John Wiley and Sons, 1966) p. 47.

[9]   Gordon Jackson, (ed.), *Isaac Watts: Selected Poems* (Manchester: Carcanet, 1999) p. xxi.

[10]   James Sutherland, *A Preface to Eighteenth Century Poetry* (Oxford: Clarendon Press, 1948) p. 148.

Watts and the Dissenting Tradition

Isaac Watts was an Independent Congregational minister, part of the Dissenting tradition which had Puritan roots but allowed for further emphasis upon the congregation. During Watts's lifetime Protestant Dissent ran in fierce opposition to the 'divine right' of Kings and 'popery', and many Dissenters were incarcerated. Independent, Congregational churches were encouraged to choose their own ministers and create a congregation with relative autonomy from the Church of England. Horton Davies describes an increased 'sociable aspect' in the Dissenting churches, which placed emphasis on hymns and congregation participation. Watts hymns such as 'When *I* survey the wondrous cross' injected a new subjectivity to fit with the emphasis on congregation and Christian community.[11] The emphasis on community in the Dissenting tradition can be seen further in Watts's assertion of the importance of living an industrious life. One must live a life of action, which is therefore useful to one's community. The importance of industry and of 'useful' life can be traced to Calvin's assertion of St. Paul's notion of industry. David Stannard (1977) notes Calvin's emphasis on an honourable occupation:

> [T]o Calvin the Pauline denunciation of 'disorderly persons' applied [...] to indolent and worthless persons, who employ themselves in no honourable and useful occupation.'[12]

The Puritans required usefulness for one's life within a community and held contempt for the individualistic mode of worship and hermit recluse. It was the Puritan's duty to live and to work usefully in the world, within the community and amongst fellow people. William Perkins, a Puritan divine, as Stannard records, spoke against monks, who:

> [...] challenge to themselves that they live in a state of perfection, because they live apart from the societies of men in fasting and prayer: but contrawise, this kind of living is damnable.[13]

The cultural legacy of the Puritans and Calvinism of her day no doubt influenced Dickinson, but as a woman poet attempting to forge a life of writing for herself, it was also necessarily utilised. Having identified for herself a vocation in writing, this could also be validated in accordance with Protestant values of being 'useful' and 'industrious'. This 'usefulness' also offered Dickinson a release from the expectations of her own society. The importance she places upon having a vocation and a useful life can be seen in her letters, where she is disdainful of women who desire only that their lives be 'taken up' in due course by a respectable

---

[11] Horton Davies, *Worship and Theology in England: From Watts and Wesley to Martineau, 1690–1900* (Cambridge: William B. Eerdmans Publishing Company, 1996) pp. 99–100.

[12] David E. Stannard, *The Puritan Way of Death: A Study in Religion, Culture and Social Change* (Oxford: Oxford University Press, 1977) p. 25.

[13] Ibid, p. 26.

male suitor.[14] It is no coincidence that anxiety about being useful extends also to achieving 'faith' in a particular God. To achieve that kind of 'clarity' is *the* human struggle, the labour which defines the pilgrim's journey. This struggle in Dickinson (and Watts) is also the poet's 'occupation', as she terms her life in Fr 466. As will be discussed in detail in Section Three, Dickinson's use of bee imagery conveys such concern with the validation of work.

Born to Dissenting parents, Watts belonged to and moved within Dissenting circles.[15] Donald Davie positions the 'axiomatic' thinking he sees in Watts's hymns as connected with this family background and also his position as an Enlightenment thinker.[16] Dissenters, Calvinist and Puritan in heritage rejected the paraphernalia of Anglicanism and Catholic sensuousness. As Horton Davies explains:

> The use of the surplice, the kneeling for the reception of Holy Communion, the signing of the cross in Baptism, the blessing of the ring in marriage - those inevitable targets for the Puritan blunderbuss - were thought to be not only the outward and visible signs of Anglicanism's attachment to the past but tributes to its tolerance and sympathy with other branches of the Catholic Church. (Davies, p. 20)

Watts's hymns are peppered with terms for the human condition such as 'worm', which make it clear that he had a Calvinist's view of natural depravity and of inherited sin. However his position as a Dissenter makes it likely that he (as Dickinson does in 'Some keep the Sabbath') would reject the surplice and the bondage of doctrine which it signified. A Dissenter's position in relation to the Established Church was one of the outsider. New modes of expression often arise out of a state of exile and Watts's position as a Dissenter was no doubt pivotal in the production of his new 'simple' hymns. The occupation of writing against inherited religious values pervaded Watts's verse as much as it did his prose. Michael Watts (1978) observes:

> Watts objected to the monopoly which Jewish psalms occupied in Christian praise, 'with confessions of sins you never committed, with complaints of sorrows which you never felt; cursing such enemies as you never had; giving thanks for such victories as you never obtained; or leading you to speak ... of things, places, and actions you never knew.'[17]

---

[14]   See L: I, p. 210. June 1852, to Susan Gilbert: 'It does rend me, Susie, the thought of it when it comes, that I tremble lest at sometime I, too, am yielded up'.

[15]   For further information on Watts's Dissenting heritage, see David Fountain, *Isaac Watts Remembered* (Harpenden: Gospel Standard Baptist Trust Ltd, 1974) pp. 3–15. Watts's father was a member of Nathaniel Robinson's 'Independent Church' in Southampton and later became a Deacon. He was incarcerated in 1673 for being a Dissenter. This experience influenced Isaac Watts's upbringing and subsequent views on religion.

[16]   Donald Davie, *The Eighteenth-Century Hymn in England* (Cambridge: Cambridge University Press, 1993) p. 35.

[17]   Michael R. Watts, *The Dissenters: From the Reformation to the French Revolution* (Oxford: Clarendon Press, 1978) p. 312. Watts cites H. Davies, *Worship of the English Puritans* (1948) pp. 176–7.

The use of simplified language and rhythms in Watts's hymns displays a clear attitude of defiance against religious practices which offer only vicarious experience. The injection of a more autonomous voice conveys in Watts's hymns a desire in to undermine views of the divine which support the exclusive power of a few over many, as in the 'divine right' of Kings. It is this attitude of inclusivity and autonomy which Dickinson perhaps retained from the popular 'simple' tunes so familiar with her friends, family and town community.

Critical Perceptions of Dickinson's Use of Watts

The influence and presence of Watts in Dickinson's world is evident in the fact that his works and teachings were widely available in nineteenth-century New England Congregationalist circles which Dickinson and her family would have been a part of.

Julian's *Dictionary of Hymnology* (1892) gives us an outline of the dissemination of hymnals in New England, and we can see that a volume entitled *Watts and Select Hymns* published in 1823 held a prominent place there.[18] Noted American Congregationalist hymnographers roughly contemporary with Dickinson and no doubt also influenced by Watts's hymns were: Phoebe Hinsdale Brown (1783–1861), Samuel Wolcott (1813–1886), James Henry Bancroft (1819–1844), Emma. C. Willard (1787–1870), Eliza Lee Follen (1787–1860) and Eleazer. T. Fitch (1791–1871), amongst others. Connections between Dickinson's hymn-poems and the hymns of contemporary women Phoebe Hinsdale Brown and Eliza Lee Follen will be discussed in the following chapter. Watts's most prolific work, *The Psalms of David imitated in New Testament Language together with Hymns and Spiritual Songs* (first published in 1707 and reprinted in 1832 in Boston by Loring, Lincoln and Edmunds as *Psalms, Hymns and Spiritual Songs*) gave him centre stage in New England Congregationalist circles. Watts's name became synonymous with congregational hymn singing which gained popularity during this time. The Evangelical Protestant revivals (in Dickinson's circle these were predominantly Congregationalist[19]) which accommodated versions of Calvinist, Trinitarian doctrine had also a Puritan heritage, and Watts's hymns were used to assist these revivals. Henry Wilder Foote (1961) argues that whilst the emergence of Leonard Bacon's volume *Psalms and Hymns* thirteen years later in 1845 was important, the earlier voice of Watts resonated strongly.[20] Johnson's biography of Dickinson (1955) tells us that both Watts's *Christian Psalmody* and *The Psalms,*

---

[18]   John Julian, *Dictionary of Hymnology* (New York: Dover Publications, 1907) p. 57.

[19]   For an account of the Congregational societies and church practices familiar to Dickinson and her family, see Alfred Habegger, *My Wars Are Laid Away in Books: The Life of Emily Dickinson* (New York: Random House, 2001) pp. 27–36 and pp. 114–20. Hereafter '*MWL*'.

[20]   Henry Wilder Foote, *Three Centuries of American Hymnody* (Connecticut: Shoe String Press, 1961) pp. 213–15.

Hymns and Spiritual Songs were owned by Dickinson's father Edward, and were 'sheepskin bound, inscribed with his name, and readily at hand for Emily's perusal.'[21] However Dickinson's name appears alongside that of her mother's, Emily Norcross Dickinson, in a volume of Watts Psalmody. The green gilt copy of *Psalms carefully suited to the Christian worship,* passed on from mother to daughter is evidence of the place Watts's verse occupied in her emotional as well as spiritual landscape.[22] Women hymnists of Dickinson's grandmother's generation, such as Phoebe Hinsdale Brown – who, as discussed in the following chapter, was also a fellow member of the Monson Praying Circle – would undoubtedly have owned a similar volume of Watts. Thus Watts occupies a place within Dickinson's matrilineal heritage. The Dickinson family library also held a copy of Rufus Griswold's *Sacred Poets of England and America* (1848) which includes six of Watts's devotional poems. The pervasive nature of Watts's influence on her can also be seen in her letters. One written when she was by then in her late forties recalls hymn phrases from Watts which she remembered from childhood, a time when she would have attended church regularly.[23] Richard Sewall (1976), Benjamin Lease (1990), and Alfred Habegger (2001), amongst others, have each provided suggestions for Dickinson's contact with Watts's didactic poetry for children, his moral philosophy, as well as his popular hymns.[24] However, it is clear that Watts's hymnody was a dominant resource for piety in the generations of Dickinson's mother and grandmother. It is this connection which makes Dickinson's allusions to Watts, and her alignment with hymn culture, decidedly more illuminating than has previously been accounted for in decades of criticism on the subject.

---

[21]   T.H. Johnson, *Emily Dickinson; An Interpretive Biography* (New York: Atheneum, 1955) pp. 84–5.

[22]   The volume listed in Harvard's record of the family library is Isaac Watts, *Psalms carefully suited to the Christian worship in the United States of America : being an improvement of the old version of the Psalms of David.* (New York: Williams and Whiting, 1810).

[23]   See L: II, pp. 593–4. To Mrs J.G. Holland. Dickinson recalls a line from 'When I survey the Wondrous Cross.'

[24]   Richard B. Sewall, *The Life of Emily Dickinson*, vol. 2 (London: Faber and Faber, 1976) p. 352. Sewall cites both Frederick Tuckerman *Amherst Academy: A New England School of the Past 1814–1861* (Amherst, MA: 1929) and E.W. Carpenter and C.F. Morehouse, *The History of the Town of Amherst, Massachusetts* (Amherst, 1896) for an Amherst Academy reading list which included Isaac Watts's *The Improvement of the Mind* (1741). Lease cites various family members recalling lines from Watts, as also cited in St. Armand, p. 158, and confirms that the Dickinson household library had copies of Watts's *Church Psalmody* and *Psalms, Hymns and Spiritual Songs* (*RMB*, pp. 50–53). Habegger suggests in *MWL* that Dickinson might have learned some of Watts's *Divine and Moral Songs for Children* at her church's Sabbath School during the 1830s (pp. 100–01). He also states *Watts and Select* as being Dickinson's church's hymnal in the 1830s (pp. 118–19) and that Watts's philosophical work, *The Improvement of the Mind* (1741), was one of the key texts at Amherst Academy during her time there (on and off for seven years, from 1840–1847) (pp. 142–3).

Another factor which may affect our view on Dickinson's relation to Watts is that certain religious groups were reassessing his theology and using him as an ally. Watts's psalms and hymns expressed the Calvinist and Trinitarian views of his education[25], but Unitarians were interested in his later works that presented, as they saw, a precedent for conversion to Unitarian views. George Burnap argued that Watts's later prose and poetical works illustrated a clear conversion to Unitarian views of one, unified God:

> While he was acknowledging that the Trinity amounted to nothing more than one God in one person and two divine powers, thousands and thousands were appending a Trinitarian doxology to the Psalms of David on his authority, – "To God the Father, God the Son, and God the Spirit, three in one," when at the same time he himself had given up the personality of the Holy Ghost, and acknowledged that there was no Scriptural authority for addressing a doxology to it at all, any more than there is for addressing a doxology to God's arm or eye![26]

The fact that Unitarians were interested in 'revising' Watts's work to fit with their own theological beliefs might have furthered Dickinson's interest. Her literary mentor Thomas Wentworth Higginson was a Unitarian minister, and she no doubt would have been familiar with Unitarian views and the controversy they proliferated within the Protestant Evangelical Revival culture of the 1830s and 1860s.

During the mid-nineteenthcentury period of revival, middle-class, 'cultivated' Episcopalians eschewed the scholastic use of texts such as Watts's *The Improvement of the Mind* (1741) which espoused using the intellect to support an orthodox religious way of life. They may have disapproved of the use of texts such as this because, as Habegger argues, they perceived them as reflecting a 'tasteless' land with its 'factories, equality and independence' (*MWL*, p. 143). Dickinson's engagement with Watts is therefore more complex than her simply alluding to him as an establishment figure, as a dominant voice in orthodox Evangelical worship. The fact that his work was associated with an increased sense of 'equality and independence', which certain strata of the community disdained, provides further insight into her sense of him. In allusion to Watts, Dickinson also 'lowers' her own poetic register well below the genteel poetry of domesticity issued by many of her contemporaries. In this way her hymnic poems have more in common with the

---

[25]   Particularly the Doxologies – hymns dedicated to the existence of the Holy Trinity comprised of the 'father, son and holy spirit,' *Hymns and Spiritual Songs* (1707), Book III, Doxologies; hymns 26–45, pp. 541–8 in *PH* and the Trinitarian aspect of his version of the Psalms in *The Psalms of David Imitated in the Language of the New Testament, and Applied to the Christian state and worship* (1719).

[26]   George Burnap, *Popular Objections to Unitarian Christianity Considered and Answered*, 5th edn (Boston: Crosby, Nichols and Company, 1855) p. 166.

antebellum hymnist Phoebe Brown, than with the poems of contemporaries such as Alice and Phoebe Cary. This point is discussed in detail in Chapter 5.

Critics are agreed upon the resonance of Watts's hymns in Dickinson's poetry. It can be registered stylistically in the following: her use of common hymnic metre (4-3, 4-3); imperfect rhymes; compacted stanzas 'containing' the metaphor; harsh or abrasive register of language; 'simple' language combined with puzzling syntax; and a tension between abstractions and material things. Wendy Martin (1984) offers an informative illustration of her transformation of the rigid 4-3 4-3 hymnic common metre into 'slant rhymes, lively rhythms and colloquial language,' and identifies what she sees as being Dickinson's 'mocking' of the 'rigid regularity' and 'pious certainty' in Watts's hymns.[27] In contrast, Christanne Miller's section on the hymns of Isaac Watts in *Emily Dickinson: A Poet's Grammar* (1987) focuses on Watts's 'loosely irregular verse'.[28] She identifies important 'irregular' characteristics in other poets as well as in Watts's hymns. However, the widely held expectations of hymns, that they should be both 'consistent in theme' and 'progressive in the development of ideas' is underestimated here. The comparative analysis of Watts's hymn ('And must my body faint and die? / And must this soul remove? / O, for some guardian angel nigh, / To bear it safe above!) with Dickinson's poem ('That after Horror - that 'twas us,' Fr 243) provides useful insights into the wide-ranging influence that Watts provided for Dickinson. Dickinson was interested in Watts not merely, as other critics have argued, as a patriarchal figure whose modes she could reject and rebel against, but somewhat more crucially, because his verse provided an example for the breaking of rules; grammatical rules, rules of prosody, and also rules of taste, both literary *and* religious. Miller focuses on Watts's 'harsh sounding phrases' and argues that when placed alongside his verse, Dickinson's own loose rhymes and cryptic metaphors seem 'less unusual' (Miller, p. 142).

Miller's discussion of the American Plain Style is useful as it demonstrates how the authority invested in the speaker could also allow room for deviance against God, and was therefore a potentially deviant space in writing; 'even when it most anarchically expresses the perception of the individual, it maintains the guise of saying little' (Miller, pp. 144–5). Helpful connections are made between Dickinson's various grammatical 'deviations' and twentieth-century feminist theories of language which espouse the negotiation of phallocentric, patriarchal language, as in the work of Julia Kristeva, Luce Irigaray and Helene Cixous. The ideas in this influential section of Miller's book (pp. 160–86) are instructive. However, as this book will show, they can be taken further with the supporting historical/cultural context for Watts to show how this may have fed Dickinson's attitude to the divine.

In her illuminating essay 'Rhetoric or Not: Hymnal Tropes in Emily Dickinson and Isaac Watts' (1988) Shira Wolosky argues that Dickinson's interaction with

---

[27]   Wendy Martin, *An American Triptych: Anne Bradstreet, Emily Dickinson, Adrienne Rich*, pp. 138–9.

[28]   Christanne Miller, *Emily Dickinson; A Poet's Grammar* (Cambridge, MA: Harvard University Press, 1987) pp. 141–3.

Watts's work goes beyond the 'formal conventions' of metre, rhyme, punctuation, grammar and images. She observes that Dickinson 'manipulates unique phrases, openings, and idioms' found in Watts's hymns, and provides five comparative examples.[29] However, this essay also fails to offer a rigorous analysis of the cultural contexts of Watts's hymns and the different modes and purposes for which they were written. As a result, Wolosky's treatment of Watts omits the material basis necessary to demonstrate exactly how Dickinson's interest in Watts might go beyond such formal concerns (Wolosky, p. 232). She writes that Dickinson's intention to subvert the doctrinal assertions in Watts with the use of hymnal modes and tropes is not straightforward in its execution, and that Dickinson's use of Watts is therefore problematic. She includes various examples of such 'modes and tropes', such as Dickinson's challenging use of synecdoche (where whole is substituted for part or vice versa). She argues that Dickinson disassociates synecdoche from its doctrinal framework of symbolising a part and whole in co-existence. That is to say, the framework which positions an individual and God as being inseparable, and attaining 'wholeness' through death (Wolosky, pp. 227–8). In contrast with previous treatments of the influence of Watts, it is Wolosky's uncertainty about Dickinson's apparent subversion of Watts which is refreshing and provides impetus for studies such as this.

Martha Winburn England (1966) gives an informative account of Jonathan Edwards's promotion of Watts in his Northampton church in the mid-eighteenth century. Edwards was an influential preacher and England shows how his influence served to reinforce Watts's 'monopoly' over hymns for worship in the nineteenth century and beyond.[30] She argues that Dickinson's relation to Watts's hymnody was always to her an example of 'how she never would write' (England, p. 120). She sees Dickinson as persistently rebelling against Watts's 'instructive' moralism, as epitomised by his 'How doth the busy bee,' which became a cultural idiom for morality through industry in the nineteenth century. Significantly, England identifies the bee (along with her recurring consideration of the figure of Moses) as an image which Dickinson uses in order to parody Watts directly. She cites Dickinson's 'Valentine' poem as the first example among a further many, for which she provides a list of poem numbers as they appear in Johnson's collection (England, pp. 122–3). The scope of this image in Dickinson's poetry indicates the extent of her series of challenges towards Watts's Puritanism. However, England's view of Dickinson's relation to Watts is informed ultimately by her view of Puritans:

> She was a Puritan with a Puritan's attitude toward the Establishment, which is by definition a desire to purify it and recall it to the right ways. In her life, Watts had pre-empted control of the Establishment, and she saw a great deal that seemed wrong with Watts. (England, p. 120)

---

[29]   Shira Wolosky, 'Rhetoric or Not: Hymnal Tropes in Emily Dickinson and Isaac Watts', *The New England Quarterly* 61 (1988) 214–32 (pp. 216–17).

[30]   Martha Winburn England and John Sparrow, *Hymns Unbidden: Donne, Herbert, Blake, Emily Dickinson and the Hymnographers*, pp. 113–14.

England's account of Dickinson's estimation of Watts might be less accurate than was first thought. There is much in Watts that Dickinson could have taken seriously. Some of the ways Dickinson may have interpreted his position as a Puritan in relation to the establishment needs to be clarified. England ultimately sees Dickinson as 'referring to his [Watts's] uprightness to define her angle of variation,' (England, p. 121) and this 'uprightness' is connected for England with Watts's Puritanism. However, if by 'establishment,' we encompass traditional or normative literary and religious expressions of devotion, then Watts provided Dickinson with much scope for learning not only the art of 'sinking' language, and of parody, but also of autonomy and choice in relation to the 'establishment.'

Through a Glass, Darkly: Representation and Obstruction of the Divine in Watts and Dickinson

One way in which a speaker's relation to the divine is presented in Watts's hymns is through the use of imagery connected with sight. Watts's hymns convey a subjectivity that involves not only ability to perceive the divine but also that which 'obstructs' a view of it. This reflects the new subjectivity of hymns during the eighteenth century, whilst it also articulates a Dissenter's attitude towards the formalities of Anglican worship. One the one hand his voice articulates Dissent by bemoaning an obstructed view of the divine but on the other he equally asserts a spiritual vision of clarity based on opposition and linear narrative. During Dickinson's lifetime, not only Watts's hymns, but also his philosophical and theological prose pieces led to his name being predominantly almost synonymous with harsh Puritan doctrine. The clear definitions of heaven and hell depicted in Watts's *The World to Come* (1738) support this view. In 'Discourse twelve - The Nature of the Punishments in Hell,' Watts takes for his inspiration the scriptural passage from Mark 9:46 'where their worm dieth not, and the fire is not quenched'. This passage is reproduced at the beginning of a section which includes the following cautionary prose:

> There will also be raging desires of ease and pleasure which shall never be satisfied, together with perpetual disappointment and endless confusion thrown upon all their schemes and their efforts of hope ... But if we should suppose these sensualities die together with the body, yet this is certain, the soul will have everlasting appetites of its own, i.e., the general desire of ease and happiness, and of some satisfying good; but God, who is the only true source of happiness to spirits, the only satisfying portion of souls, is forever departed and gone; and thus the natural appetite for felicity will be ever wakeful and violent in damned spirits, while every attempt or hope to satisfy it will meet with perpetual disappointment. (*The World to Come*, pp. 305–6)[31]

---

[31]   Isaac Watts, *The World to Come: Or Discourses on the Joys or Sorrows of Departed Souls at Death and the Glory or Terror of the Resurrection to which is Prefixed an Essay toward the Proof of a Separate State of Souls after Death* (1738) (London: Richard Evans and (Edinburgh: John Bourne) 1814) p. 294.

Outlined here is a clear religious vision conceived in terms of a series of binaries; good/evil, body/soul, hope/disappointment, salvation/damnation. Ultimately, this description attempts to describe, not only a path towards God, but also the nature of God. Getting to God for Watts involves a series of choices between opposites, and this vision is clearly defined in each of his works, whether psalm, hymn, devotional poetry or prose. However, despite this sense of clarity in the way to achieve/perceive God, many of Watts's hymns describe the speaker's frustration at not being able to view God completely, invoking the Pauline image of obscured light in Corinthians 13.12, 'For now we see through a glass, darkly; but then face to face: now I know in part; but then shall I know even also as I am known'. Although this conveys the separation of humanity from God, which is bound by mortality and corruptible physicality, Watts's complaint can also be seen in terms of the general feeling of resentment by Puritan Dissenters towards the Anglican Church and rituals that intervene between God and man and interrupt direct communication. Erikson observes:

> As a Christian, he [the Puritan] longed for an intimate experience of grace, a chance to touch and be touched by God directly [...]. He saw the ritual and ornamentation of the Church service as so much foliage obstructing his view of God, the intricate hierarchy of the organized Church as little more than an elaborate filter through which his expressions of piety had to be restrained. To the extent that he had any policies at all, then, the Puritan wanted to restore the church to the simplicity it had known in the days of the Apostles: he wanted to choose his own words in prayer, to worship in a plain setting, to scrape away the decorations and insignia, the rules and formulae, which had formed like a crust over the primitive core of Christianity.[32]

Watts makes many attempts to articulate the Puritan desire for unmediated relation with God through Pauline imagery favoured in Puritan aesthetics. However, there is almost always a tension in his hymns between the need to lament a partial view of God and the desire for the knowledge of grace, and sight of heaven expressed in the didactic rational discussions about God and Christian life set out in his prose. Being able to 'see' the outcome of the spiritual pilgrimage, having hope in reaching Paradise is what defines faith, and is central to many of Watts's hymns, as is the imagery of the Book of Exodus. The most famous example is 'There is a Land of Pure Delight,' which recounts Moses' view of Canaan from Mount Nebo before his death, as found in Deuteronomy 34.1–12:

> There is a land of pure delight,
> Where saints immortal reign,
> Infinite day excludes the night,
> And pleasures banish pain.
> [...]

---

[32] Kai T. Erikson, *Wayward Puritans: A Study in the Sociology of Deviance*, p. 47.

O! Could we make our doubts remove,
Those gloomy doubts that rise,
And see the Canaan that we love
With unbeclouded eyes!

Could we but climb where Moses stood,
And view the landscape o'er,
Not Jordan's stream, nor death's cold flood,
Should fright us from the shore. (*Hymns and Spiritual Songs*, II, 66:413–14)[33]

For Watts, Moses represents hope in reaching the promised land, the spiritual landscape of heaven. Despite not reaching it in earthly terms, this land awaits Moses. Moses is invoked in this hymn as inspiration for living in hope, despite the 'gloomy doubts' which arise to challenge faith. In her treatment of the same biblical narrative in the poem below Dickinson focuses on the knowledge of never attaining that hope. (Moses, and this scene, is alluded to again in Fr 179 and Fr 1271, and as 'old Moses' in Fr 1342). She portrays God's treatment of Moses as being in the manner of a childish contest in which 'boy should deal with lesser boy':

It always felt to me - a wrong
To that Old Moses - done -
To let him see - the Canaan -
Without the entering -

[...] God's adroiter will

On Moses - seemed to fasten
With tantalizing Play
As Boy - should deal with lesser Boy -
To prove ability - (Fr 521)

In showing Moses the promised land but then not allowing him to reach Canaan, God appears in this characterisation as the playground bully and 'tantaliser'. The idea of hope appears as a cruel affliction to mortals such as Moses in this poem, which conveys the idea that 'sight' (and the declaration of 'sight') is problematic to the enjoyment of the journey of one's life. The very idea of being able to perceive 'Canaan' undermines, in the speaker's view, both God's credibility, and also that

---

[33] Isaac Watts, *The Psalms, Hymns and Spiritual Songs of the Rev. Isaac Watts, D.D. To which are added Select Hymns from other Authors; and Directions for Musical Expression* (Boston: Samuel T. Armstrong and Crocker and Brewster, 1832) pp. 413–14. 'A Prospect of Heaven Makes Death Easy,' Hymn no. 66. in *Hymns and Spiritual Songs, Book II.* (Hymns and Psalms will be cited hereafter with an abbreviation of the text [e.g. '*HSS*' or '*POD*'], book and/or hymn/psalm number, followed by page reference for the above collection ('*PHSS*') in which both *Hymns and Spiritual Songs* (1707) and the *Psalms of David* (1719) appear.)

of those who purport to have 'seen'. Dickinson discredits the biblical narrative ('No Moses there can be') and likens it to a 'romance' to be mused upon in less 'sober' moments. The fixed knowledge or 'sight' of Canaan which is imparted by God but never fulfilled or attained is at odds with the meandering ecstasy which Dickinson's imagery of flight negotiates in other poems.

The desire to achieve clarity of vision is repeated throughout Watts's hymns and can be seen further in the hymn 'Sight thro a glass and face to face,' which is an example of the struggle with Puritan aesthetics of opposition:

> I love the windows of thy grace
> Thro' which my Lord is seen;
> And long to meet my Saviour's face,
> Without a glass between.
>
> Oh, that the happy Hour were come;
> To change my Faith to Sight!
> I should behold my Lord at Home
> In a diviner Light.
>
> Haste, my Beloved, and remove
> These interposing days;
> Then shall my passions all be love
> And all my powers be praise. (*HSS*, II, 145:458–9)

Although the hymn bemoans an obscured vision and the obstacle of 'interposing days,' the speaker declares the ability to see God through the 'windows of thy grace' and thus claims knowledge of them in order to 'love' them. 'Interposing days' expresses the distance between God and the speaker which mortality has imposed, but also alludes to the obscuring effect of the interposing objects ('Without a glass between') which make worship over-complicated. The interposing glass connotes not only time, but also the 'objects' which mediate religious experience, such as surplices and crosses, which a Dissenter would liken to the paraphernalia of the established church. Where Watts expresses a Dissenter's desire for direct communication with God, and bemoans the 'interposing' obstacles, Dickinson takes this state of temporary blindness or stasis to its limits where it is transformed into a source of inspiration.[34]

The influence of Watts is clear when reading his hymn alongside Dickinson's famous poem 'I heard a Fly buzz when I died.' The 'interposing days' in Watts present themselves as an obstacle to reaching the anticipated 'Home' of love with the Lord. Whereas the interruption of the 'interposing' fly in Dickinson's poem is

---

[34]　The theme of obfuscation and of overcoming 'interposing' obstacles is a dominant feature in the work of women hymnists and the hymns of eighteenth-century hymnist, Elizabeth Singer-Rowe. Watts knew her personally, and she is a good example of this. See Madeline Forell Marshall, (ed.), *The Poetry of Elizabeth Singer Rowe (1674–1737)* (Lewiston: Edwin Mellen Press).

not only a humorous subversion of the faith and 'wholeness through death' idea expressed in Watts, but is also a welcome salvation from such 'Sight' and a refusal of such notions of 'wholeness':

> There interposed a Fly -
>
> With Blue - uncertain stumbling Buzz -
> Between the light - and me -
> And then the Windows failed - and then
> I could not see to see - (Fr 591)

The 'windows' of faith expressed in Watts are not only unreliable in Dickinson, but when she ventures beyond the 'glass' which separates life and death, faith and heaven, she experiences only a further blindness. As the windows 'fail', an assumed darkness takes over. If the speaker can't 'see' or have faith before the moment of death, then death only comes as an end to this doubting via physical impossibility rather than as a final confirmation of Heaven or God. Both pieces echo Corinthians: "For now we see through a glass, darkly; but then face to face: now I know in part; but then shall I know even as also I am known." But Dickinson's take on the metaphor serves to highlight the further 'darkness' or doubt she experiences when contemplating such fullness or knowledge. Paradoxically, it is this aspect of darkness, of not seeing, which provides empowerment and an alternative, renewed vision for the speaker. Not being able to 'see to see' places her beyond the agony of being presented, like Moses, with a view of a promised land that is withheld. It also allows the speaker to escape the confining scrutiny of her own 'death-bed' behaviour that the poem parodies.[35] In reconstructing a death-bed scene ('The Eyes around - had wrung them dry -/And Breaths were gathering firm'), Dickinson does not envisage the death of her mortal body so much as she charts the death of her commitment to the restrictive trajectory of religious faith. The speaker takes a different path than the one offered in biblical narrative. She has dispensed with the considerations of 'seeing' God to be found in Watts's hymns. Although the poem conveys despair at the moment of physical death, as the speaker in the poem experiences her sight failing in its final throes, there is also a sense in which an unexpected perception is also achieved within the poem. The sudden introduction of the fly's buzzing noises serves to draw attention to this. It is the carrion-bound fly one associates with death for sure, but its 'buzz[ing]' presence is also equally the surprise event which signals a shift towards that which is beyond language and human definition.

---

[35]   Barton Levi St. Armand considers this poem, and other Dickinson poems, in light of popular nineteenth-century literature which focus on a person's ('death-bed') behaviour, before the moment of death, as a barometer for salvation. See St. Armand, *Emily Dickinson and Her Culture: The Soul's Society*, pp. 52–8.

Dickinson continues the theme of spiritual 'sight' in Fr 442. In opposition to Watts's lamentations, she reconfigures darkness as conducive to a prismatic spiritual vision:

> I see thee better - in the Dark -
> I do not need a Light -
> The Love of Thee - a Prism be -
> Excelling Violet -
>
> I see thee better for the Years
> That hunch themselves between -
> The Miner's Lamp - sufficient be -
> To nullify Mine -
>
> And in the Grave - I see Thee best -
> It's little panels be
> A'glow - All ruddy - with the Light
> I held so high, for Thee -
>
> What need of Day -
> To Those whose Dark - hath so - surpassing Sun -
> It deem it be - Continually -
> At the Meridian? (Fr 442)

Dickinson's view of mortality, that is, of the distance which separates her from 'Thee' is one which sustains and indeed facilitates the best 'sight.' The 'interposing days' which obstructed the speaker's view of the divine in Watts's hymn are in this poem depicted as years which 'hunch themselves' within the dark passage of time. They inhabit the dark space between the speaker and the 'Light' of knowledge of the divine. Like the 'un-saying' in mystical discourse, the darkness and unknowing paradoxically illuminate the creative impetus of Dickinson's poetical/spiritual trajectory. Obscured vision in Watts is a trope for the Dissenter's relation to the church, and Dickinson's poems exploit this as a mode of dissent also. However, her poems frequently disrupt the teleological process of reading hymn narratives such as those in Watts by reconfiguring obscured (or absence of) vision, paradoxically, as sight.

Watts uses imagery of obscured vision to bemoan the distance and obstruction the speaker senses between the 'I' and God. This can be associated with his position as a Dissenter. However he also, simultaneously, conveys sight of the divine with ease and confidence. In looking at Dickinson's poem 'Before I got my Eye put out' alongside his famous hymn 'When I survey the wondrous Cross,' we can see the way in which she critiques the comparatively easy act of 'surveying' Christ's suffering as promoted in Puritan ideology and conveyed in Watts's hymn. At the same time, Dickinson also undercuts the intensity of vision available to the poet. She paraphrases the final verse in Watts's hymn in order to rework the notion of spiritual devotion, and expresses the process in immediately provocative terms:

But were it told to me, Today,
That I might have the Sky
For mine, I tell you that my Heart
Would split, for size of me - (Fr 336)

The implication here being that it is impossible to achieve a comprehensive perception of God, represented in this poem by the sun. Moreover, she maintains that the gift of such 'vision' would be ultimately fatal; 'The News would strike me dead.' Paradoxically the 'Good News' becomes a source of potential fear, as Dickinson brings into question the validity of those who claim to have such 'vision.'

Dickinson's memory of this particular hymn from her school days is interesting as it conveys her early inclination to the idea of writing. She wrote to Elizabeth Holland in 1877, saying, 'How precious thought and speech are! "A present so divine," was in a Hymn they used to sing when I went to Church.' Benjamin Lease's observation of what he calls Dickinson's 'inaccurate' recollection of a line from Watts's 'When I survey the wondrous cross' is interesting. He fails to notice that her 'apparent' blunder (in Watts, emphasis is placed upon '*Love* so amazing, so divine' as opposed to the 'present' which is, for him, the natural world) provides us with a clue to the sentiments expressed in Dickinson's poem (*RMB*, p. 51). Dickinson's substitution of 'a *present* so divine' when discussing thought and speech is in fact not a blunder at all, but reveals a conscious association between the life of a poet and the idea of a divine gift. Her comment not only categorises the experience of the poet as being as a divine gift, with the ability to use language ('thought and speech') freely, but it also conveys that the idea of a 'divine gift' was the overall impression she had gleaned from her earlier reading and experience of the hymn. Dickinson's response to the hymn's final stanza, which claims, 'Love so amazing, so divine/ Demands my Soul, my Life, my All' is to become the poet who gives her 'All' in verse. Her vocation of 'circumference', unlike biblical notions of doing good work along the spiritual journey, does not require an identifiable end point of 'heaven' or reward. This poem's association of spiritual awe with sunlight, or the sun's glare, carries with it the connotation of masculinity that devours, or scorches the feminine. Dickinson's concerns about restrictive ideas about gender and religious faith are frequently conflated, as her letter to her then friend and future sister-in-law, Susan Gilbert, illustrates:

How dull our lives must seem to the bride, and the plighted maiden, whose days are fed with gold, [...] but to the wife, Susie, [...] our lives perhaps seem dearer than all others in the world; you have seen flowers at morning, satisfied with the dew, and those same sweet flowers at noon with their heads bowed in anguish before the mighty sun; [...] they will cry for sunlight, and pine for the burning noon, tho' it scorches them, scathes them; they have got through with peace - they know that the man of noon, is mightier than the morning and their life is henceforth to him. (June 1852, L: I, pp. 209–10)

In this letter Dickinson voices the social stigma of 'shame' which surrounds single women, by connecting this status with the degradation of being a religious doubter. However supposed 'peace' on offer to those in the 'light' is conveyed as a kind of violence ('They have got through with peace'). The masculine sun of 'noon' represents not only Christ, but also the husband, superior to his wife in the institution of marriage. By extension, morning and 'dew' are associated with femininity. The notion of 'thirst' connotes separation from such feminine space which has not yet yielded to the heat of the sun. Watts often uses 'thirst' with reference to sin, as for example in the following verse; 'Here consecrated water flows/To quench my thirst of sin.' (*HSS*, II, 119:446) Dickinson's allusion in this letter to the 'bride' or betrothed who 'gathers pearls every evening', which critiques the link in society between marriage, piety and social prominence, also carries a Wattsian tone. Her words remind us again of Watts's hymn:

> This is the field where hidden lies
> The pearl of price unknown;
> That merchant is divinely wise
> Who makes the pearl his own. (*HSS*, II, 119:446)

The poem 'Before I got my eye put out' begins with a pre-established mode of violence which echoes that depicted by Dickinson in the above letter. In the letter Dickinson formulates a metaphor for society which 'rewards' women who are drawn to marriage. In this poem the draw to the 'sun' represents the drive for spiritual knowledge, typical in a revival. Violence appears to be the speaker's reward for daring to behave as other 'creatures':

> Before I got my eye put out -
> I liked as well to see
> As other creatures, that have eyes -
> And know no other way - (Fr 336)

The gravity of the speaker's daily experience of spiritual perception is exaggerated in this poem to great dramatic effect. The notion of sight is established on two contrasting levels of intensity: the poet's penetrating gaze which sees at once too intensely and dangerously, and the sight of the many, that is to say, the 'incautious' creatures, whose weaker vision leads them to no apparent harm. Typically, Dickinson fuses the act of spiritual reflection with physical experience in order to highlight how worldly existence is a fundamental pre-requisite to any kind of enlightenment. In this, she offers a counter to the Enlightenment-based idea of 'sight' and reason evident in Watts.

Watts uses the word 'Creatures' frequently to describe the baser elements of humanity's disposition, which need to be transformed and redeemed through spiritual union with Christ. However, the separation between the speaker and the other creatures in this poem is uneasy. The apparently objective, reflective speaker of the poem who, we are told, remains outside the scene ('upon the window pane') is not capable of sustaining the aloof objectivity from the intensity with which she is faced: at the end of the poem she is resigned to align her soul (in keeping with Watts's 'my soul, my life, my all') with the locus of spiritual intensity which the sun represents. In contrast with the difficult and even violent intensity of sight in Dickinson's poem, the sight in 'When I survey the wondrous cross' comes easily and readily to the speaker, who is able to gain, simultaneously, an objective distance from the scene, which provides him with an almost immediate spiritual insight, and an automatically devotional stance:

> When I survey the wondrous cross
> On which the Prince of glory dy'd,
> My richest gain I count but loss,
> And pour contempt on all my pride.
>
> Forbid it, Lord, that I should boast,
> Save in the death of Christ, my God:
> All the vain things that charm me most,
> I sacrifice them to thy blood. (*HSS*, III, 7:478)

The hymn illustrates the point made in Galatians 6:14 that we should always remember the suffering of Christ: 'But God forbid that I should glory, save in the cross of our Lord Jesus Christ, by whom the world is crucified unto me, and I unto the world.' Dickinson utilises this hymn in order to critique of the religious 'boasting' and the Puritan's seemingly 'easy' relationship with God that she perceives in her own popular religious culture. The notion of the 'gift' of salvation is central to her poem and is a direct response to the final stanza in the Watts hymn:

> Were the whole realm of nature mine,
> That were a present far too small;
> Love, so amazing, so divine,
> Demands my soul, my life, my all. (*HSS*, III, 7:478)

Dickinson repeats 'mine' in order to reinforce her sense of incredulity. She cannot even begin to conceptualise the vastness that the 'realm of nature' implies with a superficial simplicity in Watts, let alone attempt to understand how she could be an integral part, as measured against nature's infinite scale:

> The Meadows - mine -
> The Mountains - mine -
> All Forests - Stintless Stars -
> As much of Noon as I could take
> Between my finite eyes

To look at the 'gift' of the world in all its awe is for her a painful prospect, and she contemplates each aspect part by part, just as Watts surveys the fragmented body of Christ: 'See from his Head, his Hands, his Feet/Sorrow and Love flow mingled down.'

The essential paradox of 'Before I got my eye put out' is that Dickinson, on the one hand, seems to be attacking the ease with which spiritual vision is achieved in Watts, and the orthodox Christian view of salvation that his hymns serve to reinforce. And yet on the other hand, the poem's final stanza, where the speaker places 'just' her soul (her 'life,' and her 'all') upon the window pane, re-enacts and reaffirms the essentially devotional mode at the end of the Watts hymn. She writes:

> So safer - guess - with just my soul
> Upon the Window pane -
> Where other Creatures put their eyes -
> Incautious - of the Sun -

Where others offer only a part ('eyes') of their physical selves, Dickinson *is* prepared to offer her soul, perhaps to writing. The effect of 'just' here serves to underscore the speaker's sense of incompatibility with the souls Watts would want to be saved. However she isn't prepared to declare that she has achieved an absolute vision or knowledge of immortality. Echoing the demand for 'my all' in 'When I survey the wondrous cross,' it is precisely because of the expansive nature of her consciousness and power of perception that she cannot offer *less*, or the 'Present far too small.' Although she writes from the objective distance behind the 'Window pane' that the role of the poet affords her, Dickinson offers a new mode of devotion in this poem. Her mode of devotion is to describe her own vision of Paradise which, for her, can only be apprehended in the now, looking outwards from that vision.

Given that Watts chooses to highlight the Bible's caution of vain boasting in this hymn: 'Forbid it, Lord, that I should boast/Save in the death of Christ my God,' it is interesting that Dickinson should choose this particular poem to underline her self-characterisation as being different from other 'Creatures' (that distinctly Wattsian phrase) who 'know no other way.' The notion of sight is crucial to ideas about faith in Dickinson's nineteenth century religious culture, as community-based worship placed a person's relationship with God in public view. Dickinson is eager to criticise the many who achieve respectability through being seen, and having their religiosity perceived by others, but in doing so, projects a certain amount of superiority from her own position.

Ultimately, the poem seems to be another version of the sight prescribed in Watts's hymns. What might appear to be at first a critique of religious boasting and the Puritan's seemingly easy relationship with God, actually reinscribes a religious or spiritual awe. What is more, Dickinson seems to adopt what is essentially a defence of such boasting in Watts (where the hymn's second verse forbids all boasting *'save'* in the death of Christ my God) as an acknowledgement of the unrestricted license to describe one's mode of devotion. Autonomy and choice are radically asserted by both writers here and Dickinson's poem undoubtedly exploits the license to 'boast' found in Watts. However, the awe in Dickinson's poem is arrived at also by a process of engaging with the ideas of spiritual enlightenment or 'sight' conveyed in Watts's hymn and traditional religious doctrine. The process of re-simplifying spiritual experience is necessary to Dickinson in order to describe what is essentially a journey of (self-) discovery, and the assessment of possibilities within it.

As we have now established, there is a major tension which dominates the thematic structure of Watts's hymns. Moments where spiritual vision is obstructed are held in tension with the claims he makes about the divine and the path towards God. The claim to spiritual vision in the hymn 'My thoughts surmount these lower skies' is typical of the confidence in salvation that much of his work displays:

> My thoughts surmount these lower skies,
> And look within the ve[a]il;
> There springs of endless pleasure rise,
> The waters never fail.
>
> There I behold, with sweet delight,
> The blessed Three in One;
> And strong affectations fix my sight
> On God's incarnate Son.
>
> His promise stands for ever firm;
> His grace shall ne'er depart;
> He binds my name upon his arm,
> And seals it on his heart.
>
> Light are the pains that nature brings:
> How short our sorrows are -
> When with eternal, future things,
> The present we compare!
>
> I would not be a stranger still
> To that celestial place,
> Where I for ever hope to dwell,
> Near my Redeemer's face. (*HSS*, II, 162:467–8)

The ability of the speaker in Watts's hymn to achieve spiritual transcendence is conveyed in the capacity to think beyond the realm of worldly existence ('My thoughts surmount these lower skies'). The speaker's autonomous capacity for thought is the vehicle which enables him to penetrate the 'veil' of unknowing, of the mystical, surrounding the divine. Watts fully owns this capacity ('*my*' thoughts which 'look within the vail'). Eager to achieve the ecstasy of (self-) recognition in God, the speaker's horizon for the divine is then materialised into the 'Blessed Three in One'. This is perceived within the 'springs of endless pleasure' which his mental 'sight' provides. This hymn asserts the speaker's autonomy. It is also asserts a version of the divine which recapitulates traditional Trinitarian doctrine, and is described in a decidedly phallogocentric mode and reference of imagery.

In 'I dwell in Possibility' Dickinson locates the poetic process within the realm of the spiritual, linking poetic imagination with spiritual engagement, where access to imagination brings a renewed sense of spiritual vision. She writes:

I dwell in Possibility -
A fairer House than Prose -
More numerous of Windows -
Superior - for Doors -

Of Chambers as the Cedars -
Impregnable of Eye -
And for an Everlasting Roof
The Gambrels of the Sky -

Of visitors - the fairest -
For Occupation - This -
The spreading wide my narrow Hands
To gather Paradise - (Fr 466)

This poem explicates the importance of openness, both in terms of imaginative openness to spirituality and the possibilities that a renewed vision implies, but also a more literal openness. Dickinson uses the metaphor of an open house for thinking through the space of possibilities, of letting the light in through many windows and doors, of receiving visitors and of 'spreading wide narrow Hands/ to gather Paradise.' Here Dickinson's role as poet ('occupation this') is described as 'gathering paradise,' that is gathering or capturing experience in the World. It is an act that is paradoxically dependent upon the limitations of the body, as metrical emphasis is placed upon the 'narrowness' of the hands in the penultimate line. If Dickinson's quest as a poet is to 'gather paradise,' then she relies as much as anything upon the 'narrow hands' with which she enacts it. Her interest in spiritual vision lies not in what may be recovered at the end of it, that is to say, in terms of an eternal 'truth' or 'answer' to life's questions, but rather, in the engagement with the physical world which the process of achieving it requires. The image of the Crucifixion, which the poem's final two lines evoke, implies a willed abnegation of all previously established and comparatively 'safe' modes of thinking with regard to matters spiritual. Moreover, it is necessarily required to achieve this paradise. The striking examination of detail in this poem is in stark contrast with the enlarged view of the world which Watts's hymns presents. Where the speaker in 'My thoughts surmount these lower skies' wishes to rise above the world, penetrate the 'veil' and obtain absolute vision of the divine and 'endless pleasure', Dickinson's gaze is both outward and inward and these two modes are mutually generative in the poem. The line 'Of Chambers as the Cedars/Impregnable of Eye' suggests an ideal space of multiplicity, of possibility, where the poet can possess the whole world. The cover which the many cedars together in the forest affords her, serve to resist the destructive gaze which may potentially seek the poet out. That potential gazing eye is also the phallic desire to define and name, which is equated here with the comparative linearity of 'prose'. From the vantage point of multiplicity the speaker in this poem experiences no limitations, hence what is potentially an enclosure ('Roof") becomes the limitless expanse of 'Sky'.

Although Watts claims a partial or obstructed view of the divine in some instances to articulate a Dissenter's antagonistic relation to the 'foliage' of the

Established church, the teleological thrust of his narratives is centred on the notion of absolute vision and knowledge. Whereas for Dickinson, to 'see darkly' is ultimately a mode of revelation, as she asserts, 'Apprehensions - are God's introductions - / To be hallowed - accordingly -' (Fr 849). The ability to comprehend the divine is 'introduction' enough.

'Give Me the Wings of Faith to Rise': Poetics of Autonomy and Choice

If the articulation of obstructed sight, which also claims an unobstructed view of the divine, is held in tension in Watts's hymns, then the claim to spiritual transcendence which imagery of flight implies in his work is less ambivalent. Watts's use of wing and flight imagery conveys a Dissenter's sense of autonomy with regard to faith and a confidence in poetic expression of the divine. Biblical instances of the wing motif are common, conveying at different points the love and care of God, and the hope of human transcendence to reach God.[36] Wing imagery in Watts is connected with both spiritual transcendence and autonomy to assert a subjective account of the divine. For Watts, this autonomy is connected with the linguistic and lyrical expression ('sublime flight') available to the hymn writer. Motifs of the Wattsian sublime are images such as wings, air or sky, and verbs which describe the spiritual 'sight' of the divine. The act of experiencing commune with the divine is described in terms connected with seeing. John Hoyles argues that the association of spiritual flight and transcendence with reason in Watts's hymns serves to connect the 'sublime' with Enlightenment philosophy of his age that championed reason as the route to real wisdom and spiritual transcendence:

> Watts's adaptation of the Hermetic tradition was influential. It made available to a wider public a Christianised neoplatonism, shorn of its cosmic intricacies, refined out of its Metaphysical framework, and capable of carrying a stereotyped form of lyrical piety, which lingered on in the effusions of the Victorian hymn-writers.[37]

The wing motif appears frequently in Watts's hymns, as well as in many other hymns. Hoyles identifies it as an image which most clearly highlights Watts's adaptation of the Hermetic tradition and notes that it appeared in his work as early as 1694 in a tribute to Casimire. Hoyles also notes that this use of wing imagery carried influence into nineteenth-century hymnody; this can certainly be seen in many hymns from this period. (Hoyles, p. 204) Watts cannot be seen himself as hermetic or mystical as he draws from the tradition poetics of sublimity without any commitment to the ideas of man being made in the image of the 'kosmos'.

---

[36]   At least eight examples of the word 'wings' to connote limbs for flight, the image appears amongst other places, in Exodus 19:4, Proverbs 23:5 and Isaiah 40:31, and especially in Psalms; 36:7, 55:6, 139:9.

[37]   John Hoyles, *The Waning of the Renaissance 1640–1740: Studies in the Thought and Poetry of Henry More, John Norris and Isaac Watts*, p. 205.

However, as Hoyles notes, 'only in so far as he wants to 'grow wings and soar into the air' (Hoyles, p. 204). As will be discussed in Chapter 5, the wing motif is frequently employed by nineteenth-century American women hymnists and Dickinson's use of the motif signals an engagement with this tradition, which the wide use and availability of Watts's hymns during this period undoubtedly helped to make prominent.

One of the most striking biblical examples of wing imagery is in psalm 55, which, like many of the psalms, is addressed 'to the chief musician, on strings, for instruction':

> Give ear to my prayer, O God;
> and hide not thyself from my
> supplication.
> [...]
> My heart is sore and pained
> within me: and the terrors of death
> are fallen upon me.
> [...]
> And I said, Oh that I had
> wings like a dove! for then
> would I fly away, and be at rest.
> Lo, then would I wander far
> off, and remain in the wilderness.
> Se'lah.
> I would hasten my escape from
> the windy storm and tempest. (Psalm 55, 1,4, 6–8)

The psalmist prays for wings as an escape route into 'the wilderness,' away from the pain and terror inflicted upon him by deceitful friends. He does not ask to be alongside God, but simply that God hear his pain. He wishes to be away from the violent city dwellers, and above all to be 'at rest.' However, Watts's version of this psalm emphasises the speaker's disposition and ability as a vessel to transmit sound:

> With inward pain my heart-strings sound,
> I groan with ev'ry breath;
> Horror and fear beset me round
> Amongst the shades of death.
>
> O were I like a feather'd dove,
> And innocence had wings,
> I'd fly, and make a long remove.
> From all these restless things.
>
> Let me to some wild desert go,
> And find a peaceful home;
> Where storms of malice never blow,
> Temptations never come. (*POD*, 55:136)

This piece emphasises the speaker's ability to articulate himself to God, and also the speaker's remarkable self-reflexivity and esteem; if 'innocence had wings.' Moreover, the Bible version's 'wandering' in the 'wilderness' is here more clearly defined and is domesticated into Watts's own vision of a 'peaceful home'. Watts's version champions a division between the 'restless things' and himself, whereas the biblical psalm is less certain about the place of peace which is envisaged. Watts's persona as a hymn writer and his vision of peace or heaven is conveyed boldly. Such comparison with the King James version of the psalm illustrates the transmission of the wing motif into Watts's language. It highlights how Watts's wing imagery serves to articulate self-reflexivity and to outline his own idea of the finite heaven/ideal space he anticipates and envisions in his hymns. As will be discussed further on, Dickinson's use of wing imagery conveys a less clearly defined journey.

Watts's use of the hymn form serves to re-emphasise the linear structure he writes within, that is, within the framework of Protestant theology and a commitment to reason. Both Protestant theology and Enlightenment championing of reason imbue Watts's hymns and moral verse with a didacticism which Dickinson found cause to parody. The speaker's conceptualisation of God in Watts's hymns is necessarily unambiguous – knowledge about the presence of God is asserted and there is a clear upward movement in the speaker's articulation of himself towards God. The presence of wings in Watts's hymns signals the speaker's ability to achieve spiritual transcendence and commune with the divine. The speaker's knowledge of God confirms the ability to 'rise'; reason's part in such transcendence is rendered inconsequential as the all-consuming force of God's presence is articulated through the speaker's perception of Him.

In 1706, Watts's *Horae Lyricae, Poems Chiefly of the Lyric Kind* was published, comprising of three books. It signalled Watts's increasing desire to reconcile artistic, lyrical expression with devotional piety. This shift was apparently inspired by the hymns and devotional verse of Elizabeth Singer Rowe, to whom a poem is dedicated, in book two of the collection.[38] Indeed, the second poem in book one of the collection, 'Asking Leave to Sing,' sets the tone for the volume by imploring 'indulgence of my tongue:'

> Yet, mighty God, indulge my tongue,
> Nor let thy thunders roar,
> Whilst the young notes and vent'rous song
> To worlds of glory soar. (*HL*, I:3)

The poem describes a relation between the divine and the poet who seeks the Muse's wings and 'slender reed' to sustain the 'daring flight' of the linguistic

---

[38] *PW*, p. 266. Poem 'To Miss Singer (Now Mrs Rowe)' from *Horae Lyricae*, Bk II. Watts declares in the poem; 'Twas long ago I broke all but the immortal strings.' All citations for *Horae Lyricae,* hereafter referred to as '*HL*', followed by book number and page reference for the above collection in which *HL* appears.

artistry which enables a heaven on earth. Achieved through God's grace, this poetic flight enables a 'heaven below' which is inscribed by the pen:

> If thou my daring flight forbid
> The Muse folds up her wings;
> Or at thy word her slender reed
> Attempts almighty things. (*HL*, I:3)

Watts's collection, *Hymns and Spiritual Songs* (1707), which was published swiftly the following year, is also in three books. Even after the perceived shift in the focus of Watts's writing the emphasis remains on defending poetic expression. The second book in the hymnal comes with the heading 'Composed Upon Divine Subjects'. The scope for Watts's self-reflexivity is apparently wider in this book, as what constitutes a 'divine subject' is slightly more loose than the paraphrasing of scripture which the first book does. Therefore, it is no surprise that the subject of wing-wearing is more frequent in this book than the other two. Watts's appeal is to see God and Christ in Heaven with the aid of wings provided by the Holy Spirit:

> Descend from heav'n, immortal Dove,
> Stoop down and take us on thy wings,
> And mount and bear us far above
> The reach of these inferior things (*HSS*, II, 23:387–8)

The hoped for 'sight' and vision is then described in detail, as Watts is carried upon the wings of his own poetic flight:

> O for a sight, a pleasing sight
> Of our Almighty Father's throne!
> There sits our Saviour crown'd with light,
> Cloth'd in a body like our own.
>
> Adoring saints around him stand,
> And thrones and powers before him fall;
> The God shines gracious through the man,
> And sheds sweet glories on them all.
>
> Oh what amazing joys they feel
> While to their golden harps they sing,
> And sit on ev'ry heav'nly hill,
> And spread the triumphs of their King!
>
> When shall the day, dear Lord appear,
> That I shall mount to dwell above,
> And stand and bow amongst them there,
> And view thy face, and sing, and love? (*HSS*, II, 23:387–8)

Although Watts adds this caveat in the final stanza, of eventual transcendence which is hoped for but not yet reached, his 'sight' of heaven, and claim to transcendence, has been envisioned and achieved within the hymn. The wings appealed for in the first verse have been put on metaphorically, in order to retrieve the view of heaven and express it in verse for the communal, many singers. Watts's hymn invokes the 'I-Thou' relation and vertical reciprocity of traditional prayer in order to transcend 'inferior things' and to confer status upon his own 'vision' of heaven, which is itself a recapitulation of hierarchical structure. The 'Saviour crown'd with light' resides above his group of 'adoring saints'. The hierarchical structure of Watts's view of heaven is derived here from St. John's in *Revelations*, for example; 'Immediately I was in the spirit: and, behold, a throne was set in heaven, and one sat on the throne' (Rev 4.2) and 'round about the throne were four and twenty seats: and upon the seats I saw four and twenty elders sitting, clothed in white raiment; and they had on their heads crowns of gold' (Rev 4.4). Wings are frequently appealed for in hymns by Watts, such as 'Give me the wings of faith to rise' which, as in 'My thoughts surmount these lower skies', the speaker desires to rise above the world and penetrate the veil which separates the divine from the speaker:

> Give me the wings of faith, to rise
> Within the veil, and see
> The saints above, how great their joys,
> How bright their glories be! (*HSS*, II, 140:456)

Whereas the speaker in Watts's hymns desires absolute knowledge of the divine which resides above the world and represents a trajectory to follow, Dickinson uses wings to symbolise a material immanence. This is derived from physical experience as opposed to the divine interchange between self and a knowable, perceivable God. Wing imagery is also used dramatically in the poem 'Easter Wings' by the metaphysical poet George Herbert, whom Dickinson read, as a symbol of his capacity to 'rise' towards God and to become more like God through suffering: 'For, if I imp my wing on thine,/Affliction shall advance the flight in me.'[39] The poem is presented in two stanzas with lines gradually decreasing in length forming the shape of wings. Thus, the act of writing and spiritual transcendence are connected visually upon the page. Being bestowed with wings illustrates a shift from physical being to spiritual and angelic transcendence. Herbert's (and also Watts's) desire for wings is clear. However, Dickinson's use of wings differs from Watts as the speaker frequently acquires them herself, performing a self-baptism. The yearning and struggle for wings that we get in Watts is not apparent in Dickinson. In fact, wings are referred to flippantly as one of many items in a list of apparatus associated with spiritual transcendence and orthodoxy religion. Indeed, a poem by Dickinson containing an example of what Manning might categorise as exhibiting 'kindergarten

---

    [39] John Tobin, (ed.), *George Herbert: The Complete English Poems* (London: Penguin, 2004) p. 38. Herbert's poem 'Virtue' appears in Griswold's *Sacred Poets of England and America* (1848).

expressions,'(Manning, p. 88) is the one below, in which she uses images from the natural world around her to construct her own place of worship:

> Some keep the Sabbath going to Church
> I keep it, staying at Home -
> With a Bobolink for a Chorister -
> And an Orchard, for a Dome -
>
> Some keep the Sabbath in Surplice -
> I just wear my Wings -
> And instead of tolling the bell for Church,
> Our little Sexton - sings.
>
> God preaches, a noted Clergyman -
> And the sermon is never long,
> So instead of going to Heaven, at last -
> I'm going, all along. (Fr 236)

This poem wittily contrasts an affectation of child-like naivety against the serious paraphernalia associated with traditional forms of religious worship. Where the sound of the 'tolling bell' in the poem is elongated and sombre, the sprightly vitality of the bird's singing is placed in sharp contrast. The speaker wears wings already, signaling her apparent state of transcendence and freedom from the constraints of the surplice and the spiritual and physical restriction it represents. Such inclination to non-decoration in worship echoes the Wattsian, Dissenter's distrust of obstruction, and can be seen elsewhere in Dickinson. For example; Fr 325, where 'symbols' and 'wardrobe' are 'needless' at sacrament, and Fr 328 where the ones who 'overcame' 'wear nothing commoner than Snow -/ No Ornament - but Palms -'. In these poems, true communion and victory lies in being able to overcome not only opposition and difficulty, but also the outward, worldly (artificial) ciphers of salvation and spiritual life. Where transcendence for others usually implies a deferred or anticipated state, Dickinson's is located in the present. She states here that she believes in the journey towards salvation: 'I'm going all along,' but it is a parallel path to that which is prescribed by Puritanism, which traditionally involves the withholding of physical experience until the greater spiritual union with God is achieved through death. The path in Dickinson's poem is one that privileges the fullness of physical experience. The poem conveys with humour the individual approach to spirituality encouraged by Watts, in which it is possible for the 'noted Clergyman' (God) to preach or communicate directly with the speaker of the poem. The speaker here is also able to experience 'Heaven' on a daily basis ('all along'). This idea can be located in a poem from *Horae Lyricae*, where Watts states that:

> Heaven is my home, and I must use my wings;
> Sublime above the globe my flight aspires:
> I have a soul was made to pity kings,
> And all their little glitt'ring things;
> I have a soul was made for infinite desires. (*HL*, I: 50)

Where Dickinson appears to adopt Watts's autonomous view of worship by constructing her own place in the world and in poetry for spiritual reflection. Equally, she also remains sceptical about any achievable mystical transcendence. Transcendence for Dickinson means rising above what is accepted or defined as a given truth. That is to say, it means remaining open to possibilities in ways of thinking. Dickinson could find readily in Watts this equation of wing wearing with spiritual transcendence, and also with poetic expression. However, as the previous chapter explored in connection with definitions of mysticism and alternative metaphors for the divine, immanent relationality places any achievable transcendence within the context of worldly experience. Dickinson's use of wing imagery signals bodily, material immanence rather than Wattsian spiritual flight which has an implicit telos.[40] As will be discussed in Chapter Six, Dickinson's use of bee imagery connotes a diverse relationality, thus making connection between poetry and industry, industry and revery, more explicit.

Watts frequently makes explicit his reflections upon the nature of writing hymns. His vocation (and skill) as a hymn writer is inferred in many hymns, thus connecting the work of the hymnist with the Protestant work ethic. Whilst warning against idle pursuit and of 'vain boasting,' Watts's often considers the nature and quality of his particular skill, and paradoxically reproduces a version of such boasting within the hymn itself that exacts self-validation. Moreover, the hymn below conveys a form of self-consecration where, despite the appeal to God, the speaker chooses to dedicate his life to God through writing. The conversion is measured in terms of the speaker's response to different types of music/writing:

> Mine ears are rais'd when Virgil sings
> Sicilian swains, or Trojan kings,
> And drink the music in;
> Why should the trumpet's brazen voice,
> Or oaten reed, awake my joys,
> And yet my heart so stupid lie when sacred
>   hymns begin?
>
> Change me, O God; my flesh shall be
> An instrument of song to thee,
> And thou the notes inspire;
> My tongue shall keep the heavenly chime,
> My cheerful pulse shall beat the time,
> And sweet variety of sound shall in thy praise
>   conspire.

---

[40] S.P. Rosenbaum's concordance to Dickinson's poems shows that Dickinson used 'wing(s)' or 'winged' more frequently than 'flight,' further highlighting the poet's emphasis on the physicality of spiritual experience. See S.P. Rosenbaum, (ed.), *A Concordance to the Poems of Emily Dickinson* (New York: Cornell University Press, 1964), each entry is presented alphabetically.

> The dearest nerve about my heart,
> Should it refuse to bear a part
> With my melodious breath,
> I'd tear away the vital chord,
> A bloody victim to my Lord,
> And live without that impious string, or show my
>   zeal in death. (*HL*, I: 11–12)

Self-consecration comes at the point of the speaker's decision to reconcile the division between a joyous response to the fruits of his Classical learning and the comparatively less stimulating experience of singing and hearing hymns. As found typically in Watts's verse, the speaker's responses to the music are described in bodily terms ('ears,' 'flesh,' 'awaken' and 'lie'). This emphasis on the physical aspect of spiritual experience demonstrates Watts's commitment to a simple and easily understood language for the wide usage of his hymns. It also lends itself to readings which cannot accommodate the awkward adjacency between piety and graphic imagery. Such graphic imagery as the bloody tearing out of heart strings in the final stanza, makes the 'sublime ridiculous' (Manning, p. 88.), slapstick, even. Watts's use of language serves his desire to make hymns easily accessible, but it also conveys his autonomy with regard to devotional language. It is this autonomy that gave Dickinson the freedom to be critical of the principally organising structures. Such autonomy and choice can be seen in poems where she self-baptises, in relation to her status and position, from child or 'wife' to the singular, self-defined poet (such as Fr 194 'Title divine, is mine/ The Wife without the Sign -' and Fr 353 'I'm ceded - I've stopped being Their's'). The poem below, which is about a bird's initial experience of taking flight, can also be read as the experience of a spiritual journey which is self-generated. Invoking wings again, 'feathers' this time, Dickinson highlights the element of risk that such a journey of becoming involves:

> She staked her Feathers - Gained an Arc -
> Debated - Rose again -
> This time - beyond the estimate
> Of Envy, or of Men -
>
> And now, among Circumference -
> Her steady Boat be seen -
> At home - among the Billows - As
> The Bough where she was born - (Fr 853)

Dickinson's pun on 'arc' alludes to the journey of faith that led Noah to safe ground and spiritual fulfilment. It is also the arc or trajectory of flight which the bird gains by risking losing her feathers, and her life, if the attempt at flight is unsuccessful. The willingness to lose that which we have and see ('feathers') for that which we cannot see, but which is ultimately more fulfilling (flight, and a place in omniscient 'circumference') is of course a metaphor for religious faith. However, remembering the explicit connection Dickinson makes between 'Circumference' and her 'business' of poetry, (SL, p. 176) the bird's object of being 'at home among the billows' (shifting the metaphor from air to water) echoes the confidence in poetry displayed by Watts's wing-wearing speaker; 'Heaven is my home, and I must use my wings;/ Sublime above the globe my flight aspires.' (*HL*, I:50) Whereas the object conveyed in Watts is to achieve spiritual transcendence, which is communicated through the writing of hymns, this poem describes the process of achieving the selfhood Dickinson experiences through the vehicle ('steady Boat') of writing. In this way, Dickinson's poem invokes the woman poet's experience, perhaps specifically that of Elizabeth Barrett Browning, whom she admired. Where Watts claims spiritual transcendence and vision, Dickinson observes and negotiates that which defines, constrains and 'estimates' her claim to herself and of 'circumference,' which is itself 'beyond the estimate/ Of Envy, or of Men-'.

'"Hope" is the Thing with Feathers': Transcending the Word

Although Watts is confident of the 'sublime flight' and degree of creative autonomy which his poetics allow, he also derives comfort from the Bible. In the hymn below, he locates his spiritual enlightenment precisely within the 'written word' of the Holy Scriptures:

> Laden with guilt and full of fears,
> I fly to thee, my Lord;
> And not a glimpse of hope appears,
> But in thy written word.
>
> The volume of my Father's grace
> Does all my griefs assuage:
> Here I behold my Saviour's face
> Almost in ev'ry page.
>
> (This is the field where hidden lies
> The pearl, of price unknown;
> That merchant is divinely wise,
> Who makes the pearl his own.)
>
> (Here consecrated water flows,
> To quench my thirst of sin;
> Here the fair tree of knowledge grows,
> Nor danger dwells therein.)
>
> This is the Judge that ends the strife,
> Where wit and reason fail;
> My guide to everlasting life,
> Through all this gloomy vale.

Oh! may thy counsels, mighty God,
My roving feet command;
Nor I forsake the happy road
That leads to thy right hand. (*HSS*, II, 119:446)

Moreover, the reflection produced by the 'volume' of Scripture is described in plain, physical terms, where the 'Saviour's face' is perceived by the speaker 'Almost in ev'ry page.' The spiritual sight which is conveyed in this hymn is seemingly uncomplicated by doubt, interruption or opposition. It is in contrast with the frequent tendency to avoid assertions of complete vision/knowledge in Dickinson's poems. And yet, on closer inspection the speaker's confidence is also never fully attained. 'Glimpse' of the first verse and 'almost' in the second do not articulate the absolute vision that the hymn is at pains to portray. Watts attempts to correlate the written word of the Holy Scriptures with 'knowledge' in the fourth verse, which is distinct from the 'wit and reason' which 'fail' in the fifth verse. In direct contrast to this hymn we can see that Dickinson uses the same common hymnic metre to write about her experience of the Bible, and how little it provides her with the 'guide to everlasting life' proclaimed in Watts's hymn. In contrast with Watts, the 'antique volume' cannot account for the speaker's sense of spirituality, nor provide a mimetic moment or horizon for the speaker that the frequent evangelical revivals in Amherst were supposed to encourage. She declares:

The Bible is an antique Volume -
Written by faded Men
[...]
Boys that "believe" are very lonesome -
Other Boys are "lost" -
Had but the Tale a warbling Teller -
All the Boys would come -
Orpheus' Sermon captivated -
It did not condemn - (Fr 1577)

In this poem Dickinson comically portrays biblical stories as 'tales' with characters and settings associated with 'civilised' notions of rank ('Brigadier' and 'Homestead'). They are also derived from literary history, involving notions of courtly or 'civilised' behaviour ('Troubadour') which might be found in other kinds of 'antique volumes.' She seems to be saying here that spirituality itself has become 'civilised' and the interpretations of the bible given in sermons has such an effect that does not 'captivate' in the same way that poetry can. The invocation of Orpheus places emphasis upon lyrical art, and is also placed in contrast to 'men' who wish to use religious dogma in order to 'condemn' others. The story of the bible and of spiritual experience is decidedly gendered in this poem, as it is 'boys' who are either 'lost' or 'lonely' in their relation to belief. The alternative to such a method of interpretation is offered at the end of the poem, in terms of there being not only a lyrical art to interpreting scripture, but also a preferred method of articulation in 'warbling.' The word 'warbling' here is significant in that it suggests the bird imagery which Dickinson often invokes when writing about worship (as we have seen for example, in poems Fr 236 and Fr 853). It also carries with it connotations of the female singer.[41]

In contrast to the assertion in the first stanza of the hymn by Watts above, where 'not a glimpse of hope appears/But in thy written word,' the Dickinson poem below conveys a new version of hope which is distinct from the written biblical text, and is the 'the tune without the words':

> "Hope" is the thing with feathers -
> That perches in the soul -
> And sings the tune without the words -
> And never stops - at all -
>
> And sweetest - in the Gale - is heard -
> And sore must be the storm -
> That could abash the little Bird
> That kept so many warm -
>
> I've heard it in the chillest land -
> And on the strangest Sea -
> Yet, never, in Extremity,
> It asked a crumb - of Me. (Fr 314)

This poem conveys the ideal of Christian hope and the comfort it gives. The bird is a metaphor for the hope of salvation that 'kept so many warm'; always reliable to call upon; silent and perching. However, the use of the past tense in the second and third stanza ('kept' and 'heard') and the plodding metre of the poem (4-3 4-3 with the exception of the first line which encourages pause for thought at 'Hope') invites a parody of such meekness and virtue. Moreover, whilst (in the past) offering altruism and comfort, this feathered version of hope, perching in the soul, does not require any thought or participation; 'never, in Extremity,/ It asked a crumb - of Me.' However, the silent and enduring 'hope' also represents the point at which the division between 'I' and 'Thou' is collapsed; the angelic 'thing' with 'feathers' is within 'Me' which provides spiritual sustenance and is self-generating. Despite the fact that 'hope' is described as that which 'perches' it is ultimately another form of Dickinson's non-static metaphors, a poetics of flight;

---

[41]   For discussion of the connection between bird imagery and women poets, see Cheryl Walker, *The Nightingale's Burden: Women Poets and American Culture Before 1900*, p. 15 and pp. 21–2. Walker explains the transmission of the Philomela story into nineteenth-century culture as the nightingale, the sister (Philomela) who was raped by her brother-in-law Tereus, had her tongue cut out, but conveyed the crime in tapestry to her sister. Eighteenth-century hymnist Elizabeth Singer Rowe frequently employs the image of Philomela (also her pen name) to invoke the singer in her hymns, see Madeline Forell Marshall, (ed.), *The Poetry of Elizabeth Singer Rowe (1674–1737)*.

it is anticipatory, possessing the potential to explode outwards and take up the business of 'Circumference' (See Fr 853 above).

Although both readings of a parody of Christian hope and exposition of the potentialities of the self are available, the bird metaphor and its associated imagery could not be dispensed with by Dickinson. This is due to its strong connection with singing and poetry, and the dialectic between transcendence and experience which metaphors of flight generate. A commitment to expressing the 'tune without the words' is central to her antagonistic relation to the inner life which Christianity prescribes. It also offers a powerful counter to the hierarchical 'I-Thou' relation available in traditional hymn culture. Dickinson's poetics of flight thus conveys a diverse relationality which describes negotiations of these two elements of hymn culture.

By analysing the work of Isaac Watts alongside Dickinson's poems, the way in which her ideas about faith and spirituality have been formed in a dialogic way can be made more visible. Her dialogic voice comes out of the space between the acceptable mode of religious discourse and the process of her engagement with it. Watts offered Dickinson a way of measuring her own experience of spirituality against the dominant beliefs of religious communities within her own society. The seemingly paradoxical attitude she has towards him, in that she appears, on one hand, to be reasserting the modes and tropes of hymnody which she aims to subvert, whilst on the other hand, drawing upon the imagery and convention of address in hymns as a basis for 'a continuing dialectic' (St. Armand, p. 158), can perhaps be seen as a reflection of Dickinson's perception of Watts. It is more than possible that she saw him not only as the most popular hymnist of her day, but also as a figure whose work was necessarily innovative, radical and borne from a climate of religious and political dissent. Her connection with Watts offers the reader a reassessment of spirituality and world that is constructed out of a desire to radically alter pre-established modes of expression and ultimately exclusionist representations of spirituality. By moving through imagery in Watts which is connected with the 'I-Thou' model of relation in hymns, such as imagery of sight, the extent of his own protest as a Dissenter bemoaning an 'obstructed' view of the divine can be observed. His innovative use of wing imagery demonstrates a desire for poetical (as well as spiritual) flight, and a developed sense of autonomy and choice with regard to worship. By analysing Dickinson's engagement with the motifs of sight and flight in Watts's hymns we can see the way in which Dickinson engages with Watts as a model for Dissent, and also as a model for autonomy and choice within orthodox religion. Whilst Watts's hymnody, in the main, represents the hierarchical structure of the 'I-Thou' that Protestantism prescribes, the modes of self-validation and the championing of poetic expression that his use of wing imagery signals also provides Dickinson with an important model for the poetic transcendence of religious orthodoxy. Watts's 'sublime flight' remained rooted to the hierarchical and patriarchal premises of the speaker-God relation prescribed by Protestantism. However, Dickinson's dialogic response transforms the hymn as a heterologous, discoursal space in which to challenge traditional, phallogocentric depictions of God and assert a radical alternative to conventional religious expression. By aligning herself with hymnody, Dickinson chooses a politicised space for the project of redefining spirituality which is also within the context of a highly popular genre. Hymnody was also a 'respectable' genre for women writers.

This close examination of Watts puts into clearer perspective the subjective voices and reconfigured speaker-God relation to be found in the work of female hymnists in Dickinson's social milieu. It also provides a clearer backdrop for the assault on static metaphors for the divine in Dickinson's poetry. Dickinson was reluctant to reject the influence of Watts in favour of more 'modern' or explicitly secular forms. She was also willing to call her poems 'hymns'. In this we can interpret what must have been a conscious decision to express herself through the echoes of her own matrilineal heritage. This heritage of spiritual women had hymnody and Watts at its core. Therefore, in her own way, she emphatically unites a Dissenter's autonomy and choice with the ideal of relation and community.

Chapter 5
'The Prospect *oft* My Strength Renews':
Spiritual Transport in the Hymns of
Phoebe Hinsdale Brown and
Eliza Lee Follen

Despite the popularity of Watts and the wide reaching influence of his hymns in nineteenth-century New England, Dickinson's experience of hymnody would of course not have been restricted to Watts. Criticism on Dickinson and the area of hymnody as an influence upon her poems has focused exclusively upon Watts.[1] Although illuminating work has been done on connections between Dickinson and other contemporary women writers, nothing so far has been done on the relation between Dickinson's 'religious' poetry and that of the women hymn writers of her era.[2] We know that Dickinson shared correspondence with Helen Hunt Jackson and was eager to learn of her contemporaries, seeking, as she did, information on the subject from Thomas Wentworth Higginson.[3]

Alfred Habegger's important essay 'Evangelicalism and its Discontents: Hannah Porter versus Emily Dickinson' (1997)[4] places Dickinson's resistance to orthodox

---

[1]   The two most important essays in this area which are discussed in Chapter 4 of this book are; Shira Wolosky, 'Rhetoric or Not: Hymnal Tropes in Emily Dickinson and Isaac Watts,' *The New England Quarterly* 61 (1988) 214–32 and Martha Winburn England, 'Emily Dickinson and Isaac Watts,' pp. 113–48 in Martha Winburn England and John Sparrow, *Hymns Unbidden: Donne, Herbert, Blake, Emily Dickinson and the Hymnographers.*

[2]   See Elizabeth Petrino, *Emily Dickinson and Her Contemporaries: Women's Verse in America 1820–1885* (Hanover, N.H.: University Press of New England, 1998) which analyses mainly Helen Hunt Jackson's influence on Dickinson. Paula Bennett's study, 'Emily Dickinson and Her American Woman Poet Peers', in *The Cambridge Companion to Emily Dickinson* (ed.), Wendy Martin (Cambridge: Cambridge University Press, 2002) pp. 215–35, focuses on Post-bellum contemporaries such as Lucy Larcom, the Cary sisters, Harriet Prescott Spofford and Rose Terry Cooke. Although contemporaries such as Lucy Larcom and Alice Cary also wrote popular hymns, Martin does not choose this as a focus. See also Jay Ladin, 'So Anthracite to Live: Emily Dickinson and American Literary History', *The Emily Dickinson Journal*, 13:1 (2004) 19–50.

[3]   L: II, p. 480, September 26, 1870. Dickinson wants to obtain Maria White Lowell's poems published posthumously in 1855. She also refers to Helen Hunt Jackson's poems; 'Mrs Hunt's Poems are stronger than any written by Women since Mrs Browning, with the exception of Mrs Lewes.'(George Eliot) (L: II, p. 491).

[4]   Alfred Habegger, 'Evangelicalism and its Discontents: Hannah Porter versus Emily Dickinson,' *The New England Quarterly* 70: 3 (1997) 386–414. See also *MWL*, pp. 28–31.

religion within the context of the Evangelical climate, people and institutions which 'laboured to convert' her. He examines the influence of specifically female communities set up by and for women, with the example of Hannah Porter's Praying Circles. Crucially, Habegger measures Dickinson's poetic dissent in relation to this climate and confirms that Dickinson was in 'direct communication' with Porter (Habegger, p. 402). He views Dickinson's relation to the women of the Monson Praying Circles who also taught her at Mount Holyoke as one of defiant resistance: a 'silent, a non-act, a turning away,' against those who aimed to convert her (Habegger, pp. 386–7). Hannah Porter represented an 'invasive community of devout women' whom Dickinson had to 'stand off' (Habegger, p. 414). It is clear that the activities of Praying Circles, like those of the Monson Praying Circle which had Dickinson's grandmother Betsey Fay and the hymnist Phoebe Hinsdale Brown as founder members, bore influence on Dickinson's writing. Such gatherings fostered the exchange of theological ideas and opinions, and significantly, the production of hymns. Although she did resist conversion, Dickinson was far from resisting the preoccupation with theological concerns which occupied members of Hannah Porter's Circle and those earlier at Monson. Nor did she resist the desire to develop her own subjectivity on spirituality which was inevitably a product of such circles. In Dickinson's case, this subjectivity became a vehicle for poetic expression. Her familial and educational connections with Praying Circles gave Dickinson access to an important precedent and wider context for a female hymn culture, one that reflected social and political concerns.

The modes and imagery of women's hymns which also partially occupied the genre of morally didactic hymns for children, were, like those written by Watts, very popular in religious worship. In order to get a greater understanding of Dickinson's heritage of female hymnists, we must consider the work of two women who represent the antebellum era of Dickinson's childhood, and whose publications were widely known during Dickinson's lifetime; Phoebe Hinsdale Brown (1783–1861) and Eliza Lee Follen (1787–1860). Drawing from women's hymnody of this period allows for the early and lasting influence on Dickinson's development as a poet who engaged with hymn culture in various ways throughout her life. Although both women were solidly aligned to religious groups (Protestant Evangelical and Unitarian respectively) their hymns often circumnavigate versions of the divine as espoused in the doctrine of those religious groups. In their works, the struggle to reconcile experience and subjectivity with doctrinal narratives produces an altered hymnic space in which dissent is visible and produces a dynamically re-envisaged version of the divine which deviates from hierarchical structures. Moreover, their work is representative of a community of women hymnists that the repeated invocation of hymn culture to be found in Dickinson's work and letters cannot be separated from. Any discussion of Dickinson's relation to hymnody would be unsatisfactory without an examination of the hymns written by women in her social milieu, especially those produced within the context of a specifically female community in which theology was debated. As we shall see, the concern with the act of writing which is present in many of the hymns by Phoebe Brown and Eliza

Follen presents an example of women who, like Dickinson, considered both the vocation and 'industry' of writing as well as its transporting effects and means of articulating/achieving spirituality.

The voices of Brown and Follen present an alternative to the dominant discourses that obfuscate female subjectivity and position a woman's relation to the divine in an inextricably hierarchical way. Their hymns provide context for the mystical and heterologous, non-linear and anti-hierarchical writing on spirituality evident in Dickinson's exaggeratedly hymnic poems from the Civil War era. The self-reflexivity about writing and depiction of selfhood as defined through relation to the world evident in their hymns is invoked in Dickinson's poetry. Whilst not attempting to work within or offer an overarching definition of 'antebellum women's hymnody' (not least because of the differences between the religious affiliations of the women discussed here), it is helpful to show ways in which Brown and Follen were unconventional. The hymn form in both instances pressurises subjectivity to highlight ruptures within and challenges to the teleological reading of hymns which privilege and recapitulate phallogocentric depictions of the divine.

Although imagery of flight is common in devotional literature, the expectation of teleological linearity in orthodox religion is ruptured when transport, flight and journey are deprived of a telos or end point of transcendence above worldly existence. Rather, the imagery of transport, flight and journey used in the hymns by Brown and Follen, and in Dickinson's poems, convey the transcendence of orthodox religion. Perceiving journey as transport and process, not as a teleological and linear movement, bears similarities with the notion of community in feminist theology, which emphasises process and experience as part of community. Often in hymns by women the point of consecration is deferred or delayed and this feature bears affinities with mysticism. The tendency in Dickinson's poems to defer meaning, definition or climax has similarities with hymns by antebellum era women. They also serve to open out and extend the hymn structure which traditionally encloses the speaker-God relation in a narrative from which moves from conflict to resolution. Although hymns were increasingly being used for private use during the nineteenth century as Hadden Hobbs observes,[5] their performative, outward quality is undoubtedly at work in Dickinson's poems also.

Dickinson's distinctively hymnic poems of the 1861–1865 Civil War period (those which most allude to a rhythmic regularity) convey the poet's awareness of the place of hymns in war time and the cultural association and uses of hymns to reinforce patriotism and promote social cohesion. Such traditional use of the hymn had served to redefine hierarchical structures implicit within orthodox religion, such as God-man-woman, and in turn provided support for the separate-spheres ideology which placed woman's position as the moral centre within

---

[5]   June Hadden Hobbs, *I Sing For I Cannot Be Silent': The Feminization of American Hymnody, 1870–1920* (Pittsburgh: University of Pittsburgh Press, 1997) pp. 173–4. Hobbs describes Fanny Crosby's use and memory of hymns during private devotional moments of prayer.

the home. As already established, this view of hymns as promoting patriotism, social cohesion and the opportunity for a woman to express the feminine homely rhythms which reinscribed the separate spheres ideology meant that hymnody became culturally acceptable mode of writing for women. There are of course many examples of women hymnists who did not replicate or produce 'feminine homely rhythms', a noted example is Julia Ward Howe's abolitionist hymn 'Battle Hymn of the Republic' which reinforces cohesion in terms of achieving victory in war. However, antebellum women hymnists were challenging such cultural assumptions before the 'feminization' of American hymnody in the latter part of the century.[6] It is surprising given the mythology surrounding the female hymnist how few collections of hymns written by women in America during the nineteenth century there are; moreover those which do exist have never been updated.[7] Critical analysis of women's hymn writing in America is also sparse.[8]

Susan Van Zanten Gallagher (2006) argues that hymns written by women of the antebellum era challenge the separate spheres ideology rather than reinforcing it, by depicting domesticity as being far from ideal and heavenly, but rather, as toil and hardship (Gallagher, p. 236). In a similar way, the disruption of the linear, teleological speaker-God relation in hymns by women of the antebellum era provides an interesting parallel with Dickinson's versions of it. Critics such as Jackson (2005) and Sanchez-Eppler (1993) have argued that Dickinson's poems challenge the reader's expectation of culturally prescribed notions of femininity in

---

[6]   'Feminization' is used by Hadden Hobbs to describe the way hymn writing became an acceptable and popular mode for women to write from 1870 onwards. However, women's position in the production of hymns in antebellum-era America was still limited in comparison with their British counterparts. See Mary De Jong, "'Theirs the Sweetest Songs': Women Hymn-Writers in the Nineteenth-Century United States," in *A Mighty Baptism: Race, Gender and the Creation of American Protestantism*, (ed.), Susan Juster and Lisa MacFarlane (Ithaca and London: Cornell University Press, 1996) pp. 141–67.

[7]   John Julian's inclusion of a biographical sketch of Phoebe Brown, namely the 'history' behind the composition of 'I love to steal awhile away' contributes to such mythology (Julian, p. 185). The British Library holds only two collected volumes of hymns by women and one bibliographical dictionary; Emma Raymond Pitman, *Lady Hymn Writers* (London: T. Nelson and Sons, 1892), Arthur E. Mills, *Women Hymn Writers and their Hymns* (London: Epworth Press, 1953) and Charles Eugene Claghorn, *Women Composers and Hymnists: A Concise Bibliographical Dictionary* (London: Scarecrow, 1984). J.R. Watson's essay 'Quiet Angels: Some Women Hymn Writers,' in *Women of Faith in Victorian Fiction: Reassessing the Angel in the Home* (Houndmills: Macmillan, 1998) (ed.), Anne Hogan and Andrew Bradstock, draws upon material from E.R. Pitman's collection (pp. 128–44).

[8]   Susan Van Zanten Gallagher's chapter, 'Domesticity in American Hymns 1820–1870,' in *'Sing Them Over To Me Again: Hymns and Hymnbooks in America* (Alabama: The University of Alabama Press, 2006) (ed.), Mark E. Knoll and Edith L. Blumhofer, pp. 235–52., and Hadden Hobbs's book are important steps in rectifying the gap in the history of nineteenth-century American women's hymnody.

their appropriation/refraction of both the sentimental and domestic.[9] In a similar way, Dickinson's representations of spirituality and use of the hymn form can also be seen as challenging the discourses which construct a woman's relation to the divine through the role of the traditional female hymnist. The work of the female hymnist was sought by editors to reinscribe the equation of feminine spirituality not only with the domestic and sentimental but with the teleological, logocentric narratives of an implicitly hierarchical orthodox religion, whether Unitarian or Protestant Evangelical in emphasis. Examination of American women poets who wrote hymns during and after the Civil war era, such as Alice and Phoebe Cary,[10] proves interesting because of their engagement with metaphors of domesticity to situate female spirituality. However, as Jackson has argued, Dickinson, in turn, also challenges the reader's perception of such stereotypes. (Jackson, p. 222.) The challenge to the connection between domesticity and female spirituality appears to be more prominent in hymns written by women during the antebellum era, and there is also less frequently a concern with ideas of nationalism which became more prevalent in hymn writing during and after the Civil War period. Antebellum hymnists Brown and Follen offer a precursory context for Dickinson's representations of spirituality which challenge both the use of hymns in war and also employ a re-interpretation/reclamation of hymnic space. Therefore, it is their work rather than that of later hymnists which provides us with insight into Dickinson's relation to hymn culture and development as a poet.

Tracing the Circle: Brown, Follen, Watts and 'transport'

> I shall send you Village Hymns, by earliest opportunity. I was just this moment thinking of a favorite stanza of your's, "where congregations ne'er break up, and Sabbaths have no end." (March 27, 1853, to Austin Dickinson, SL, p. 101)

Dickinson would have been familiar with hymns by Brown and Follen: Asahel Nettleton's *Village Hymns for Social Worship* (1824), which includes several of Brown's hymns alongside those of Watts, was commonly used in Dickinson's social milieu. Dickinson's playful reference to the hymnal in a letter to her brother Austin is indicative of the fact that hymns were used as a tool for moral guidance.

---

[9]   Jackson sees 'This Chasm, Sweet, upon my Life' (Fr 1061) as a challenge to the reader's perception of what the 'Chasm' would be; 'The materials the lines work upon are not simply the materials of conventional sentiment, but the discourse positioning that sentiment in relation to the reader.' Virginia Jackson, *Dickinson's Misery: A Theory of Lyric Reading*. p. 222. Karen Sanchez-Eppler argues in *Touching Liberty: Abolition, Feminism and the Politics of the Body* (Berkeley: University of California Press, 1993) that Dickinson's poems collapse the differences between liberty and bondage as upheld in abolitionist writing of the period, thus redefining the domestic realm.

[10]   Each of these writers are featured in *Lyra Sacra Americana: Or, Gems from American Sacred Poetry* (ed.), Charles Dexter Cleveland (London: Samson Low, Son and Marston, 1868) p. 62. 'Nearer Home' by Phoebe Cary explores home as a trope for heaven.

Her partly accurate recollection of a line from Simon Browne's 'Frequent the day of God returns', often the hymn of choice for a Sunday, takes its place in *Village Hymns* under the heading 'Times and Seasons'. The didactic nature of some of these hymns is evocative of the literature Dickinson would have been exposed to during her early years and particularly during her time at Amherst Church's Sabbath School. It is here that the instructional songs, poems and hymns of Isaac Watts were used. Watts's *Divine and Moral Songs for Children* was a popular choice, and Follen's *Hymns, Songs and Fables for Young People* (First Published in 1831) bears similarities with Watts's text in structure but displays a (perhaps unfavourable to the Calvinist school) Unitarian's ideology. Although some people in Dickinson's society in Amherst may have found anything associated with Unitarianism objectionable because of its 'heretical' stance in relation to orthodox and Calvinist views of the Trinity, the Unitarians had some eminent members. The Unitarian's revival of Watts, and Dickinson's awareness of Unitarianism (T.W. Higginson was an ex- Unitarian preacher) might lend itself to the supposition that she would also be familiar with Follen as a significant Unitarian woman writer. Prose pieces such as Brown's *The Tree and Its Fruits, Or, Narratives from Real Life* (1836) were undoubtedly familiar to Dickinson. The Calvinist-influenced lessons of 'solitude' and warnings against vice which are repeated throughout the text would make it a favourite choice for a school with older students. The family connection with Brown through Betsey Fay's Praying Circle makes it likely that she was familiar with her work.[11] Both Brown and Follen, like Dickinson after them, would undoubtedly have been influenced by the hymns of Isaac Watts, given his enormous presence in New England during the early and mid-nineteenth-century Evangelical revivals. They would also know of the popularity of his hymns for children within the Sunday School Movement and also within Unitarian churches. Brown and Follen's hymns date from the early 1830s, Dickinson's early childhood. This places them alongside Watts in the period to which Dickinson looked back as a time when the comfort of Christian faith was the closest to her. The letter to Abiah Root in 1846 (L: I, pp. 30–31, as quoted in Chapter One of this book, pp. 12–13) conveys nostalgia for the early childhood in which she supposedly experienced Christian faith; a faith taken over by a decidedly poetic calling.

The hymns of Brown and Follen connect Dickinson with childhood and therefore also with the period before poetry became an established element in Dickinson's world and identity. Although Dickinson mocks religious faith in letters, her memory and experience of hymns perhaps provided the link between the poetic, adult self and the childhood self of 'perfect happiness.' Given the emphasis which was placed upon religion in school education in the nineteenth

---

[11]   See Alfred Habegger, *My Wars are Laid Away in Books: The Life of Emily Dickinson* (New York: Random House, 2001) p. 100. (*MWL*) Although Habegger does not consider the hymns of Follen or Brown, he stresses the emphasis on juvenile literature at Dickinson's Sabbath School during the 1830s, where Watts's *Divine and Moral Songs for Children* (1715) was used. He notes the Dickinson family's connection with Brown, on pp. 28–31.

century, hymns were likely to become incorporated into one's personal history. It is likely that other hymns such as those written by Brown and Follen were carried along with, and revisited by, Dickinson just as much as Watts's. The fact that Dickinson's mother passed her copy of Watts's psalmody on to the poet means that memories of Watts's tunes were inevitably bound with memories of her mother. In his discussion of the Monson Praying Circle which Emily's maternal grandmother Betsey Fay often hosted and had Phoebe Hinsdale Brown as a member, Habegger views this 'maternal inheritance' as setting up 'pressures and expectations' for Emily. However, the precedent of an organised group which generated creative output which included hymns and a sixty-page journal also provided Dickinson with an important model for her own work ethic, despite the fact that she eschewed a religious conviction such as theirs. (*MWL*, p. 28)

Each of these hymn writers participated in religious groups and movements which became communities that produced writing and theological discourse, whatever their initial purposes were. Janet Gray points out the wider importance of such groups for women writers in nineteenth-century America:

> Women wrote in the context of their participation in groups and movements
> whose purposes extended beyond literary production. (Gray, p. xxx)

However, as women's participation in public debate became more acceptable due to their engagement with the causes of abolitionism and the treatment of Native American Indians, so membership of such groups became a way for women develop their own writing and speaking. In other words, commitment to the original cause gave way to the purpose of literary production itself. Many women were involved with the Sunday School Movement during the early to mid-nineteenth century, Follen and Brown among them, both of whom produced didactic and instructional hymns and prose for children and adults. Examining Dickinson's use of the hymn and imagery for spirituality or 'transport' alongside that of such antebellum women hymnists helps to create an historical context for Dickinson's use of the hymn as a form of dissent. It also provides additional supporting material through which to assess Dickinson's relation to the hymn form beyond metrical deviation and subversion of Watts's use of biblical tropes.

One such trope is that of flight, or transport.[12] Brown and Follen use this imagery to indicate a personal state of heightened religious awareness, thus pre-

---

[12]   The notion of 'transport' here is distinct from the Romantic sublime, with its implicit gender division through which the Romantics related to a feminised nature as the source of poetic inspiration. See Margaret Homans, *Women Writers and Poetic Identity: Dorothy Wordsworth, Emily Bronte and Emily Dickinson*. For a reading of Dickinson and conceptions of the sublime, see Gary Lee Stonum, *The Dickinson Sublime* (Madison: The University of Wisconsin Press, 1990). Stonum argues that underpinning Dickinson's 'thematics of uncertainty' is 'an unwavering commitment to the sublime' (p.189). However, the roots of Dickinson's anti-teleological mode, which goes beyond 'uncertainty', can be seen clearly in this female tradition of women's hymn writing.

shadowing Dickinson's use of it to indicate her more mystic spirituality and non-linear, non-hierarchical style of thought and experience as reflected in her poems. The idea of transport can be seen in the emphasis both Brown and Follen place upon the notion of journey and experience; the 'gentle wing' which traces the ways in which the Holy Spirit 'flies' in Brown's hymn or the 'pathless fields of air' which the soul takes in Follen's hymn, as opposed to focusing on the centre of God or end point of the spiritual journey.

The experience of, or desire for, spiritual flight or transport is commonly expressed in hymns and devotional literature. This frequently takes the form of imagery of flight which connotes transcendence of the world and a clearly defined heavenly destination, as we have seen in the hymns of Isaac Watts. Depictions of angelic flight in nineteenth-century devotional literature by women became a means through which the authors could rupture and/or recapitulate cultural stereotypes of the angelic feminine as the domestic locus of spiritual goodness, most famously promulgated by Coventry Patmore's poem 'The Angel in the House' (1854). Flight imagery, and imagery of transport serve as fortifying alternatives to the motif of the journey or 'voyage of faith', a notion common in hymn narrative and part of the 'myth of progress' in Protestant theology. Flight which is *not* predetermined by an end point and supported by a teleological narrative provides a counter to such myths which serve to define and confine all present time, space and self, in relation to a greater end point of difference. June Hadden Hobbs explains how the journey of faith is crucial to development of identity and 'those who cannot move are denied adult selfhood and mature spirituality' (Hadden Hobbs, p. 129). Moreover, the pattern of 'loss and gain' associated with the spiritual journey is equated frequently with the woman's position, where a 'deal' is made involving the 'loss of immediate, sensory gratification in favour of a huge spiritual reward somewhere down the road; the repression of human nature to achieve a new, improved, regenerate nature; the sacrifice of relationships and endurance of affliction to reach a goal' (Hadden Hobbs, p. 129). Alternative emblems for the divine which navigate such restrictive narratives can be found in hymns by women, who like Dickinson, employ metaphors which suggest non-linearity.

Like Dickinson's poems, nineteenth-century female hymnody negotiates this pattern of loss and gain in different ways. In contrast with the journey motif, the idea of 'transport' refers to a mode of spiritual ecstasy which is akin to mystical experience. Such 'transport' invokes flight and complicates the linear, teleological movement of speaker/God and God/speaker found in masculine hymnody, and the 'loss and gain' formula which is implicit, to produce an essential non-linearity which is a main characteristic of Dickinson's poetry. Comparable to such non-linearity is what Hadden Hobbs describes as the notion of 'relationship' evident in late nineteenth-century Evangelical hymns written by women. Gospel hymnody would not have been acceptable to those in Dickinson's class and would not have been used on Sunday mornings until much later. However, the ways in which Dickinson's bee imagery links ideas of spiritual transport with physicality and inter-connectedness anticipates the 'transport' associated with Christ in Evangelical hymnody. In these the hymnist challenges the concept of having to undertake an isolated spiritual journey by identifying with Christ and articulating a strong desire for communion. (Hadden Hobbs, pp. 134–5.) Editors of Fanny Crosby found it necessary to censor her portrayal of such 'transport', which she used rather than spiritual journey, to connote meeting with Jesus:

> [...] 'our wonder, our transport, when Jesus we see' to 'our wonder, our victory, when Jesus we see' missed the point. Transport is what the evangelical experience requires, and transport depends, finally, on the articulation of figures of speech that compare spirituality to sexuality, particularly to the sexual experience of women. [...] The mystical experience that Crosby called 'transport' is crucial to the authenticity of gospel hymns for evangelicals. (Hadden Hobbs, pp. 173–4.)

Transport, then, becomes a state of ecstatic pleasure which is not dependent upon a journey with a clear trajectory and telos, but defined through relation in the here and now. This is the version of 'transport' found in Dickinson, where it acquires affinity with mystical discourse, because of the ways in which Dickinson's bee imagery (a favourite trope for such 'transport') emphasises physical experience and sexuality as a mode of spiritual immanence. Dickinson's version of 'transport' thus also connects with the idea of community observed by Gray and Hobbs because it is dependent upon interaction and experience in the world. Although not exuberant in the ways Dickinson's bees are, Brown and Follen's hymnic imagery articulates an alternative spirituality which is similarly defined through relation. Their hymns provide an important precursor for the depiction of spiritual experience which is not dependent upon linear thinking and a rigidly defined 'I-Thou' relation, and so each poet deserves some specific consideration here.

Phoebe Hinsdale Brown

Phoebe Hinsdale Brown lived for some time in Monson, nearby to Dickinson's maternal grandmother Betsey Fay Norcross, was a founder member of Hannah Porter's praying circle and therefore an important member of the 'invasive community of devout women' Habegger describes. Many other members of Dickinson's mother's family became converted and involved with Monson's First Congregational church, including Emily's Aunt and cousins ('Evangelicalism and its Discontents' pp. 406–7). Brown was possibly the most famous woman hymnist of her time, as the multiple and repeated publication of 'I love to steal awhile away' indicates.[13] Brown's hymns were included in Nettleton's *Village Hymns* (1824)

---

[13] John Julian, (ed.), *Dictionary of Hymnology*, p. 185. Julian notes the hymn's popularity and cites several instances of its inclusion in collections, for example; Nettleton's *Village Hymns* (1824), *Leeds Hymn Book* (1853), and Cleveland's *Lyra Sacra Americana* (1868). Other hymns by Brown appear in many other collections, such as Nason's *Congregational Hymn Book* (1857), *Parish Hymns* (1843), Linsley and Davis's *Select Hymns* (1841) and Hastings's *Spiritual Songs for Social Worship* (1832).

which was widely circulated in New England and in Dickinson's community. At least as popular as Brown's hymns was the mythology surrounding her life of hardship, as Julian's entry on Brown includes biographical material included in Nettleton's collection which describes her disadvantaged social position at length. (Julian, p. 185.) Habegger's biography of Dickinson (2001) is in part concerned with the religious climate underscoring Dickinson's social interactions in its examination of the church affiliations of Dickinson's friends and relatives from contemporary congregational records. Although it also traces the decay of Protestantism and its doctrines alongside Dickinson's poetry, the connection between Dickinson's development as a poet and the work of contemporary women hymn writers and female religious communities is not explored.

Brown's hymns contain an unavoidable ambiguity which led her in some cases to have to edit them in order that they be suitable for publication, conform to a satisfactory hymn narrative and fit with the rationale of particular hymnals.[14] Likewise, each tale within her collection *The Tree and its Fruits, or, Narratives from Real Life* (1836) (written within an Evangelical Protestant context) strains to reach a climax whereby Christian morality prevails and the sinner is grateful for the changes or conversions which have taken place. Many of them echo the moral seriousness and orthodox harshness of Watts's *The World to Come* (1738) or even *Divine and Moral Songs for Children* (1715). Although Brown's hymns appear to conform to the moral didacticism conveyed in this collection of tales, there are striking moments where they lack the spiritual clarity and resolution one would expect to find in Evangelical hymnody of the Great Awakening, where religious conversion was a primary concern. Indeed one of the first of Brown's hymns to appear in Asahel Nettleton's *Village Hymns for Social Worship Selected and Original: Designed as a Supplement to Dr Watts's Psalms and Hymns* (1824)[15] is included under the category heading of 'Missionary Meetings,' conveying the extent to which the 'performance' value attached to hymns supplied their context. Four of Brown's hymns appear in this collection and can be identified by a capital letter 'B' next to the hymn number. The fact that Phoebe Brown's hymns were placed in a collection which was to be a supplement to Watts's hymns suggests that such hymns would, in the eyes of the editor, bear a close connection with the style and missionary, didactical mode of Watts. Indeed, three of the four hymns included in this collection share Watts's concern with reaching or communicating with God, and also the plodding common hymn metre which is the hallmark of his

---

[14]   John Julian, (ed.), *Dictionary of Hymnology*, p. 185. Brown was asked to alter several hymns in order that they be included in collections such as Elias Nason's *The Congregational Hymnbook For the Service of the Sanctuary* (Boston: John. P. Jewett and Co., 1857).

[15]   Asahel Nettleton, (ed.), *Village Hymns for Social Worship Selected and Original: Designed as a Supplement to Dr Watts's Psalms and Hymns* (Hartford: Printed by Goodwin and Co., 1824). As Dickinson's reference to it in her letters suggests, and as records show, a copy of this collection was owned by the Dickinsons. Hereafter abbreviated as '*VH*' followed by hymn and page number.

hymns. Brown's hymns also bear a remarkable resemblance to those written by Watts in their concern with the writing process, which in Watts, is the method of achieving spiritual transcendence.

The metaphors of journey and flight which are common in devotional literature (George Herbert's 'Easter-Wings' is a notable example) appear frequently in Brown's hymns, and not only in those written for sailors which carry particular resonance with the idea of the voyage. Under the heading of 'missionary meetings,' the hymn 'Go, messenger of love, and bear,' conveys a concern with the capacity of religious writing to transport, and, it is hoped, transform, the listener:

> Go, messenger of love, and bear,
> Upon thy gentle wing,
> The song which seraphs love to hear,
> And angels joy to sing.
>
> Go to the heart with sin opprest,
> And dry the sorrowing tear;
> Extract the thorn that wounds the breast,
> The drooping spirit cheer.
>
> Go, say to Zion, "Jesus reigns" -
> By his resistless power,
> He binds his enemies with chains;
> They fall to rise no more.
>
> Tell how the Holy Spirit flies,
> As he from heaven descends -
> Arrests his proudest enemies,
> And changes them to friends. (*VH*, 496:371–2)

The teleological movement from composition to transport to hoped-for conversion in this hymn appears upon initial reading to be straight forward, compounded by the Wattsian strength of its assured common metre. It is hoped that the 'song,' that is the hymn being composed, will bear witness to the triumph of Jesus over enemies who 'fall to rise no more.' However, the leap that the hymn makes between the method and manner of the song is disjointed, and at odds with the oppositional nature of the narrative doctrine of Jesus's dominant 'power'. In contrast, the song's 'gentle wing', which is aligned with the Holy Spirit in the final verse, conveys a much less combative, linear objective than the two middle verses. Furthermore, the final 'resolution' of conflict in the final verse, that enemies should be 'change[d] to friends,' sits uneasily alongside the fatal bondage Jesus is described as inflicting upon his enemies in the third verse. So there is an identifiable unresolved tension in this hymn between the 'gentle wing' of the 'song' and the uncompromising drive towards conversion which it aims to portray. The hymn itself ostensibly flies upon this 'gentle wing', transporting the 'opprest' in the same way as the Holy Spirit 'flies.' Yet rather than transforming the listener and conveying images of absolute power, the third and final verses draw attention to those moments when the individualised action of Jesus/God is described ('Jesus reigns'-/'he from heaven descends-'). Such action separates the speaker from the divine and leaves the reader/listener to contemplate the consequences of such action. Brown's writing itself takes over the privileged position of 'messenger,' bearing wings akin to the 'Holy Spirit' which also 'flies.' Therefore, although the verse attempts to describe the drive towards conversion that the hymn intends to implement, the transformative, teleological journey from sin to anticipated conversion is subsumed by the transporting, rapturous effects of the writing itself. This spiritual force seeks to soothe the sorrow of those 'opprest' and 'tell' of the Holy Spirit's 'flight' and restorative capacity without actually describing it. Furthermore, Brown's directives ('Go', 'Tell') imbue the hymn with a continuous and immediate mode of action which avoids descriptions of the point of ultimate conversion. It thus suspends definition of the divine in a similar way to the manner in which Dickinson insists in the poem 'A Transport one cannot contain' (as discussed below).

Brown's hymn addresses the Missionary and in that sense describes its aim to bring comfort and impart knowledge ('dry the sorrowing tear'/ [...] 'Tell how the Holy Spirit Flies'). However, she writes within the dominant discourse of Protestant Evangelical conversion, describing the hymn's journey toward the reader/listener without describing an end point of completion. In this way, the hymnist's experience of writing the hymn is conveyed more strongly than the experience of conversion itself. Hymnic space, traditionally colonised by hierarchical definitions of the divine is reconfigured in Brown's hymn to allow an openness which includes the speaker's subjectivity and self-reflexivity about the nature of her 'winged' hymn. The categorisation of such a hymn as a paean to the Protestant Evangelical missionary ('Go, say to Zion, "Jesus reigns"') or to sentimentalism ('changes enemies to friends') is complicated by the speaker's overt awareness of its mode of operation. The speaker's foregrounding of the hymn's religious context belies an anxiety about the effectiveness of the resolutions the hymn strains to bear. The powerful act of writing, of unleashing subjectivity ('Go, messenger of love, and bear') and of extending it outwards, is the hymn's primary concern. The genre's association with communal experience supports Brown's ambition for her words, by harnessing that subjectivity and propelling it towards relation; an immediate relation between self and world which is both intimate *and* multiple and diverse. The space between the religious tradition Brown writes within and her own spiritual experience is thus conveyed within and through the transporting act of writing of the hymn.

The transporting aspect and effect of writing appears frequently in Brown's hymns. Another example is 'How sweet the melting lay,' which appeared in Cleveland's *Lyra Sacra Americana* in 1868, under the heading 'Morning Prayer Meeting:'

> How sweet the melting lay
> Which breaks upon the ear,
> When, at the hour of rising day,
> Christians unite in prayer.

The breezes waft their cries
Up to Jehova's throne;
He listens to their bursting sighs,
And sends his blessings down.

So Jesus rose to pray
Before the morning light;
Once on the chilling mount did stay
And wrestle all the night.

Glory to God on high
Who sends his blessings down,
To rescue souls condemn'd to die,
And make His people one. (*Lyra Sacra Americana*, pp. 28–9)[16]

Considered by the editor as appropriate to connect with prayer meetings, this hymn describes the experience and act of praise and worship. However, the phrase 'melting lay' is self-consciously poetic and invokes a connection between the sound of hymns being sung communally and, once again, the speaker's ambition for the hymn itself. In describing the scene, Brown's hymn also extends praise outward, the scene of a transported community of worshippers transporting the writer herself in the process of writing. Far from describing a tightly constructed group or cohesive core, the 'united Christians' are connected by praise which is described in terms of fluidity and elasticity, which is at turns 'melting,' and 'breaks;' 'breezes waft their cries,' and their sighs are 'bursting.' Brown's connection of the physical act of singing and producing sound with the biblical trope of water (connotative of the holy spirit) confers a strength of movement and power to her own writing and also undermines the importance of the linear, reciprocal movement between speaker and God found in traditional hymnody. Although the fact that God 'sends his blessings down' is repeated in verses two and four, the strikingly poetic description of the communal activity and experience of worship which unites Christians is the dominant aspect of the hymn. The continual need for praise and for unification which the hymn describes is not reached at the end; there is no explicit point of resolution. Rather, unification is conveyed as an ongoing process ('who sends his blessings down/to rescue souls condemn'd to die/and make His people one') where God's action ('sends') is always present and continual. This serves to forge a continuity of experience over the biblical account of the past, where Jesus 'once' rose, and wrestled on the 'chilly mount.'

In this hymn Brown articulates and performs her own version of praise, which, as its fluid description of communal praise implies, is the self (subjectivity) in relation. Far from offering a sentimental and idealised version of Christian unity

---

[16]   Charles Dexter Cleveland, (ed.), *Lyra Sacra Americana: Or, Gems from American Sacred Poetry* (London: Samson Low, Son and Marston, 1868) 'XXII Morning Prayer Meeting,' by Phoebe Brown, pp. 28–9.

and union with the divine, Brown's hymn situates the act of praise within the context of a negotiation with daily life and struggle, as Jesus himself did 'wrestle all the night.' Brown gives credence to her own act of writing by comparing it with the actions of Jesus, who, like her, (in the hours when work is done or before a day of work begins), 'rose to pray before the morning light.'

The theme of requiring time to one's self in order to achieve spiritual solace is continued in the hymn 'I love to steal awhile away', where Brown connects spirituality with struggle more forcefully. This, Brown's most famous hymn, was altered for its inclusion in Nettleton's *Village Hymns* (Julian, p. 185.). Alterations were made by Nettleton, including the significant omission of three stanzas.[17] It appears in *Village Hymns* as:

> I love to steal awhile away
> From every cumb'ring care,
> And spend the hours of setting day,
> In humble, grateful prayer.
>
> I love in solitude to shed
> The penitential tear,
> And all his promises to plead,
> Where none but God can hear.
>
> I love to think on mercies past,
> And future good implore;
> And all my cares and sorrows cast
> On him whom I adore.
>
> I love by faith to take a view
> Of brighter scenes in heaven;
> The prospect oft my strength renews,
> While here by tempests driven.
>
> Thus, when life's toilsome day is o'er,
> May its departing ray
> Be calm as this impressive hour,
> And lead to endless day. (*VH*, 285:219–20)

However, as Van Zanten Gallagher has shown, the three removed stanzas were those which implied a fierce critique of domesticity:

> Yes, when the toilsome day is gone,
> And night with banners gray,
> Steals silently the glade along
> In twilight's soft array,

---

[17]   S.W. Duffield describes Nettleton's 'compression' of this hymn in his history of Brown. S.W. Duffield, *English Hymns: Their Authors and History* (New York: Funk and Wagnalls Co, 1886) pp. 242–47 (p. 244).

I love to steal awhile away
From little ones and care,
And spend the hours of setting day
In gratitude and prayer.

[...]

I love to meditate on death!
When shall his message come
With friendly smiles to steal my breath
And take an exile home? [18]

As the original stanzas in this version, and the remaining original second stanza from the Nettleton version show, the much sought bliss of 'solitude' is only found occasionally, and then it is to shed tears. As Gallagher argues, this hymn 'posits an alternative domestic space in heaven that will release the homebound woman from 'life's toilsome day" (p. 245). Far from an idealised version of heaven at home, Brown's hymn offers a critique of domesticity as comprised of inevitable toil rather than bliss. As with many hymns the structure includes repetition of 'I love,' which although attempting to impose subjective voice onto the narrative of a woman's 'Private Devotion' the narrative it struggles to convey is problematic. Moreover, despite the fact that the speaker in this hymn appears anxious to convey satisfaction in achieving such solitude, it is the struggle and pains to achieve it which comes through primarily, just barely suppressed by the guiding, directive repetitions. Indeed, in order to make the hymn narrative even more forceful and less ambiguous than the version in *Village Hymns*, Charles Dexter Cleveland's treatment of the hymn appears with the significant change in verse four from 'the prospect *oft* my strength renews' back to 'the prospect *doth* my strength renew' as Brown herself had written in the original.[19] The fact that Cleveland felt it necessary to make such a substitution is telling, as this subtle change alone dramatically affects a reading of the hymn as offering a depiction of assured spiritual satisfaction ('doth') where 'oft' is far less certain. The fact that such 'small' changes were deemed necessary in many ways emphasises the symbolic value of the hymn, and the extent of the cultural investment in them.

---

[18]   Susan Van Zanten Gallagher, 'Domesticity in American Hymns,' p. 245. Gallagher's source for the pre-edited version of Brown's hymn is Charles S. Nutter and Wilbur F. Tillet, (eds), *The Hymns and Hymn Writers of the Church: An Annotated Edition of The Methodist Hymnal* (New York: Methodist Book Concern, 1911) Hymn # 498.

[19]   Ibid, p. 245, Gallagher cites the original stanza which includes 'doth'. Charles Dexter Cleveland, (ed.), *Lyra Sacra Americana: Or Gems From American Sacred Poetry*, p. 29. 'I love to seal awhile away' is numbered xxiii and appears under the title 'Private Devotion.' Later reprints of *Village Hymns* also retain this less ambiguous 'doth'. (For example, New York: J.M Fairchild and Co., 1858) (p. 223).

The space between the speaker and the attempt to convey a traditional religious narrative of the divine is highlighted in another hymn by Brown, which appears under the heading 'the penitent' in *Village Hymns* and with a reference to Luke's gospel, vii, 36–50. The hymn alludes to the story of Mary Magdalene washing Jesus's feet; a narrative of penitence popular in Evangelical circles. In this way the hymn corresponds with the expectations of a hymnal conceived as a companion to Watts. 'As once the Saviour' invokes traditional hierarchical notions of God-man-woman by conveying the female supplicatory position in relation to the elevated Christ. Its subject is thus 'suitable' for a woman hymnist:

> As once the Saviour took his seat -
> Attracted by his fame,
> And lowly bending at his feet,
> A humble supplicant came.
>
> Asham'd to lift her streaming eyes
> His holy glance to meet,
> She pour'd her costly sacrifice
> Upon the Saviour's feet.
>
> Oppress'd with sin and sorrow's weight,
> And sinking in despair,
> With tears she wash'd his sacred feet,
> And wip'd them with her hair.
>
> "Depart in peace," the Saviour said,
> "Thy sins are all forgiv'n!"
> The trembling sinner rais'd her head,
> In peaceful hope of heav'n. (*VH*, 90:69)

Upon first reading the hymn's metrical pace pushes the narrative of penitence along on what is seemingly unshakable ground: the supplicant is 'asham'd' and lowly, but redeems herself in the eyes of Christ with her tearful penitence; her tears and hair 'wipe' the feet of Christ as he then 'wipes' her sins away, concluding with the directive, 'Depart in peace.' However, there are points at which Brown's rendering of the biblical scene deviates from the depiction of Magdalene's supplication in the Gospels, and the hymn's positioning of the penitent in relation to the figure of Christ is both shifting and paradoxical.

On the one hand, the hymn appears to connect Magdalene with Christ. The distance between them is narrowed by the very first word of the hymn, 'as,' which immediately makes a connection between Magdalene's actions and Christ's. This has the effect of conferring status upon her own action to seek salvation and connection with the divine. Conversely, the hymn also articulates the penitent's distance from Christ; conveying her difficulty in meeting His eyes, anticipating the Pauline imagery of obscured vision (frequently employed by Watts, as shown in Chapters Two and Four). However, in the second verse subjective knowledge of the penitent's inability to 'meet' Christ's 'holy glance' interrupts the simple narration begun in the first verse, thus privileging this moment as the central concern. The hymn declares that the penitent is 'ashamed' and that the sacrifice of tears (which is not tears, but expensive oil in Luke's Gospel) was 'costly,' conveying an intimate knowledge of the penitent's suffering. Christ's 'glance' is fleeting, momentary, and almost arbitrary. Moreover, the swiftness with which Christ's forgiveness is conveyed in the final verse suggests an implausibility which is then confirmed in the final line 'in peaceful hope of heaven,' where knowledge, faith or certainty are substituted with a decidedly less firm statement of 'hope.' That said, the supplicant's experience of 'hope' in the hymn is also consistent with the Pauline version of partial sight; even saved sinners are not supposed to be presumptuous, and the final 'hope' she is given is one of the divine three elements in the trio of 'faith, hope and charity'. The fact that the final word of the hymn is 'heaven' suggests a journey towards it, and the supplicant is also addressed directly by Christ, placing the speaker in a position of relative elevation. However, the shifting and paradoxical position of Christ in relation to the female supplicant exposes paradoxes within traditional biblical discourse. The hymn's moments of identification with Magdalene's suffering in verses two and three place the dominant biblical discourse which equate female sexuality with sin and salvation with fear and condemnation ('trembling sinner'), alongside contemplation of intimacy with Christ. In this way, the hymn posits a view of Christ's love as having the potential to transform not only the 'sinner' but also narratives of female sin whilst also recapitulating a 'traditional' narrative of penitence. However, the hymn's final verse is far from the satisfactory resolution to be found in the penitent narratives in Watts's hymns in which, for example;

> Life and immortal joys are given
> To souls that mourn the sins they've done;
> Children of wrath, made heirs of heaven,
> By faith in God's eternal Son. (*HSS*, II, 125:449)

Dickinson frequently derided such reliance upon biblical text as a way of reaching understanding about the divine; for her 'The Bible is an antique Volume/Written by faded Men' (Fr 1577). In a similar way, although the manifest content of her work is pious in a way that Dickinson's is not, Brown implicitly questioned the relation between rational approaches to the divine and emotional response to/through the 'presence' of the Lord. Her hymn 'Assembled at thine altar' begins with a plea for a greater understanding of the divine through the intellectual pursuit of 'study' of the bible ('Thy word') and through 'duty,' which is both the act of reading and the enactment of the instruction of a dutiful life which the bible provides. However, the requirement in the second verse shifts from the speaker's participation to a desire for the Lord's presence ('Thy presence we implore'), which in turn would instruct the speaker on prayer and on how to 'love and praise Thee more.'

> Assembled at thine altar, Lord,
> We lift our hearts in prayer,
> Study the pages of Thy word,
> And learn our duty there.

Grant us Thy Spirit's guiding ray;
Thy presence we implore;
Dear Saviour, teach us how to pray,
To love and praise Thee more.

So will our worship here below
Resemble that above,
Where saints unclouded glory view,
And sing redeeming love. (*The Congregational Hymn Book,* p. 550)[20]

This hymn is a humble statement of 'our' inadequacy unless illuminated by God's grace and is therefore consistent with orthodox themes fit for the service of the sanctuary. It also conveys a struggle. The speaker conveys her own imperfect ability to both perceive the divine and to enact praise ('To praise thee more') and thus also implicitly criticises her own ways of knowing or reaching the divine. Unlike the moments of obscured vision described in Watts's hymns as a physical distance from a perceivable God, the speaker's sense of obscured vision is not predicated upon a temporal, physical impossibility (the 'interposing days' of Watts's hymn) but rather, on a cognitive absence and inability to perceive the perfection of the divine with such clarity in the first place. The hymn Brown produces is merely a cloudy and clouded 'resemblance' of the heavenly worship or 'duty' prescribed within the rational 'word' in the first verse. Indeed, the speaker in Brown's hymn is not only unsure about her own relation to heaven's example of how to be devout, but is equally uncertain about the divine being represented. At the point of the hymn's composition, the presence of the divine is neither felt nor identified and the 'guiding ray' is not brought down to the speaker to enter into the relationship of love and 'praise' she desires.

Brown's hymns convey a struggle to reconcile the traditional modes of expressing religious devotion usually found in traditional hymnody with the experiences of the divine felt and conveyed in and through her writing. Moreover, the culturally prescribed version of the devotional woman hymnist and biblical narratives and doctrines of sin and salvation in Protestant Christianity which position the female as inferior/sinful become obstacles to be negotiated. As a result, despite their inclusion in hymnals to assist revivals, Brown's hymns frequently portray a sense of struggle with traditional configurations of the divine, such as the 'guiding ray' that has not already illuminated the path for the speaker in the final hymn discussed above. Moreover, blindness and searching for the path without such illumination becomes integral to spiritual experience in her hymns. Brown's hymns depict an experience of spirituality which exposes the limitations of orthodox ways of knowing God and their correlative narratives. In this way her hymns present a precursor to the rupturing of expectations of hymn narrative in Dickinson's poetry. Although Dickinson's poetics 'ride' subjectivity in a way that Brown's congregational hymns could never overtly claim to, the co-existence of

---

[20]   Elias Nason, (ed.), *The Congregational Hymn Book, For the Service of the Sanctuary* (Boston: John. P. Jewett and Co., 1857) p. 550. Hymn # 786 by 'Brown.'

tradition and experience in the work of both produces new metaphors and ways of expressing the divine. Like Brown, Dickinson uses the hymn form and imagery associated with hymn culture, in the same way as she uses domestic imagery, to challenge the reader's inclination to equate a given knowledge about hymns with what is actually presented in the poem.

Moreover, the emphasis which Brown's hymns place upon the act of writing and the explicit and implicit connection they forge between this and experience of the divine anticipates the self-generative and autonomous spirituality of Dickinson's poetry, of which 'Some keep the Sabbath going to Church' (Fr 236) is a marked example. Brown's descriptions of communal worship and praise as fluid and transporting (for example, in 'How sweet the melting lay') also provide an important precursory example of anti-teleological depictions of spirituality as the self in relation, which Dickinson's bee imagery conveys (as will be discussed in the following chapter). Her hymns provide Dickinson with a model for representing biblical narrative as incomplete or unsatisfactory. The speaker's attempt to reconcile immediate experience of the divine with biblical narrative and the notion of salvation through penitence is left unresolved. As a result we hear dissent in the representation of the domestic sphere as heavenly. These inherent problems rupture and challenge the teleological and 'simple' framework of the hymn. The space which Brown's hymns thus make visible is exploited in Dickinson's poems and transformed in into a heterologous space. The dominant 'framework' of religious narrative and the 'I-Thou' formulation is subordinated by its dialogic relation to the force of Dickinson's subjectivity. The formal structure of Dickinson's hymnic poems encodes the discourses of traditional hymns, whilst subjectivity is expressed always alongside, in relation to those discourses. The relation between tradition and experience which is presented in Dickinson's work opens up a space for the divine to be continually re-traced and re-imagined.

In poem Fr 316 the scene Dickinson describes replicates the speaker-God relation evident in Brown's hymns, particularly in 'As once the Saviour took his seat,' where the 'humble supplicant/Ashamed to lift her streaming eyes' is echoed in the 'awkward - gazing - face' of the speaker. However, from the outset, Dickinson's poem explicitly exposes the linear structure of reciprocity between the divine and speaker as being problematic. The expectation of hymn narrative is simultaneously delivered and ruptured in the poem's first two lines, compounded by the hymnic common metre which dissolves in stanzas two and three:

> If I'm lost - now -
> That I was found -
> Shall still my transport be -
> That once - on me - those Jasper Gates
> Blazed open - suddenly -
>
> That in my awkward - gazing - face -
> The Angels - softly peered -
> And touched me with their fleeces,
> Almost as if they cared -

I'm banished - now - you know it -
How foreign that can be -
You'll know - Sir - when the Saviour's face
Turns so - away from you - (Fr 316)

Immediately 'lost,' *because* found - Dickinson turns the notion of the lost sheep on its head. Divine grace and salvation are figured in terms of a human relationship in which the speaker is cruelly chosen ('found'), then spurned ('banished'). This inversion of 'lost' and 'found' is used elsewhere by Dickinson, in poem Fr132; 'Just lost, when I was saved!'). However, the 'transport' gained from the experience is that which produces the poem. Thus, the creative experience is privileged over the orthodox notions of spiritual union with God that 'Jasper Gates' and 'Angels' connotes. Moreover, the speaker delights in being 'lost'. The position of being 'banished' enables the poem to come into being, and for subjectivity to be expressed. In other words, the fact that the Jasper Gates stand open (whether she chooses to venture near them or stay away) produces a knowledge of the self which surpasses the 'experience' of divinity being prescribed. 'Transport' in this poem is the speaker's ability to transform loss into creativity. The notion of 'transport' Dickinson connects with the divine in 'A Transport one cannot contain' (Fr 212) can be connected directly with the notion of transport described in this poem. This poem exploits the expectation of hymn narrative (being lost and then found) to produce a reconfigured notion of transport which does not depend upon religion's definitions of spiritual transcendence through the doctrinal revelation of an afterlife. The speaker's 'transport' exists and renews itself within the poem, even though she remains 'banished', as if to provide evidence against the conventional believer's idea of being 'lost' which the poem's initial 'If' immediately brings into question.

Eliza Lee Follen and the 'Useful' Hymn

The struggle to conform to traditional narratives of conversion or penitence found in Brown's hymns is also found in Eliza Lee Follen's work. Similarly, there is also a self-reflexivity about writing, and the idea of selfhood through relation is described in terms of flight and transport. Follen wrote prose, poems and hymns prolifically, as well as hymns and songs for children. The daughter of the Unitarian minister Samuel Cabot, she was herself a Unitarian, and knew Thomas Wentworth Higginson (Dickinson's literary mentor and an ex-Unitarian minister) as well as the Cary sisters.[21] It is likely that Dickinson would have known of Follen's work,

---

[21]   Despite the volume of her work there are currently only ten entries in the British Library Catalogue. Wesley T. Mott, (ed.), *Dictionary of Literary Biography: The American Renaissance in New England*, third series (Boston: Gale Group, 2001) p. 141. Mott notes that Follen went to William Ellery Channing's (Unitarian) federal Street Church in Boston and knew T.W. Higginson and Alice and Phoebe Cary. Also that she was known for her anti-slavery writings. Her papers are in Massachusetts Historical Society, Boston.

as her *Hymns, Songs and Fables for Young People* was popular and reprinted several times during Dickinson's childhood years and beyond, during the ante-bellum period (1825, 1831, 1846 and 1851). A collection of her poems appeared in 1839, entitled *Poems*, which included her own versions of psalms as well as hymns which initially appeared in various hymn collections, magazines, and books on Christian worship for children (Julian, p. 380). Whilst in England in 1854, Follen issued another collection for children, entitled *The Lark and the Linnet*. She was certainly a household name in Boston during the mid-nineteenth century. However, despite her nineteenth-century popularity she has received little critical attention. Janet Gray includes three of Follen's poems with a short introductory commentary in her 1997 edited collection of American women poets of the nineteenth century (Gray, pp. 3–6), and has produced an as yet unpublished commentary on some of Follen's poems. There has been very little if nothing at all written on her hymns, and moreover, nothing at all on comparisons between Dickinson's poems and the influence of Follen as a woman hymnist.

Follen's allegiance to Unitarianism might lead readers to expect rather different representations of the speaker-God relation in her poems from that found in Brown's Protestant Evangelical hymnody. However, like Brown, Follen had an uneasy relation to the traditions of her church, an unease which can be traced in her poems. Unitarianism was seen by Protestant Evangelicals as heretical because of the denial of the trinity. The rejection of the trinity and divinity of Christ in favour of the 'uni'-personality of God in Unitarian doctrine, together with the use of cryptic language when describing the divine as favoured by antebellum Unitarian preachers, might be expected to have an effect upon Unitarian hymnody. However, as Howe notes, the hymns of Isaac Watts and traditional Christian symbols were still being used in addition to new hymns.[22] Therefore, the desire for new ways to convey the speaker-God relation in hymnody was countered by the reluctance to do away with the certainties of the Protestant tradition. Such 'certainties' were perceived in Watts. Follen's work reflects this aspect of transition within Unitarian hymnody, but also exploits it to her advantage.

The moral didacticism of Watts's congregational hymns and songs for children fitted with the importance placed upon education in Liberal Unitarian and abolitionist circles such as Follen's. Her collection, *Hymns, Songs and Fables for Young People* (1851) is written primarily for children, but it also bears a dedication to parents. Her husband Charles Follen, writing on behalf of his wife, states in the Preface to the first edition that:

---

[22]   Daniel Walker Howe, *The Unitarian Conscience: Harvard Moral Philosophy 1805–1861* (Cambridge, MA: Harvard University Press, 1970) pp. 170–71. Howe cites Henry Ware Jnr., 'Notes,' p. 59. (from *Works,* 1830) pp. 354–55. He also cites two 'interesting' Unitarian hymnals; *Singers and Songs of the Liberal Faith* (ed.), Alfred Putnam (Boston, 1875); and *Hymns for Public Worship* , (ed.), J.S. Buckminster (Boston, 1808).

[...] the approbation of parents, she does aspire after, and most earnestly desire;
this and this, alone, will satisfy her; without this, she would be the first to
pronounce it an unworthy offering.[23]

The mode of this preface, which emphasises the volume's usefulness to parents,
should be borne in mind when reading Follen's hymns, as they often struggle to
produce a satisfactory educative voice. For example, in 'On Prayer', emphasis is
placed upon the 'wandering' action of the dove as much as it is upon the biblical
narrative of God's promise to Noah; moreover, the dove's return signals only a
compromise ('pledge of peace with heaven') rather than a statement upon the
existence of heaven (*HSF*, p.16). The role of educator provided a legitimate mode
for literary output for women, as Charles Follen's remarks reassure the reader.
And yet, it is difficult to categorise the 'lessons' within these hymns as they often
display a struggle with opposition, and a fluid, less didactic approach in their
descriptions of God.

The majority of the hymns in this collection bear the hallmark of Isaac Watts
in that they often follow the hymnic common metre which makes them easy to
sing, recite and learn. They also follow the straight-forward didactic diction and
Christian sentiment of Watts's *Divine and Moral Songs for Children* (1715).[24]
A good example of this is Follen's hymn simply entitled 'Hymn,' which, in the
Wattsian tradition, takes flights in poetic register by placing the smaller elements of
nature ('fly') happily alongside the traditionally more elevated ones, as epitomised
here by the waterfall:

> It was my Heavenly Father's love
> Brought every being forth;
> He made the shining worlds above,
> And every thing on earth.
>
> Each lovely flower, the smallest fly,
> The sea, the waterfall,
> The bright green fields, the clear blue sky,-
> 'Tis God that made them all. (*HSF*, pp. 14–15)

---

[23]   Eliza Lee Follen, *Hymns, Songs and Fables for Young People* (Boston:
W.M. Crosby and H.P. Nichols, 1851) Preface, p. ii. Hereafter referred to as '*HSF*' followed
by page number.

[24]   The influence of Watts is undeniably present in Follen's work, but not exclusive;
prolific British women hymnists such as sisters Ann and Jane Taylor were also influential
for American hymnists writing for children. The Taylor sisters produced many hymns
independently as well as numerous jointly produced hymnals for children, such as *Hymns
for the Nursery* (1806), *Hymns for Infant Minds* (1809), *Original Hymns for Sunday Schools*
(1812). (Julian, p. 1116.) They were published widely in the United States prior to the work
of Follen or Brown, as the many editions of *Hymns for Infant Minds* indicates, to name just
a few: Philadelphia: Johnson and Warner, 1811; New York: Samuel Wood, 1814, Newburgh
[N.Y]: Benjamin F. Lewis & Co, 1818 and Boston: Samuel T. Armstrong, 1819.

Comparing Watts's 'Praise for Creation and Providence' in his collection *Divine and Moral Songs for Children* (1715), we can see a similar movement in diction where a description of God's creation of 'mountains' and 'seas' is reduced, somewhat ludicrously in the third verse to 'filling the earth' with 'food:'

> I sing the almighty power of God,
> That made the mountains rise,
> That spread the flowing seas abroad,
> And built the lofty skies.
>
> I sing the wisdom that ordain'd
> The sun to rule the day;
> The moon shines full at his command,
> And all the stars obey.
>
> I sing the goodness of the Lord,
> That fill'd the earth with food;
> He form'd the creatures with his word,
> And then pronounc'd them good. (*PW*, p. 319)[25]

Both hymns include a version of the obligatory verse on God's omniscient judgement of the child-reader as one would expect in hymns of this genre; in Follen's hymn, God 'sees and hears me all the day' and in Watts; 'He keeps me with his eye.' Although in this aspect both writers conform to Christian moral codes for childhood obedience, the mode in which the Creator creates and exists in Watts's hymn in relation to the child-reader is conveyed somewhat differently than in Follen's. Follen's God is described as creating, and bringing 'every being forth' through love, whereas Watts's God 'ordains' through 'wisdom' and 'goodness'. Watts's description of the power of divinity is altogether more authoritarian. When 'love' does appear in Watts's hymn, it is within the form of 'beams,' rather like the phallic 'beams of light' he frequently employs in other hymns to connote God's presence. Furthermore, where Follen describes a familial relation between God and child ('He guards me with a parent's care/When I am all alone'), Watts's speaker is described as a mere inhabitant of God's realm and as God's possession:

> In heaven He shines with beams of love,
> With wrath in Hell beneath;
> 'Tis on his earth I stand or move,
> And 'tis his air I breathe. (*PW*, p. 319)

It could be said that the differences between Watts's hymn of praise for creation and Follen's are to some extent cultural; that the poetics in each are influenced by

---

[25]   Isaac Watts, 'Praise for Creation and Providence,' from *Divine and Moral Songs for Children* in *The Poetical Works of Isaac Watts* (Boston: Little, Brown and Company, 1866).

Enlightenment rationalism, and sentimental, liberalised Christianity respectively. Nevertheless, both are within the framework of Christian instruction for children and supposedly operating under the same theological assumptions and moral intentions of that framework. One could argue that Follen's hymns are simply inferior in quality and lacking in the technical skill of Watts. However, one cannot dismiss Follen's differences and her particularised uses of imagery as a series of failures. What makes Follen's hymns so interesting to look at alongside Dickinson's poetic responses to orthodox Christian notions of the speaker/God relation in traditional hymnody, is that they frequently provide similar and unexpected turns within the hymn structure. They delineate a space for the divine to occur and be enacted through metaphors of flight. Even amongst her hymns for children, expectation of, and desire for, the divine is articulated by negotiating rather than reproducing phallogocentric representations of God. In a way which is comparable to Brown's searching in the absence of illumination, Follen's hymns describe the spiritual journey in terms of a flight which is necessarily 'pathless'. Both metaphors, not without risk, invoke the ecstatic vastness and potential which subsumes loss of direction.

Writing the Pathless Flight

On closer examination, Follen's hymns often fall short of the usually 'uncomplicated' nature of hymns written for children. In a similar way to Brown's hymns which describe a self-reflexivity on the act of writing, of constructing praise, Follen's hymns also privilege the act of writing. For example, in the hymn 'On Prayer,' the prayer is depicted as a dove whose repeated attempts at being heard by God displays an exemplary tenacity for the child-reader's human faith. The human spirit's attempts to commune with God is described as a 'pathless' flight:

> As through the pathless fields of air
> Wandered forth the timid dove,
> So the heart, in humble prayer,
> Essays to reach the throne of love.
>
> Like her it may return unblest,
> Like her again may soar,
> And still return and find no rest,
> No peaceful, happy shore. (*HSF*, p. 16)

The fact of the flight being 'pathless' suggests at once an ideal space which transcends the normative paths of right and wrong which dominate so much morally instructive juvenile literature. The notion of ideal space is connected here with the unrestricted play of thought and feeling which one would associate with childhood, which both 'fields' and 'wandered' connote. However, this ideal space is constructed within the hymn and the 'wings' of the hymn transport the speaker beyond the bounds of 'I-Thou' into an expansive relation with both world and self. Both the dove (prayer) and the heart are expressed in feminine terms and the hymn's third and final verses make the associative connections between gender roles and those prescribed within orthodox religion.[26] Feminine obedience and timidity are qualities which need to be overcome despite the command of God:

> But now once more she spreads her wings,
> And takes a bolder flight,
> And see! the olive-branch she brings,
> To bless her master's sight.
>
> And thus the heart renews its strength,
> Though spent and tempest-driven,
> And higher soars, and brings at length
> A pledge of peace with Heaven. (*HSF*, pp. 16–17)

Invoking the Biblical story of the dove's return to Noah after the flood, signalling the promise of dry land and the fruition of God's promise to Noah and also the justification of his faith, Follen's hymn aims to illustrate the importance of maintaining Christian faith. However Follen's gendering of the heart, and the self/ 'master' along with the dove within the hymn, takes the scene beyond Christian allegory (Follen follows her source with the dove, as it is gendered in Genesis 8.9 'But the dove found no rest for the sole of her foot, and she returned unto him into the ark […]'). Faith is described by its 'length,' and there is an uneasy, lengthy tension between the spirit/prayer and its attempted destination, 'Heaven,' which it aims to make a 'pledge of peace' with. Heaven is masculinised and a desired reciprocity is not reached satisfactorily by the hymn's closure. Follen implores and encourages boldness and endurance ('bolder flight'/ 'higher soars') in the distinctly feminine heart/prayer within the hymn, in order that peace may, 'at length,' be achieved. Moreover, it is hoped that this peace might 'bless her master's sight,' suggesting a mutually restorative outcome from such perseverance. Not only is the spirit of prayer and its movement within the hymn gendered, but it is autogenetic and capable of producing the blessing for the self/onlooker which is described as masculine, and capable only of 'sight.' The spirit of prayer in the hymn is presented as an alternative to the bodily, physical act of sight which frequently frustrates the speaker in many hymns by Isaac Watts. The activity of prayer is described within this hymn as a struggle between gendered aspects of the human self and the divine; between the feminised prayer ('dove') and the masculine spirit that requires and awaits a response. In this way, the hymn's models of the spirit reverse and destabilise Protestant assumptions and Biblical representations of the female as an anticipatory receptacle awaiting the masculine, redemptive spirit which fills and completes her/it. In this way Follen is not only able to align herself

---

[26] For Biblical emphasis on woman's status below men, see: Gen. 3. 16., I Cor. 11.3–16., I Cor. 14. 34.

with the masculine role of Noah, but is also able to effectively re-gender the mind to accommodate this duality, which appears as type of a pre-Freudian bisexuality.

Similarities can be seen between Follen's description of prayer in this hymn and those of Dickinson's in poem (Fr 483). The poem appears, at first reading, to be about the speaker's experience of feeding a bird and of afterwards hearing its song of thanks to her:

> Most she touched me by her muteness -
> Most she won me by the way
> She presented her small figure -
> Plea itself - for Charity -
>
> Were a Crumb my whole possession -

The initial indeterminacy described by the speaker with regard to the origin of the sound, 'Twas as Space sat singing' combined with the gendered term for such 'to herself - and men - ' encourages a connection to be made between the bird, the singer of praise, and the poet herself. This describes the desire for reciprocity implied in the hymn form. Although Dickinson repositions the stereotypes of feminine Christian devotion to construct herself as both the masculine onlooker and also simultaneously the receptacle of spiritual revelation, the poem articulates a transcendent moment when the 'bird' communicates with the speaker. The speaker adopts the role of master, initially, and is seduced by the bird's 'muteness' and diminutive, pathetic figure which is 'presented' to her in ceremonious fashion. It invokes the Eucharistic rite of taking the bread of Christ's body, which the bird takes rapidly and returns to the 'Sky.' The fact that the bird is already in a state of transcendence as it is capable of producing praise, knows what it wants, and is not delayed in taking its desired nourishment, suggests further parallels with the poet-speaker. Moreover, to the speaker's surprise, it does not bend in supplication and thanks, despite the speaker's initial estimation gathered from its comparative size. The fact that the speaker declares initially that it was 'most..by..' and 'most.. by..' suggests a conclusion that the speaker ended up being 'most' surprised and touched by the realisation of the song of praise after the event. The desire for reciprocity in Follen's hymn 'On Prayer' which also describes prayer as a bird, is dramatically reworked and enacted in Dickinson's poem by the subtle conflation of bird and poet.

Beyond Vision: Communicating the Divine in Follen's Hymns

In 'The Spirit Giveth Life,' the nature and practice of the hymn form as a mode of communication comes into play explicitly, where the speaker asks a series of questions about how God is visible. Importantly, the inquiry focuses on the speaker's responses to the sounds she hears about her. Her perception is the vehicle for possible transcendence or commune with the Spirit. However, as becomes increasingly clear as the hymn progresses, the distinction between the active sounds within the hymn and the supposedly passive listener become decidedly blurred, conferring active, divine power upon the 'questioning' speaker herself:

> What was in the viewless wind,
> Wild rushing through the oak,
> Seemed to my listening, dreaming mind
> As though a spirit spoke?
>
> What is it to the murmuring stream
> Doth give so sweet a song,
> That on its tide my thoughts do seem
> To pour themselves along?
>
> What is it on the dizzy height,
> What in each glowing star,
> That speaks of things beyond the sight,
> And questions what they are? (*HSF*, pp. 17–19.)

The initial boldness of the first stanza, which sets the hymn up to be an enquiry into the manifestation of God in nature, breaks up towards the last line's uncertainty of 'as though' a 'spirit spoke.' Where Watts would have perceived God unequivocally, Follen's speaker is more intent on pursuing likenesses of her own voice as a starting point for her enquiry. The 'murmuring' of the stream and the speaker's thoughts are conflated in the second stanza; moreover, the speaker's thoughts are 'poured into' nature's stream, communication apparently already established and a 'dizzy height' of sorts is already reached. In order to 'speak of things beyond the sight' Follen's choice of language points towards the rhapsodic and the non-verbal in nature, which in turn echoes the speaker's experience of God. References to the hymnic mode are frequent, where it is invoked by sounds in nature, the 'sweet song' of the stream, the ocean's 'roar,' and 'echoes,' and also the omniscient 'delicious melody' perceived by the feminine moon:

> What in the gentle moon doth see
> Pure thoughts and tender love,
> And hears delicious melody
> Around, below, above?

The 'melody' of the divine is all-encompassing and decidedly connected with femininity ('gentle,' 'pure' and 'tender') and yet at the same time has the power to 'bid the savage tempest speak' in the following verse.

Here Follen attempts to present a gender-neutral divine Spirit. The 'ever-living mind' recalls Romantic pantheism in a manner which is similar to the opening lines of Shelley's poem 'Mont Blanc;' 'The everlasting universe of things/ Flows through the mind, and rolls its rapid waves'. However, the grandness this implies is counterbalanced with a depiction of the 'ever-living mind' as diminutive; 'This little throb of life'. This phrase invokes the gendered, coy mode of the supplicatory female, as utilised often by Dickinson. Paradoxically, in its attempt to accommodate a reading which would satisfy the didactic Christian motive proclaimed in the collection's Preface, or a Romantic sensibility, the hymn increasingly retreats from 'saying' the secrets of the divine which the speaker boldly asserts and 'hears' autogenetically throughout most of the hymn:

> It is the ever-living mind;
> This little throb of life
> Hears its own echoes in the wind,
> And in the tempest's strife;
>
> To all that's sweet, and bright, and fair,
> Its own affections gives;
> Sees its own image everywhere,
> Through all creation lives.

Moreover, the 'little throb' is described as having to 'bid' reciprocity (a 'solemn tone') from the large, imposing 'everlasting hills.' Thus, Follen conveys through metaphors of size the tension between the speaker's experience of spirituality versus the old, 'solemn' hymns of Christian and masculine Puritan orthodoxy. The all-encompassing 'delicious melody' of the hymn's earlier verses is presented with an obstacle ('hills') within and against the sky of possibilities ('boundless arch of azure'). The realm of possibilities presented in the hymn extends also to new languages ('accents all its own') and fresh ways in which the divine can be communicated:

> It bids the everlasting hills
> Give back the solemn tone;
> This boundless arch of azure fills
> With accents all its own.
>
> What is this life-inspiring mind,
> This omnipresent thought?
> How shall it ever utterance find
> For all itself hath taught?
>
> To Him who breathed the heavenly flame,
> Its mysteries are known;
> It seeks the source from whence it came,
> And rests in God alone. (*HSF*, p. 19)

The inclusion of the word 'solemn' is striking as it is placed in direct contrast to each of the other descriptions of sound in the hymn. Moreover, the concluding verse admits all 'mysteries' to Jesus without having declared them as such throughout the hymn.

Such 'mysteries' are evidently and keenly felt and described by the speaker herself. Whilst questioning, ultimately, how the 'Spirit/'mind' shall find 'utterance,' Follen simultaneously describes how the Creator 'speaks' through his creation.

In this she ascribes divinity to the act of writing this hymn, and in which the speaker-mind speaks both to herself and to others of her experience of God. The depiction of God as breathing the 'heavenly flame' is no doubt an allusion to Pentecost and the Holy Spirit's tongues of flame on the apostles, invoking the ways in which the spirit informs, and breathes life into, the natural world. Such Pentecostal imagery leads the hymn to a strong climax and the plurality of the Trinity allows Follen this ending. Simultaneously however, the inclusion of 'Him' in this final verse appears, almost perfunctorily, and connection between the various evidences of God in the previous verses and 'Him' in the final verse is somewhat flimsily constructed. 'Him' does not satisfactorily contain or conclude the multiplicity of God as depicted by the hymn's emphasis on various and multiple strains and sounds. The hymn struggles to reconcile experience of and communion with God which is not gendered, with the child's entrance into Christian worship which conceives of God as 'Him.'

Follen's hymn to the 'Spirit' of God to some extent reinscribes the increasing popularity in the nineteenth-century to locate God in nature, and to articulate experience of God in terms of the natural world. However, her conspicuous concern with gender, as evidenced by the gendered terms for God and the devotional human which are reworked in her hymns for children, sets her apart from the Protestant Evangelical context within which she writes. It also sets her apart from Unitarian and Transcendental thinking. Follen's depiction of the 'Spirit' in this hymn makes movements towards the tenets of secularised religion, perhaps as a cover for the concern with gender which takes 'the Spirit' beyond a depiction of a genderless 'over-soul.' The experiential aspect of the speaker's encounter with the divine in this hymn provides connections with Dickinson's representation of spirituality which is similarly experiential. There are parallels to be drawn between Follen's 'spirit' or 'omnipresent thought' and the speaker's experience of hearing 'Space sat singing to herself- and men' in Dickinson's poem, Fr 483, as discussed above. Both Follen's hymn and Dickinson's poem ultimately describe the divine spark of poetic inspiration which emanates from nature but also from the within the self. Writing and spiritual experience are for both inseparable.

Crucially, by representing God in terms of being a presence within nature and also within the self, Follen's hymns challenge assumptions about gendered relations and descriptions of the divine. With their emphasis on other senses such as touch and hearing, there is an absence of 'sight' which sets her work apart from the decidedly more easy relation between God and man described in Watts's hymns. The rigid teleological distinctions and polarities between self and God, light and darkness, good and evil, are much less easy to define in Follen's hymns, despite the popular conception of them being didactic and instructional, as evidenced by their success during the nineteenth century. Follen's Unitarianism perhaps gives shape to the 'unipersonality' of God which permeates both nature and the self at once. However, her description of the divine in nature is both contradictory and dialectically charged. This is in part due to the influence of the genre, of educational texts such as Watts's songs and hymns for children, but even more to a desire to articulate her own experience of the divine.

Towards Transport not Transcendence

The imagery examined in Follen's hymns conveys an idea of transport that is not confined to achieving transcendence in general abstract terms (a struggle that Watts's hymns often convey). Rather, it 'transports' readers beyond such notions of transcendence, above the confining spaces of religious orthodoxy. Paradoxically perhaps, whilst appearing to be more palatable for the young reader, both Brown and Follen's depictions of the spiritual relation to God have more in common with the complex and rich suspension of oppositional thinking on the divine articulated in Dickinson's poems than with the linear relation to God presented in Watts's didactic hymns. For example, this poem by Dickinson, dated 1861, parodies the excitement that 'lift[ing] the lid' on the spiritual realm has the potential to generate:

> A transport one cannot contain
> May yet a transport be -
> Though God forbid it lift the lid -
> Unto its Ecstasy!
>
> A Diagram - of Rapture!
> A sixpence at a Show -
> With Holy Ghosts in Cages!
> The Universe would go! (Fr 212)

One is reminded of the fervour surrounding religious gatherings during the revival or even the mid- nineteenth-century enthusiasm for spiritualism. 'Though God forbid it' underscores the element of transgression involved in experiencing Ecstasy, a transport which is no longer contained. And yet, the accompanying stanza describes the necessity of not holding forth ('lift[ing] the lid') on matters spiritual; spirituality is at odds with the commercial market which 'Show' represents and drags spirituality into the realm of the visible, and into the arena of mere entertainment. A 'Diagram' of 'Rapture' is a contradiction; it is the potential for flight, the imagination, incarcerated for the benefit of the mere spectacle, one such as 'Holy Ghosts in Cages' invokes. And yet, Dickinson not only 'contained' her own spiritual discourse within poetry to give out to friends and relatives, but also constructed it within the confining form of the hymn, as the 4-3 common hymn metre of this poem illustrates. Not only is the non-saying of mystical experience ('transport') conveyed in a communicable melody, but also within a form associated with communal experience. 'Transport' can be seen as a trope for mystical experience because it designates a trajectory, and emphasises journey, as opposed to defining a goal or terminus, a heaven or hell. By engaging with a hymnal trope of flight in this poem, Dickinson makes the limitations and dead-ends of hymn culture visible, and by doing so is able to take spiritual discourse some way beyond those limitations, leaving space for an openness which cannot be 'contained.' The denunciation of religious charlatans in this poem not only condemns orthodox 'descriptions' of spirituality produced by various religious groups and individuals, but also acts to leave cognitive space open. By generating space in this way, Dickinson allows the reader to consider what exactly is meant by 'transport,' 'ecstasy' or 'rapture'. The poem thus enacts and reproduces heterologous space in which Dickinson's experience and agency acts upon the structure of religious tradition to make it 'say the absence' of what it 'designates'.[27] As the speaker's thoughts are presented in relation to orthodox modes of knowing, the poem provides the reader with absences and gaps upon the subject of the divine which remain unfilled.

Comparing Dickinson's work to that of antebellum women hymn writers such as Brown and Follen provides a fruitful mode of enquiry to ascertain the examples of women's versions of the divine and of worship which inevitably influenced her poems on religious and spiritual themes. It also provides ways in which to gauge Dickinson's relation to culturally sanctioned versions of a woman's relation to the divine in the figure of the female hymnist. Various modes of the hymn form which draw upon notions of childhood correction, morality and development are employed in Dickinson's poems to register comparative 'disobedience' and also from depictions of the recuperative/legitimised self found in much devotional literature of the period. As discussed in Chapter 2, the cultural influences of the Evangelical revival and the new position for women precipitated by women's rights movements made the hymn a legitimate platform for the women writer. Writing hymns combines the inner, reflective mode of sacred devotional writing (largely of the seventeenth century) with the public, communal activity of congregational hymn singing. Dickinson's engagement with the hymn form, like Brown and Follen before her, is both social and political.

The attempt to conform to culturally prescribed narratives of salvation, redemption and penitence imposed by orthodox religion provides the woman hymnist with an opportunity to convey a spirituality which is expressed in terms of dissent. The fact that the hymns of both Brown and Follen often do not fit comfortably into such narratives conveys, simultaneously, an alternative version of and relation to the divine. Whilst operating within a culturally prescribed role of the female hymnist, the modes of expression evident in the hymns of both Brown and Follen are implicitly at odds with the logocentric mode and values of the doctrines they have been presumed to reassert unambiguously by hymnal editors such as Asahel Nettleton and Elias Nason and compilers like Charles Dexter Cleveland. Rigidly constructed versions of the divine frequently fail to offer the necessary 'renewal' for Brown and Follen. However, although experience of home or nature is not the panacea their affiliated religious cultures prescribe, the consciousness of the 'work' of the writing process which their hymns convey suggests that writing itself become the source of constant renewal of the self. As the following chapter will show, the negotiation of heterologous space in Dickinson's 'bee' poems is exploited fully in the connection the imagery forges between autonomy and community, between the role of the poet and the Protestant work ethic.

---

[27] Michel de Certeau, 'Mystic Speech,' in *The Certeau Reader*, (ed.), Graham Ward, pp. 188–206 (p. 205).

PART 3
Experiments in Hymn Culture

Chapter 6
Tracing Dickinson's Bee Imagery

'Repairing Everywhere Without Design'?

> Fame is a bee.
> It has a song -
> It has a sting -
> Ah, too, it has a wing. (Fr 1788)

Thus far the book has traced aspects of the hymn culture in Dickinson's social milieu and has suggested ways in which the anti-teleological and mystical spaces found in Dickinson's poetics have been formed dialogically, in relation to this culture. The 'I-Thou' model of relation, the connection between individual and community and also the aspect of usefulness and worthy work of the hymn have been taken into account. However, Dickinson's use of bee imagery serves to bring each of these aspects of hymn culture to the fore, and connects each aspect firmly with poetry and the role of the poet. A re-vision of the traditional bird imagery found in hymns by women to denote spiritual transport, Dickinson's bees describe the paths to revery. Her bee imagery illustrates the connection in her poetics between this metaphor and the role of the poet, and in doing so makes explicit the imperative connection between two poles of orthodox Puritanism: of 'industry' and 'revery'. By connecting the Puritan work ethic with poetry, Dickinson not only confers the status of spiritual vision on her writing (as did the traditional hymnists such as Watts) but also forges a defence of her own position as a woman poet. Her bee imagery incorporates the Puritan rhetoric on industry and idleness that surrounded mid-nineteenth-century debates on the work ethic in relation to the woman question.[1] In this way, Dickinson also challenges ideas about 'usefulness' through casting her own vocation and subjectivity as a poet as a metaphorical bee that creates whilst also being 'idle'. Furthermore, the suspension of opposition in Dickinson's use of bee imagery allows for community and the individual to co-exist and resonate without one being subsumed by the other.

---

[1]   In his chapter on feminist versions of the work ethic, Daniel T. Rodgers describes the critique of 'idle womanhood' in feminist works, such as *My Wife and I* (1871) by Harriet Beecher Stowe. In the novel, Stowe criticises the conventions that forced middle-class women into marriages which fostered and perpetuated purposelessness in otherwise capable women of 'faculty'. Daniel T. Rodgers, *The Work Ethic in Industrial America 1850–1920* (Chicago: The University of Chicago Press, 1974) pp. 182–209.

Dickinson's use of bee imagery draws upon significant cultural associations of the bee such as ideas of community and also the name and genesis of the poet.[2] Importantly, the bee offers Dickinson an imagery of flight which is both able to 'transcend' religious orthodoxy and remain rooted in the experiential, worldly realm. The bee signals the anti-teleological approach to the divine in her work which is also compatible with feminist thinking on anti-patriarchal representations of the divine.

Crucially, cultural associations come into bearing when images are conveyed in an 'emblematic' fashion and are exposed to create dramatic impact as well as the poet's deviation from or concurrence with such moral, political, social and spiritual associations and assumptions. Dickinson's use of the bee to connote transcendence is inventive not only because of the 'jaunty' or quirky qualities her bees often display, but also because of their association with spiritual community, communal life and the relation of the individual (bee) to the (hive) community. Bees are also connotative of flight and can therefore be connected with other hymn motifs such as birds and angels. Dickinson's poetry includes many references to insects, such as flies, spiders and butterflies, and also to birds, which also have an emblematic quality to them. The bee is of special interest here because of the many occasions when it is connected specifically with tunes, melody, singing, and therefore also poetry, and Dickinson her self as poet. Moreover, not only did Dickinson refer to herself as 'bee' in letters, but, her final bee poem invokes fame and its troubling but transcendent nature; 'Fame is a bee/ It has a song - /It has a sting -/Ah, too, it has a wing.' (Fr1788) It is no coincidence that the qualities Dickinson's bees are frequently imbued with are remarkably similar to the ways in which Dickinson's poetic persona has been described by various critics. For example, in poem Fr 304, the bee who 'invites the race,' then 'Dips - evades - teases - deploys -' enacts the post-modern literary style which critics have seen Dickinson's work as anticipating.[3]

Whilst most Dickinson critics agree on the absence of a discernable pattern or design in her corpus of poems, Dickinson's use of the bee and its variations provides evidence of a sustained engagement with particular images which assume an emblematic or tropic quality. This chapter will demonstrate how Dickinson's poems reassert shape and continuity, somewhat paradoxically, through the sustained energy of dynamic changeability which the bee imagery in her poems represents. Although the representations of many of Dickinson's poetic images have this dynamic changeability, the bee is perhaps the finest 'emblematic' example.

---

[2]   'Bee' was a name for the poet, such as the 'Athenian Bee' for Plato. The story of bees settling on the lips of the poet when young was given for the association of producing words like honey. The name was also given to Sophocles (the 'Attic Bee'), Pindar, St. Chrysostom and St. Ambrose. E. Cobham Brewer, (ed.), *A Dictionary of Phrase and Fable* rev. edn (London: Cassell and Company, 1958) p. 113.

[3]   See Mary E. Galvin, *Queer Poetics: Five Modernist Women Writers* (Connecticut: Greenwood Press, 1999) Galvin discusses Dickinson in terms of her 'trickster' quality, evading meanings divisively.

The bee is a dominant, rich and complex image in Dickinson's corpus of poems,[4] which carries associations with forms of religious worship, such as the communal singing of hymns. It therefore offers many opportunities to trace how Dickinson interrogates, subverts and challenges some of the modes and assumptions associated with orthodox religion. The bee also provides Dickinson with a different version of the traditional bird imagery popular in hymns and devotional literature which connote the soul's flight into heaven or communion with God. Her uses of the bee place emphasis on multiplicity and sexuality which are central to the notion of immanence as transcendence in many of Dickinson's poems. They describe a mode of being in the divine which is very different from the linear journey and 'I-Thou' mode of relation in traditional hymns. The bee's associations with social cohesion, labour, but also rebellion and disruption of religious culture provides an important link between style and form in Dickinson's poems. The hymn form of her poems re-enacts the devotional aspect of religion, whilst the bee itself often caricatures or disrupts official religious culture within the verse. The image of the bee reflects Dickinson's engagement with the religious cultural legacy of her time because it also carries with it a set of implied oppositions, such as bee/hive; individual/community; part/whole; production/consumption; industry/revery; male/female and human/God. Each of these implied oppositions which the bee carries reflects back for the reader the oppositional thinking which was central to Puritan aesthetics exemplified in Watts's hymns.[5] They are the 'added information' through which we read the various anarchic bee behaviours in her poems. Dickinson's bee imagery exemplifies the heterologous space of the hymn by invoking and suspending such oppositional relations but also by rupturing them. In this way, her use of the bee image both echoes and also subverts the puritan requirement for piety in art:

> [...] for the Puritan, word and world alike were a shadowing forth of divine things, coherent systems of transcendent meaning [...] But where Romanticism celebrated the imagination as a path to spiritual understandings, the Puritan mind required piety. Believing that they would find either salvation or damnation at life's end, the Puritans demanded of all arts they cultivated – pulpit oratory, psalmody, tombstone carving, epitaph, prose or poetry in general – that they help them define and live a holy life.[6]

Dickinson's bee is a 'coherent system' for her own version of communicative action and allegiance to a self-defined spirituality. It is, simultaneously, a denial and disruption of traditional (including Romantic) forms of religious devotion.

---

⁴ By my own estimate there are at least 85 instances of the word 'bee' in Dickinson's corpus, excluding cognate words and indirect references to bees or the life of bees.

⁵ Sacvan Bercovitch's discussion of the Puritan preoccupation with polarisation, such as light/dark, good/evil, man/God (those frequently found in Watts) is instructive here. See Sacvan Bercovitch, (ed.), *The American Puritan Imagination* (Cambridge: Cambridge University Press, 1974).

⁶ Malcolm Bradbury and Richard Ruland, *From Puritanism to Postmodernism: A History of American Literature* (London: Routledge, 1991) p. 25.

More often than not, when ideas about religion, the Church, or God are brought to the fore in Dickinson's poems, the image of the bee is excessively present, performing an essential aspect of, or acting as a counter to, those ideas. The bee's noises - its humming and 'tunes' - are evocative of hymn singing, and its smaller, industrious wings offer a sub/version of the angels and ideas of spiritual transcendence found in the devotional writings of Watts and Herbert. For example, in the earlier draft of 'Safe in their Alabaster Chambers' (Fr 124) which appears in Johnson's edition, the bee in the final stanza signals triumph over the stasis and death-in-life which the religious communities of her day endure. Here those communities are represented by the actual dead; the 'meek members of the Resurrection':

> Light laughs the breeze
> In her Castle above them -
> Babbles the Bee in a stolid Ear,
> Pipe the Sweet Birds in ignorant cadence -
> Ah, what sagacity perished here! (THJ 216, 1859 version)

Paradoxically, the bee's 'babbling' connotes the divine energy which animates and is analogous to the Holy Spirit. It is also the 'sagacity' which is unintelligible to those who are focused upon formal rituals and 'safe' manifestations of spirituality.

Although there are many ways in which Dickinson utilises the bee image, analysing what appears to be the dominant modes in which the bee 'performs' in her poems is particularly useful way to gauge her shifting relation to orthodox religion and ideas about spirituality. Connected, as it is, with ideas of 'singing' or making 'tunes,' it is difficult to separate the image of the bee from the consciousness of the poems' speaker. Often the bee figure is complicit with the speaker's sensibilities, or occupies/represents a particular position (liberty, revery, multiplicity, community) that the speaker also wishes to reach. Therefore, a methodical or 'axiomatic' approach can be seen in Dickinson's exploration of spirituality via her bee imagery.

No single critical work has provided focus exclusively on the representation and use of the bee image in Dickinson's poetry. However, because of the many instances in which it does appear as a dominant image or primary focus in her poems, many critics have inevitably incorporated a discussion of the image into their analysis of other concerns or themes. As discussed earlier, Martha Winburn England's view of Dickinson's bee image as representing a challenge to the restrictive moralism of Watts's 'busy bee' is instructive.[7] However, as Thomas Johnson observes in *Emily Dickinson: An Interpretive Biography* (1955) the image also becomes a trope of ecstasy, arguing that the 'sweetness of honey which the bee gains by ravaging a flower' is '[...] a trope which she repeatedly employs in

---

[7]   See Martha Winburn England and John Sparrow, Hymns Unbidden: Donne, Herbert, Blake, Emily Dickinson and the Hymnographers, pp. 122–3.

her poems'.[8] The bee image serves as a metaphor for giving shape or pattern to one's connection to the world and therefore radically redefining what is considered as spirituality and worship. For example, in her discussion on the nature of temporality in Dickinson's poetry, Sharon Cameron (1979) notes the unexpected shift in the description of the bee from 'Buccaneers of Buzz' to the assertion of 'Fuzz ordained - not Fuzz contingent,' in poem Fr 1426. She argues that it:

> [...] rescues the bee from the triviality to which 'buccaneers of Buzz' had almost certainly doomed it. This is not such so much metaphor as it is metaphysics when, from another world, the bee is invested with priest-like powers.[9]

Cameron's view is that the poem's ability to rupture temporality allows for such a shift to occur; and yet the conception of religious hierarchical structures, rather than temporality, seems to be the most prominent dislocation here. If the bee's 'investment' of powers is not viewed as a progression from 'doomed triviality' to being 'ordained,' but the two descriptions are allowed to co-exist, then it is not time which is ruptured or struggled for in this poem. Rather, it is the representation of an alternative to hierarchical conceptions of religion and spirituality, at play in the image of the bee, which this poem typifies and conveys. Albert Gelpi's *Emily Dickinson: The Mind of the Poet* (1966) includes the chapter 'The Flower, the Bee, and the Spider: The Aesthetics of Consciousness,' in which he analyses Dickinson's use of the bee image in relation to her perception of the self as poet.[10] He connects the theme of drunkenness in Dickinson's poem 'I taste a liquor never brewed' (Fr 207) with Emerson's notion of the poet as 'inebriated by nectar[...]which is the ravishment of the intellect.'[11] Quoting Dickinson's poem, which includes the lines 'Inebriate of Air - am I -/And Debauchee of Dew', Gelpi supposes:

> It was reeling triumph to be a secret drinker while in the name of orthodox religion her father laboured tirelessly for the Temperance League. He could close the bars of Amherst, but not the 'inns of Molten Blue' where she drank with saints and was served by angels. (Gelpi, p. 134)

Gelpi does not discuss the poem in terms of the obvious bee imagery it contains, and is content to connect Dickinson's description of 'debauchery' with Emerson's

---

[8]   T.H. Johnson, *Emily Dickinson: An Interpretive Biography* (Cambridge, MA: The Belknap Press of Harvard University Press, 1955) pp. 229–30. With reference to poem Fr 1628: 'The sweetness of honey which the bee gains by ravaging a flower [...] - a trope which she repeatedly employs in her poems - is also entombed in a cell whose form and shape bear noticeable likeness to a small coffin.'

[9]   Sharon Cameron, *Lyric Time: Dickinson and the Limits of Genre* (Baltimore: The Johns Hopkins University Press, 1979) p. 9.

[10]   Apart from this short chapter by Gelpi which looks at the bee as well as other images, there have been no studies which focus exclusively on bee imagery, nor on the way Dickinson uses the image in different ways from one poem to the next.

[11]   Albert Gelpi, *Emily Dickinson: The Mind of the Poet* (Cambridge, MA: Harvard University Press, 1966) pp. 133–4 Gelpi cites Emerson's 'The Poet' in *Essays: Second Series*.

assault on the intellect to convey the idea that the poets shared a similar intellectual intoxication. However, Emerson's metaphor is concerned with the persona of the poet, whereas it is the exuberant liberty of Dickinson's intoxicated bee, 'reeling' from flower to flower, which provides the poem's focus, rather than a reflection on the role of the poet, or the 'ravishment' of the intellect, as Gelpi would have it. He then goes on to discuss the bee and flower imagery in Dickinson's work as representing two aspects of the poet-self, and offers masculine and feminine stereotypes associated with ideas of gender as explanation of the positioning of the image in her poems. There is, however, no doubt an emphasis on the divisions between masculinity and femininity in Dickinson's use of the flower/bee imagery, and Gelpi acknowledges her fluidity between the two positions:

> Emily Dickinson could think of herself as the flower or the bee, as the poet possessed or the poet possessing. Since she was no stickler for logic or rigid theory, the point is not that these concepts of the poet existed for her as distinct abstract categories but, on the contrary, that in living poetically she knew both experiences and appropriated both roles. (Gelpi, p. 139)

Although Dickinson's occupation of both genders at various points in her poems can be seen in her use of the bee image, the main focus in this chapter will be on how this fluidity relates to the representation of patriarchal religion in contrast to the representations to an alternative spirituality or mystical discourse. Gelpi does not associate Dickinson's use of the bee image with religion, except to note her inscription of lines from notable preacher Jonathan Edwards ('All Liars shall have their part' and 'Let him athirst come') alongside her poem which she entitled 'The Bumble-bee's Religion'. He thus highlights her view of the contradictory nature of religious dogma, both rebuking the bee's entrance into the flower whilst also providing an invitation to those who are thirsty (Gelpi, pp. 139–40). Dickinson usually refrained from giving her poems titles, so it is significant that one is given here. This fact, and the poem's unambiguous title, serves to connect her use of bee imagery most emphatically with orthodox religion.

The notable American preacher and important religious figure, Jonathan Edwards, provides an American example of the usage and cultivation of emblems, or 'moral images' in devotional works, which Dickinson's bee image undoubtedly invokes. In his *Personal Narrative* (1743) Edwards uses the metaphor of the 'field or garden of God' and pays particular attention to the flower:

> [s]uch a little white Flower, as we see in the Spring of the Year; low and humble on the Ground, opening its Bosom, to receive the pleasant Beams of the Sun's Glory; rejoicing as it were, in a calm Rapture; diffusing around a sweet Fragrancy; standing peacefully and lovingly, in the midst of other Flowers round about; all in like Manner opening their Bosoms, to drink in the Light of the Sun.[12]

---

[12]   Daniel B. Shea, 'The Art and Instruction of Jonathan Edwards' Personal Narrative,' in *The American Puritan Imagination: Essays in Revaluation*, (ed.), Sacvan Bercovitch, pp. 159–72. (p. 169.) Shea cites Jonathan Edwards's *Personal*

Here Edwards positions the flower as the receptacle which receives the divine light of the sun. In this the passage reproduces gender stereotypes; the feminine, responsive supplicant of the flower 'opening its Bosom' to receive the 'Beams' of the 'Sun's Glory'. With their ability to fly and to take up various and multiple positions which destabilise gender associations, the bees in Dickinson's poems offer a refreshing alternative to the duality Edwards's metaphor inscribes. The bee also provides a counter to the notion of God as being distinctly separate from humans which the hierarchical metaphors also convey in *Personal Narrative*. However, the bee emblem in Dickinson's poetry does not only explode the hierarchical structures of organised religion; it also resists, by the fact of the metaphor of the bee's relation to the hive, the descriptions of God as espoused in the poetical works of Dickinson's notable male contemporaries such as Emerson and Whitman. Gelpi maintains that by comparison, the crafted emblems such as the bee, the flower and the spider in Dickinson's poetry do not align her with any kind of 'mysticism:'

> For all her experience of the blaze of noon and the lightning-flash, for all her knowledge of the flower's ecstasy and the bee's power, she had to reject the kind of 'mysticism' which in Emerson became mistiness and in Whitman amorphousness. She wrote neither as a visionary nor as a genius but as a craftsman making order out of the fragments of mutability. (Gelpi, p. 152)[13]

Such an association of mysticism with 'mistiness' serves to undermine the radical aspect of Dickinson's mode of 'non-saying' and use of dialogic space. At the same time it denies the possibility for shape and pattern within such a mode. Dickinson's mysticism and her 'craftsman[ship]' go hand in hand because to engage with order, the form of the hymn and the structures implied in bee imagery, and her repeated (albeit differentiated) use of it, is to highlight both absence *and* relation – two aspects of spirituality which are continually reassessed in her poetry.

The prolific nature of the bee image in Dickinson's poems means that focus in both parts of this chapter will be centred on two main ideas which are broadly associated with her critique of orthodox religion. The first is the dialectic between the individual and community, an important aspect of traditional orthodox religion, which is conveyed metaphorically in terms of the bee's relation to the hive or wider community. The second is the connection/division between ideas of industry and revery, which connote respectively ideas of production and ecstasy. Dickinson's exploration of these ideas through bee imagery can be seen, firstly, in the way she uses caricature, where the bee represents the Puritan and the Protestant work ethic. Secondly, it can be seen through the emphasis on the bee's presence in the poetical scene, usually with an excessive, disruptive and often sexualised body. The different ways in which the bee image is used can be seen as being 'emblematic',

---

Narrative, pp. 29–30, from Hopkins, *The Life and Character of the Late Reverend Mr Jonathan Edwards* (Boston, 1765).

[13] Gelpi cites Walter Jackson Bate, *John Keats* (Cambridge, MA: 1963) pp. 250–52, for similar invocations of the bee, flower and spider in the poetry of Keats.

with their performative nature taking on a liturgical quality within Dickinson's poetic and spiritual architecture. Martha Winburn England identifies 'systems of images' in Dickinson's poems, and likens these to those found in Shakespeare's plays:

> In the plays, systems of images form almost a separate plot element. In her collected poems, similar systems of images give an effect of drama. [...] They enter into conflicts. They mirror one another, change sides in an argument, combine and re-combine as in multiple valences, entering into combination with conflicting ideas, themes and emotions. (Winburn England, p. 117)

The emblematic but repositioning shape of Dickinson's bee imagery enters directly into the conflicts created by the orthodox religious culture she had grown up within, as against her own spiritual experiences as she felt them. Whilst Dickinson's relation to the bee imagery she employs is shifting, the bee's relation to the hive is unchanging. In this way, the bee presents Dickinson with a paradigm for her own predicament; the effect of creating poetically a metaphor for the divine which is both emblematic *and* multivalent, both changing *and* unchanging. Bee imagery serves Dickinson as a way to articulate the reconciliation of impossibilities and therefore also, to trace the trajectory of the divine.

Transcendentalism and Unitarianism

In keeping with her time, Dickinson's poems can be seen as reflecting and articulating the climate of challenge to the myth of American Protestant unity.[14] The bee image in her work highlights various challenges to ideas of individuality and community prevalent in orthodox religious discourse. In New England in particular there was a proliferation of different religious groups which emerged in the mid-nineteenth century period and Transcendentalism and Unitarianism undoubtedly influenced Dickinson. Both were popular in literary circles and espoused in the works she read by Ralph Waldo Emerson[15] and Thomas Wentworth Higginson, and although the extent of such influence is debatable, the fact that such 'unevangelical' thinking permeated Dickinson's literary and social sphere must be

---

[14] For detail on religious groups in New England, see Catherine A. Brekus, 'Interpreting American Religion,' in *A Companion to Nineteenth-Century America* (ed.), William L. Barney, pp. 317–33.

[15] Ralph Waldo Emerson (1803–1882) See 'The Over-Soul' where Emerson states 'that Unity, that Over-Soul, within which every man's particular being is contained and made one with all other.' Ralph Waldo Emerson, *Essays* (1841) (London: J.M. Dent and Co., 1904) pp. 197–221 (p. 198). Also Emerson's poem 'The Humble-bee' in which he sees perfect design in the bee's industry. The bee in this poem is the 'Yellow-breeched philosopher' who 'dost mock fate and care,' by discarding 'the chaff' and taking 'the wheat.' (*American Poetry: The Nineteenth-Century*, (ed.), John Hollander (New York: Library of America, 1996) p. 109.

acknowledged at this point.[16] Thomas Wentworth Higginson was a Unitarian,[17] writer and critic who became an important mentor figure for Dickinson. Both Emerson and Higginson produced works on nature and the 'revery' which might be achieved by engagement with it. Dickinson's continued friendship with Higginson, and his writings, which were to be found frequently in the *Atlantic Monthly* and the *Springfield Republican*, presented ample opportunity for her to register Unitarian thinking. She was undoubtedly familiar with Emerson's essay on 'Nature,' in which Emerson argues that the natural world provides the human observer with ways to transcend mortal reality, thus articulating the important leap from rational Unitarianism to Transcendentalism.[18]

As discussed in the previous chapter, Eliza Lee Follen's hymns and songs for children were widespread and her connection with Unitarianism was perhaps a contributing factor in her popularity. Although Unitarianism was resisted in Central and Western Massachusetts, it became an important nexus for writers such as Follen. New England Unitarianism encouraged congregational hymn-singing and English hymnographers such as the theologically liberal Dissenters Philip Doddridge, Anna Letitia Barbauld (1743–1826) and, of course Isaac Watts, were also popular.

In many ways Dickinson's poems reflect this emergent shifting relation to Protestant unity. This is counter to the view of Dickinson as being essentially a poet of reticence and introspection, whose poetry is marked by its 'virtual exclusion of the contemporary and social' and is ultimately without context.[19] Dickinson's poetics, as exemplified most strongly in her use of the bee image, delineate the individual's place within a community and society. Moreover, they directly address the poet's position as one who produces 'praise.' The idea of poetry as

---

[16] Martha Winburn England dismisses claims of Dickinson's Unitarian or Transcendental tendencies, arguing that 'There are only such elements of mysticism and transcendentalism as are common to all orthodox Hebrew and Christian thinking,' and sees Dickinson primarily as displaying a Puritan's attitude toward the Establishment.' See Martha Winburn England, *Hymns Unbidden: Donne, Herbert, Blake, Emily Dickinson and the Hymnographers*, p. 119.

[17] See Richard B. Sewall *The Life of Emily Dickinson*, vol. 2 (London: Faber and Faber, 1976). For Higginson's progression from Harvard Divinity student to 'radical Unitarian Minister' (p. 540.).

[18] David M. Robinson, 'Emerson and Religion,' in Joel Myerson, (ed.), *A Historical Guide to Ralph Waldo Emerson* (Oxford: Oxford University Press, 2000) pp. 151–77 (p. 158). Robinson cites Emerson's *Nature* to illustrate his commitment to idealism: 'Idealism sees the world in God,' 'It beholds the whole circle of persons and things, of actions and events, of country and religion, not as painfully accumulated, atom after atom, act after act, in an aged creeping Past, but as one vast picture, which God paints on the instant eternity, for the contemplation of the soul' (*Nature* 1:36).

[19] See for example, Cora Kaplan, 'The Indefinite Disclosed: Christina Rossetti and Emily Dickinson' in Cora Kaplan, *Sea Changes: Essays on Culture and Feminism* (London: Verso, 1986) pp. 95–115 (p. 98). And Lynn Shakinovsky, 'No Frame of Reference: The Absence of Context in Emily Dickinson's Poetry', in *Emily Dickinson: Critical Assessments Vol IV* (ed.), Graham Clarke (Mountfield: Helm Information Ltd., 2002) pp. 703–16.

prayer, or prayer as poetry, can be seen in the pun Dickinson makes on 'prairie' in Fr 1779: 'To make a prairie it takes a clover and one bee'. The notion of 'revery' incorporates the bee to challenge religious authority and patriarchal control in the depiction of sexuality and bodily excessiveness. In this way Dickinson uses it to articulate rebellion via sexuality. There are of course moments when Dickinson's bee is simply that: an insect she chooses to use as a metaphor for transcendence, physical pleasure or interconnectivity. However, the fact that the image has such strong resonance both in literary history and also the puritan work ethic and notion of leading a 'useful' life conveyed in many of Isaac Watts's hymns, means that it becomes, overall, more than a metaphor for these things; it becomes a trope within her own poetic 'liturgy' and is therefore also inextricably bound to her own search for, and expression of, belief.

Dickinson's Bee Imagery and Traditional Emblems

The various ways in which the bee is presented resists, partly, the impulse to see it as a definitive, one-dimensional emblem or motif. Frequently, Dickinson's metaphors deny and undermine language's power to define and it is this quality that has made her work so receptive to post-modern accounts and readings. However, because of its repeated use within her body of work, and the numerous occasions when it does seem to carry a uniform quality across the corpus from one poem to another, the bee in Dickinson's work can be seen as having a tropic quality within her own poetic liturgy. This repeated presence reveals an effort to construct an alternative to the dogma of orthodox religion. Lease concedes that Dickinson's metaphors were 'rooted in ideas that she took seriously – that we can and should take seriously'[20] but the extent to which they were 'rooted' or connected explicitly to ideas or even political persuasions is debatable. If we are to assume that Dickinson's imagery serves as material to construct a poetic world, one in which she participated whilst writing poetry, then the bee image seems a particularly poignant place to start.

The symbol in Western Christian traditions of worship has been noted as possessing potency and importance. M. Bradford Bedingfield's (2002) comments on the place of the symbol in Anglo-Saxon Christianity are relevant here:

> The relationship between the symbol and what it symbolises is real enough to belie the modern predisposition that ritualistic expression, relying as it does on symbols, is somehow unrealistic. [...] art can imbue a church with divine power, providing 'a way of entering the next world.'[21]

---

[20] *RMB*, p. 62. Lease argues that Dickinson's metaphors shouldn't be taken literally and that her central emphasis was secular and aesthetic, and cites Charles R. Anderson, *Stairway of Surprise* (p. 46); 'that figurative expressions should not be taken literally is an unexceptional position - but I would urge that Dickinson's life and art were inextricably linked to her lifelong struggle for religious belief' (p. 144).

[21] M. Bradford Bedingfield, *The Dramatic Liturgy of Anglo-Saxon England* (Woodbridge: The Boydell Press, 2002) pp. 5–6 Bradford Bedingfield cites Barbara Raw, *Anglo-Saxon Crucifixion Iconography* (Cambridge, 1990) p. 16.

Reading Dickinson's poems in such a way goes against one's impulses, and does seem to be implausible or 'unrealistic' in a similar way to that suggested above. However, given that Dickinson's mode of expression is often elliptical and evasive, the recurrence of images and the personifications she frequently employs become all the more striking when compared with the conventions of religious liturgy and religious art. In particular, the subtle shift to the mimetic in Anglo-Saxon dramatic liturgy that Bradford Bedingfield identifies – that is, the shift from the ritual to representational – is useful when thinking about Dickinson's use of imagery because her use of the bee seems to fall somewhere between these two categories (Bedingfield, p. 228). In a similar manner to the symbols used in Christian liturgy, Dickinson's images often hint at analogous events, states of being or processes which are characteristic of meaning beyond the image itself.[22]

Some discussion of this trait in Dickinson's writing can be found with reference to her other images, such as flowers.[23] Citing a list of Dickinson's botanical reading, produced largely by her education at Mount Holyoke, Petrino argues that such reading, together with her devotion to a herbarium, illustrates how she 'veered away from the age's religiocentrism, with its attendant attitudes toward gender,' but also notes how such education encouraged the scrutiny of the physical world which would prepare young women to be capable of abstract thought (Petrino, p. 105). However, just as she clearly revised the gender associations with flowers in contemporary literature, she also systematically revised the 'religiocentrism' inherent in other emblematic depictions of nature such as the bee. The image of the bee in Dickinson is ironically emblematic but also emblematic within her own poetics of the struggle to convey the essential paradox that such religiocentrism could not reconcile: the desire for community and interconnectedness with the need for freedom and liberty in poetic language.

Petrino concurs with Domhnall Mitchell's view on Dickinson's use of flowers as being that which locates her to middle class culture:

---

[22]   For explanation of liturgical symbols see Gerhard Podhradsky, (ed.), *New Dictionary of the Liturgy* (London: Geoffrey Chapman, 1967) pp. 190–91.

[23]   Elizabeth Petrino (2005) argues that Dickinson would have rejected the emblematic quality of the gentian flower as depicted in contemporary male writers such as William Cullen Bryant and John Greenleaf Whittier. Elizabeth Petrino, 'Late Bloomer: The Gentian as Sign or Symbol in the Work of Dickinson and Her Contemporaries,' *The Emily Dickinson Journal* 14: 1 (2004) 104–25. Judith Farr has argued in *The Gardens of Emily Dickinson* (2004) that Dickinson's use of flowers (both as literary tropes and also actual flowers, with Dickinson's interest in gardening) supplied her with a method of organising her poetics and even her literary and social self. Furthermore, that Dickinson's 'use' of flowers is what aligns her most decisively with the literary tradition, given the Victorian pun on 'posies' and 'poesie'. See Judith Farr, *The Gardens of Emily Dickinson* (Cambridge, MA: Harvard University Press, 2004) (p. 4). See also Domhnall Mitchell's *Emily Dickinson: Monarch of Perception* (Amherst: University of Massachusetts Press, 2000) pp. 112–77.

She ironically deploys flowers, insects, and other natural creatures to express
her wish that she could control life as she would hope to plant and tend a garden
- another aspect of her middle-class sensibility. (Petrino, p. 110)

The notion that Dickinson deployed images of the natural world, including bees,
to 'express her wish that she could control life as she would hope to plant and tend
a garden' is questionable at best when considering the various ways in which the
image of the bee is 'deployed.' Although Dickinson was in no doubt middle-class,
a desire to exert control over life cannot be taken as an indication of this fact, nor
can it be identified in her portrayal of bees, as often they invoke the abnegation of
such control. However, the various ways in which bee imagery is conveyed in the
body of Dickinson's work effectively assists readings of her critique of orthodox,
organised religion. This is because of the affinity the bee images have within the
poems with Puritanism, hymn-singing and the debates surrounding an individual's
position within a spiritual community.

The bee image is as equally established in literary (and also religious) history
as that of flowers. Unlike the flower, the bee image provides a disruption, and
a counter, to the flower's genderised, genteel-feminine associations. It carries
equally the phallic and masculine association as well as the feminine solitary-
worker, and matriarchal 'Queen Bee' connotations.[24] The image of the bee serves
to express in equal measure both masculine and feminine 'traits,' and at times
these stereotypes are manipulated in the poems to express but also undermine
and dissolve easy gender distinctions. It is perhaps because of this fluidity that
the bee is capable of reason and sound judgement, as well as 'delirium'. In the
poem 'There is a flower that bees prefer,' for example, the bee is introduced as
displaying a measured, rational response (as opposed to 'desire') with regard to
the choice of flower, which in this instance is a clover:

> There is a flower that Bees prefer -
> And Butterflies - desire -
> To gain the Purple Democrat
> The Humming Bird - aspire - (Fr 642)

The poem, which eulogises the clover as the perfect feminine specimen delays
the usual climax of ironic wit present in other poems which are concerned with
flowers as a metaphor epitomising negative stereotypes of femininity. Instead the
poem gives way to genuine affection for the clover's lowly, 'democratic' position
and for her endurance, invoking simultaneously both Christ's example of suffering
and Mary's innocence and patience in bearing her 'privilege:'

---

[24]   The 1828 entry for 'bee' in *Webster's* dictionary does not provide the sex of worker
bees, therefore we cannot be certain that Dickinson knew that they are all female. Despite
this, however, bee imagery certainly provided Dickinson with an opportunity to utilise both
the phallic, masculine association of the bee's action of gathering pollen from a flower as
well as the popular association of the Queen Bee with exclusive, matriarchal power.

Her sturdy little Countenance
Against the Wind - be seen -

Contending with the Grass -
Near Kinsman to Herself -
For Privilege of Sod and Sun -
Sweet Litigants for Life -

The bee's response to the clover is a measure of the poem's distance from a parody of the flower's innate qualities of constancy and altruism:

Her Public - be the Noon -
Her Providence - the Sun -
Her Progress - by the Bee - proclaimed -
In sovereign - Swerveless Tune -

Usually easily distracted, deference is given in this poem to the bee's estimation ('swerveless tune') of the clover's progress, here perhaps symbolising spiritual as well as physical growth. The bee in this poem is not the rebellious, pleasure-seeking wanderer, but is comparatively 'mature' and capable of sound judgement, and serves as an indication to the reader the level of esteem imparted to the clover's 'Christian' qualities.

In the epilogue to her book, Judith Farr makes a brief connection between poem Fr 610 'From Cocoon forth a Butterfly' with its references to the 'steady tide' which 'extinguishes,' and the frequent reminders of darkness to be found in eighteenth-century hymns, such as Watts's 'O God, our help in ages past' (Farr, p. 281). It is no coincidence that such a poem, in which the bee image is particularly striking because of its markedly less prominent position within the poem, should be noted for its resonance with Watts. Often in poems where the bee is present, the Wattsian association of the bee with the conflict between idleness and industry, and how that relates to spirituality, or rectitude, is also there. Dickinson's use of the bee can be seen as much more than a desire to align herself with nature, moreover, it directly confronts 'nature' as a concept which problematises gender construction. In contrast to the flower as a relatively *static* metaphor, the bee, which invokes what Farr terms 'the conflict between the need for labour and the quest for pleasure' (Farr, p. 281) is rather, an *ecstatic* metaphor. This image conveys at different turns, fluidity, multiplicity, liberty, community and regeneration: qualities which are strongly associated with spirituality in her poems which appear as disruptive to the representation of orthodox religion. As such an *ecstatic* metaphor it both occupies and delineates the heterologous hymnic space in Dickinson's poems.

The tendency to align rebellious, rowdy qualities with the bee can be seen in a letter of April 1856, to John L. Graves, where she describes the bumblebee as a 'Cockney' in 'jaunty clothes', and makes the distinction between this type of bee and the 'manly, earnest' bees of summer:

> [...] here's a *bumblebee* - not such as summer brings - John - earnest, manly bees,
> but a kind of Cockney, dressed in jaunty clothes. Much that is gay - have I to
> show, if you were with me, John, upon this April grass. (L: II, p. 327)

The 'jaunty cockney' bumblebee represents an elusive character whose
changeability resists the definitions of gender, a trait echoed in the fluid nature of
bee imagery which is here the jauntiness of the bumblebee rather than the industry
of the honey bee. Contemporary literary treatments of the bee image as worker
or 'jaunty' entrepreneur are found in both Emerson and Dickens. As Bee Wilson
observes,[25] *Bleak House* contains a section in which Dickens uses the metaphor
of the male (nonindustrious) drone in order to convey the deceptive nature of Mr
Skimpole's character. Skimpole's ability to scrounge money out of others whilst
receiving little in the way of retribution conveys the opposite of the more widely
held association of the worker bee with worthwhile industry. In Chapter 8 of *Bleak
House*, entitled 'Covering a Multitude of Sins,' Dickens describes Mr Skimpole's
rumination on the productive life of bees:

> He didn't at all see why the busy Bee should be proposed as a model to him; he
> supposed the Bee liked to make honey, or he wouldn't do it - nobody asked him.
> It was not necessary for the Bee to make such a merit of his tastes.

And the significant differences between worker bees and drones:

> He must say he thought a Drone the embodiment of a pleasanter and wiser idea.
> The Drone said, unaffectedly, '[...] I must take the liberty of looking about me,
> and begging to be provided for by somebody who doesn't want to look about
> him.' This appeared to Mr Skimpole to be the Drone philosophy.[26]

The prevalence of the notion of the 'busy bee,' and the extent to which it had
become idiomatic in popular literature during the nineteenth century is evident
here. Dickens also illustrates the distinction between industrious bees and nonindustrious drones which Dickinson, having read *Bleak House*, must have been
aware of when choosing how to represent the insect in her poems. The idea of
the morally dubious character or the association of the bee's ecstatic nature with
criminality is invoked in many of her representations of bees, as will be discussed
in the next chapter. However, her use of the image also includes criticism of
society's expectations and how one must be seen as being productive or face moral
reprehension. In her use of bees Dickinson questions the notion of productivity, as
well as the portrayal of joy, exuberance and ecstasy as being counter to orthodox
religion's emphasis on being industrious.

The notion of disorder that the bee sometimes conveys in Dickinson's poems
might also represent the female as disorder, a label which was prevalent in

---

[25]   Bee Wilson, *The Hive: The Story of the Honeybee and Us* (London: John Murray,
2004) pp. 31–2.

[26]   Charles Dickens, *Bleak House* (1853) (London: Penguin, 2003) p. 116.

Puritan New England. Susan Juster's book, *Disorderly Women: Sexual Politics and Evangelicalism in Revolutionary New England* includes a chapter on the 'Feminisation of Sin 1780–1830,' in which she outlines the ways in which women were 'othered' in a community of religious believers through their association with disorder. She writes:

> [...] disorderly qualities were seen not only to be manifest in individual women members, but to constitute the very core of the feminine character [...] 'feminine' qualities in general were redefined as disorderly even when exhibited by men.[27]

Women were seen as being the epitome of disorder, 'seducing souls and bodies away from the truth' (Juster, pp. 148–9). Dickinson's depiction of the bee often revels in disorder, presenting it as an anarchic mode of rebellion against that which oppresses and defines the woman as the enemy of truth.

The image of the bee and its life pattern has always served as a rich metaphor for writers and an opportunity for making connections between it and human political action (or inaction). As Bee Wilson explains:

> Bee politics has taken almost as many forms as human politics, shifting with the changing values of different places and times. The hive has been, in turn, monarchical, oligarchical, aristocratic, constitutional, imperial, republican, absolute, moderate, communist, anarchist and even fascist. As so often in politics, we see whatever it is we want to see. (Wilson, p. 110)

Dickinson's use of the bee shifts also, and is at times the worker honey bee, compatible with utopian socialist thinking; at other times the solitary bumblebee indicative of the excessive fuzz and buzz of society but also of her own experiences as a poet. The bee image as a metaphor for leading a useful life and also being under the rule of a Queen Bee is especially apt for Dickinson's era - in terms of both its Puritan and colonial heritage. However it is the fluidity and variety of positions available to the bee which makes it an attractive image for Dickinson and why it conveys, ultimately, her own poetic identity.

'Out of the Strong Came Forth Sweetness': Biblical and Literary Bees

In a literary sense, Dickinson's bee image is neither Classical nor Romantic; however, the range of her reading would have encompassed the following in which the bee is an important image: Virgil's *Georgics*, Milton's *Paradise Lost*, the devotional poetry of George Herbert, Isaac Watts, and William Blake's poetry. She may also have been familiar with Mandeville's *The Fable of the Bees* (1714) which has influenced many writings on the life of bees because of the emphasis which Mandeville places upon the morally dubious nature of bees. Here the 'paradise'

---

[27]   Susan Juster, *Disorderly Women: Sexual Politics and Evangelicalism in Revolutionary New England* (London: Cornell University Press, 1994) pp. 148–9.

or 'public benefit' of the hive is not constructed by the virtue of the working bees, but rather by the 'private vice' of individuals. Dickinson's 'Skimpolean' bees invoke the moral dubiousness which Mandeville associates with the individuality of bees, and assert a poetic Paradise which is similarly, hubristically, amoral. Her 'fraudulent' bees are incorporated within, and are not incompatible with, the pattern for ecstasy within her poems. However, this serves to highlight the moral judgement attached to such ecstatic behaviour as opposed to the behaviour itself.

Before engaging in a brief outline of canonical writers' use of the bee image, attention must first be turned to the Bible, one of Dickinson's most favoured sources of inspiration. Sources for the use of the bee to convey resurrection, or a bridge between life and death can be seen in many texts. The practice of 'bugonia,' the belief that dead oxen 'produce' bees and honey is alluded to in much classical literature to convey the miracle of death producing life. The biblical version is an allegory of God's power and resurrection through death. However, the actual practice of producing honey in this way was described in ancient Greek and Roman farming advice, such as in the anthology *Geoponica* (See Wilson, p. 74). The quotation from Judges 14:14 'Out of the eater came forth meat, out of the strong came forth sweetness' alludes to this. Samson gathers honey made by the swarm of bees seemingly born out of the decaying carcass of the young lion he had killed through the Holy Spirit's power. The exuberant nature of Dickinson's bees connotes a similar spiritual strength, derived from access to its own sweetness or its ability to produce sweetness.

Dickinson's schooling was predominantly classical, and the Roman poet Virgil (70–19BC) would have been familiar to her. Virgil's pastoral poem the *The Georgics* was, up until the Renaissance, one of the main sources for writing about bees (Wilson, p. 24). Virgil's main source for information on bees was books five and six of Aristotle's *Historia Animalium*.[28] It is likely that the *The Georgics*, probably Dryden's translation, widely available in the nineteenth century, may have provided a source for Dickinson's bees. The depiction in the *The Georgics* is interesting to read alongside the poems of Dickinson's which contain bees because Virgil's poem veils what is an extensive consideration of a human's place in society and the relationship to her/his environment - a similar consideration in Dickinson's poetry. In this, it is also a eulogy to the Roman people, and Dickinson's bees perhaps represent the warrior-like search for cohesion within her own 'Ecstatic nation' (Fr 1381). Mynors notes Virgil's use of Aristotle's terms of 'nare' and 'trahi' in book four of *The Georgics* which conveys the 'trailing motion of a swarm which, though composed of thousands of individuals, moveth altogether, if

---

[28] R.A.B. Mynors, (ed.), *Virgil: Georgics*, rev edn (Oxford: Clarendon Press, 1994) p. 266. Mynors notes in the commentary to lines 58–60 of book four that Virgil uses Aristotle's phrase 'ad sidera' which means 'soaring flight' to connote the bees' 'new found liberty.' Mynors comments on the swarming action of the bees - 'the first or 'prime' swarm when the hive is overfull with spring brood and the old queen issues forth with many of her people to establish a new colony.'

it move at all.'[29] It is no surprise that the image of the bee colony which is made up of many individuals and moves as one unified colony should become a metaphor for the ideal of solidarity or community, religious or otherwise. Virgil's description of the re-emergence of the bees at the end of book four is such that it effectively bridges the living and the under worlds. The bees issue forth from death, and their flight upwards from the decaying carcasses of bulls indicates and delineates a path towards heaven, that is, a new nation, and 'golden age':

> Nine mornings thence, with sacrifice and prayers,
> The powers atoned, he to the grove repairs.
> Behold a prodigy! For from within
> The broken bowels and the bloated skin,
> A buzzing noise of bees his ears alarms:
> Straight issue through the sides assembling swarms. (*The Georgics*, Book IV,
> p. 212)[30]

Depicting the practice of bugonia, this final passage from *The Georgics* reiterates the bee's origin which is death, and also simultaneously their miraculous, collective power; the 'broken bowels' and their 'straight issue through the sides' describes their physical force. Thus the bee imagery here provides a connection between death and life, where a vital life force is literally born out of the death and decay of a previously existing but now extinguished life. Significantly, at the end of Dryden's translation, Caesar's use of 'arts' in exacting his authority is invoked:

> With conquering arts asserts his country's cause,
> With arts of peace the willing people draws;
> On the glad earth the golden age renews. (*The Georgics*, Book IV, p. 212)

Dickinson's use of poetic artistry similarly envisions a new kind of heaven. Virgil's use of bee imagery is instructive to reading Dickinson's bees. In Dryden's translation they symbolise a reconfigured hope and spirituality borne from an old world (in Dickinson's case an old faith) where 'slow-creeping evil eats his way' (*The Georgics*, Book III, p. 186), and the projection of a renewed 'age' and subsequently renewed heaven.

However, other biblical instances of bees (all Old Testament) are connected with vengeance, wrath and danger and foreshadow the apocalyptic vision in the Book of Revelations. (For example; Deut. 1.44, Psalm 118.12 and Isaiah 7.18). Although Dickinson's bees do not display these qualities, the typological significance of bee imagery is undoubtedly at work in her poems. The swarming action of the bees and the state of God's vengeance being enacted foreshadows the apocalyptical visions in the Book of Revelations, which Dickinson cited as a main source of

---

[29]   Ibid, p. 266. Mynors notes in the commentary to lines 58–60 of book four.

[30]   *The Works of Virgil*, vol 3, trans. by John Dryden (Chiswick: C. Wittingham, 1822).

inspiration. (See SL, p. 172. April 25, 1862 to T.W. Higginson). The rebelliousness and disruption which the bees in Dickinson's poems display enacts the apocalyptic vision, delineating a trajectory towards a new heaven. Thus the description of the bee in poem Fr 979, which derives inspiration from the gemstone imagery in Revelations, includes an armoured Puritan in battle, a 'defender of the faith'.

Milton's use of bee imagery also invokes the typological connection with bees and the apocalyptic visions in the Book of Revelations through its emphasis on the bees' ability to rebel and disrupt. The life-force of the bee in Dickinson's poems often takes on a rebellious, excessively exuberant aspect. A significant previous example of such association of bees with the qualities of rebelliousness and defiance can be found in *Paradise Lost*, Book One, where Milton describes the throng of Satan's angels waiting to enter his court of Pandaemonium:

> Thick swarmed both on the ground and in the air,
> Brushed with the hiss of rustling wings.
> [...]
> In clusters, they among fresh dews and flow'rs
> Fly to and fro or on the smoothed plank,
> The suburb of their straw-built citadel,
> New rubbed with balm, expatiate and confer
> Their state affairs (*Paradise Lost*, Book I, 767–75)[31]

Milton draws on Virgil's notion of bees as city builders (writing of how Satan was sent 'With his industrious crew to build in Hell', *Paradise Lost*, Book I, 751) and as models of social order in *The Georgics* (Book IV).[32] The angels are gathered, in parliamentary fashion, to 'expatiate and confer/Their State affairs,' thus also depicting commonwealth ideals in keeping with Milton's politics.[33] The solitary bee is tiny but the collective, 'swarming' force of a colony ('crowd'), compounded by their ability to produce painful stings, produces a threatening image on a much larger scale. The gathering of Satan's angels and the 'hiss' of their 'rustling wings' firmly connects the industrious bee with satanic force. The 'hiss' invokes perfectly at once the rapid movement of a bee colony as well as the snake/form of Satan in *Genesis*. This is further exemplified by their ability to 'charm' the peasant in

---

[31]   John Milton, *Paradise Lost*, (ed.), Gordon Teskey (London: Norton and Company, 2005) p. 25.

[32]   Also a further allusion to Book One of Virgil's *Aeneid*, where the Carthaginians are compared to bees in spring, 'So in the youth of summer throughout the flowering land/ The bees pursue their labours under the sun.' (430–31) Thus diminishing them to insects, an effect which is also evident in *Georgics*. See Jasper Griffin, (ed.), *Virgil: The Aeneid* trans. by C. Day Lewis (Oxford: Oxford University Press, 1998) p. 19. (lines 430–37).

[33]   John Milton actively promoted commonwealth ideas in 'The Ready and Easy Way to Establish a Free Commonwealth' published in 1660, shortly before the Restoration of Charles II in the same year. *Paradise Lost* was published in 1667, although we are told he had begun to compose it in 1658. For further information, see F.T. Prince, (ed.), *Milton: Paradise Lost, Books I and II* (Oxford: Oxford University Press, 1962) pp. 204–5.

their 'mirth and dance' with 'jocund Music.' Milton's depiction of the bee in this context is perhaps useful when reading Dickinson's use of the image as it conflates the relation of power to size and also carries the association of bees with music and the 'satanic' rebellion that became a part of the Romantic sensibility.[34]

Dickinson's use of the bee trope in her letters conveys her own pointed engagement with its particular associations, but most specifically with gender. Gilbert and Gubar identify a 'master/slave' relationship which resonates throughout a lot of Dickinson's poems. To this they link Blake's 'Nobodaddy' – the notion of a domineering patriarchal figure coupled with a desire to be 'nobody,' and an abnegation of a public self.[35] One of the examples they cite to demonstrate this point comes from Dickinson's letters, and is also an example of her use of the bee metaphor in her social interactions with others, namely the unnamed masculine addressee, who has been identified by Thomas Johnson and others as Charles Wadsworth. In this letter dated around 1862, which is also grouped by Johnson into what he calls the series of 'master' letters, Dickinson employs the metaphor of the flower ('Daisy') and the Bee in order to characterise a particularly painful personal relationship. The letter displays alternative word choices which have been bracketed, and crossings out, which indicates that it may have been an earlier draft of one which may or may not have been finally sent. She writes:

> Oh, did I offend it [...] Daisy - offend it - who bends her smaller life to his (it's) meeker (lower) every day - who only asks [...] some little way she cannot guess to make that master glad - [...] Wonder stings me more than the Bee - who did never sting me - but made gay music with his might wherever I [may] [should] did go - Wonder wastes my pound, you said I had no size to spare. (L: II, p. 391)

Gilbert and Gubar call this letter an example of Dickinson's awareness of 'romantic coercion' (Gilbert and Gubar, p. 605) and use it to exemplify their ideas about Dickinson's knowledge and use of the Sun as a powerful symbol of the patriarchal other. He is the Master to whom she must bend, inevitably, and flower-like. Her use of this imagery also recalls the 'field or garden of God' metaphor in Jonathan Edwards's *Personal Narrative* discussed earlier, which depicts the flower as a supplicant and receptacle for divine light. However, her use of the bee metaphor is left uncommented upon by Gilbert and Gubar which seems odd as it is central to Dickinson's use of the master/slave metaphor which they identify, and is central to the example they give in this letter. This particular letter is an important example of Dickinson's use of the bee metaphor as it displays her knowledge of the image and its association with painful, romantic love, as also depicted in the figure of

---

[34]   See Byron's poem *Cain* for Romantic treatment of Satan as rebellious fallen angel but anarchic, intellectual force.

[35]   Sandra M. Gilbert and Susan Gubar, *The Madwoman in the Attic: The Woman Writer and the Nineteenth Century Literary Imagination* (1979) rev. edn (New Haven: Yale University Press, 2000) p. 605.

Cupid in poem Fr 1351. The bee's 'cupidity' in this poem is in reference to his ability to pollinate flowers, serving in this instance as a sexual metaphor.

The association of the bee with romantic love has its roots in Classical Greek and Latin literature, and Andreas Alciatus's sixteenth-century *Latin Emblems* (published in the seventeenth century) includes the 'Honey Thief' story in which the bee represents the pain of romantic love. When Cupid is stung by a bee, he cries to his mother Venus, who laughs and says to him, 'You too, my son, imitate this creature, for though small, you also inflict so many hurtful wounds.'[36] Although there is no conclusive evidence to confirm it, the nineteenth-century revival of interest in the emblem tradition might well have influenced Dickinson, when revisiting the image of the bee in a continuous way throughout her poetic life. Daly (1985) provides information on the revival of interest in the emblematic tradition during the Victorian period and cites the Holbein Society's publication of Henry Green's translation of Alciatus's emblems, published in London and New York in 1871 and 1872 with further reprints as being representative of such a renewed interest.[37] Furthermore, Ruth Miller's (1968) work forges comparisons between the organisation of Dickinson's fascicles and Francis Quarles *Emblems, Divine and Moral*, demonstrating a discernable narrative structure in Dickinson's work. Marietta Messmer summarises the structure Miller outlines in Dickinson's poems as being one which moves from 'acceptance through suffering and rejection to resolution.'[38] Although such a narrative is problematic in that it imposes a temporal and linear structure upon the poems, the fact that such a connection with Quarles can be made serves to bring out the emblematic quality of Dickinson's writing.

As will be discussed in part two of this chapter, Dickinson refers explicitly to the 'sacred emblems' of the 'sacrament of summer days' in poem Fr 122. This poem takes as its central concern the deceptive quality of nature's ability to present an autumn day with a blue sky which gives it the appearance of summer. Significantly, it is the bee, Dickinson's own version of a 'sacred' emblem, which is immune from this deception; it is the 'fraud that cannot cheat the Bee.' The place of emblems in religion is also brought to the fore in Edward Hitchcock's *Religious Lectures on Peculiar Phenomena in the Four Seasons* (1850), which Dickinson would certainly have read or at least been aware of. It includes a chapter entitled 'The Resurrection of Spring' which contains an illustration entitled 'Emblems of the Resurrection'

---

[36]   Peter M. Daly, and others, (eds), *Andreas Alciatus: (1) The Latin Emblems Indexes and Lists* (Toronto: University of Toronto Press, 1985) Reprint of the Padua 1621 edition. Emblem #113.

[37]   Peter M. Daly, and others, (eds), *Andreas Alciatus: (1) The Latin Emblems Indexes and Lists* Reprint of the Padua 1621 edition, 'Introduction', no page numbering.

[38]   Ruth Miller, *The Poetry of Emily Dickinson* (Middletown, Conn: Wesleyan University Press, 1968). As observed by Marietta Messmer in 'Dickinson's Critical Reception,' in Gudrun Grabher, and others, (eds), *The Emily Dickinson Handbook*, pp. 299–322 (p. 318).

that depicts emblems such as the cocoon and the butterfly.[39] In order to convey how such literature might have informed Dickinson's use of insects in poetry, Richard Sewall includes an excerpt from the poem which is Fr 162:

> The dreamy Butterflies bestir!
> Lethargic pools resume the whirr
> Of last year's sundered tune!
> From some old Fortress on the sun
> Baronial Bees - march - one by one -
> In murmuring platoon!

This, one of her earlier poems, indicates her use of the bee to depict a particular rank in the ceremonial rite of spring that is likened here to the tuneful marching of an army. As Chapter 2 noted, such simple tunes were often used in battle and form part of America's revolutionary history of the colony gaining independence, and the child gaining freedom from the parent, which no doubt permeated Dickinson's cultural background. As Kramnick observes, when the British were defeated in 1781, Cornwallis ordered his troops to sing the following song which included the lines:

> If buttercups buzz
> After the bee;
> If boats were on land,
> [...]
> If mammas sold their babies
> To gypsies for half a crown;
> If summer were spring
> And the other way round
> Then all the world would be upside down.[40]

According to Kramnick, this rhyme indicates a 'violation of all that seemed natural' (Kramnick, p. 24). Dickinson's use of the term 'baronial bee' might be seen as an indication of the paternalistic, puritan heritage of England's rule. Her desire to retain a child-like quality in her poems can be seen as a comparative desire to forge new configurations; of spirituality beyond God the Father, and independence from paternalistic notions of God or spirit. In this sense she can seen as playing with the guise of the infidel, and the rebellious child and pitting it directly against the legacy of her paternalistic puritan heritage. Therefore in this instance the bee can be said to be emblematic, in so much as it draws upon and reflects particular aspects of her religious, political and literary culture.

---

[39] Richard B. Sewall, *The Life of Emily Dickinson* vol. 2, illustration between pp. 502–3.

[40] Isaac Kramnick, (ed.), *Thomas Paine: Common Sense* (Harmondsworth: Penguin, 1984) p. 24. Kramnick notes that an account of this incident is given in Samuel Elliot Morrison's *Oxford History of the American People* (New York: 1965) p. 265.

As they appear to be influences upon Dickinson's 'emblematic' way of incorporating the bee in her poetics, Alciatus's book of emblems might also connect Isaac Watts and William Blake and provide a strong link to the emblematic tradition. Titles for Watts's *Divine and Moral Songs for Children* seem to echo some of the poetic emblems in Alciatus and comparisons were drawn between Blake and Watts by contemporary writers. Shrimpton (1976) cites B.H. Malkin's introductory letter to his *A Father's Memoirs of His Child* (London, 1806) which included a range of Blake's poems from *Songs of Innocence and Experience*, and a contrast is set up between Blake's poetic style and Isaac Watts's hymns.[41]

We know that Dickinson read and was probably influenced by the work of the metaphysical poet, George Herbert (1593–1633). Rufus Griswold's *Sacred Poets of England and America* (1850) is one obvious source, and Lease has noted that Herbert ('Mattens') was available in the *Springfield Republican* (28 October 1876) and also in the family's copy of Chambers' *Cyclopaedia of English Literature* (*RMB*, p. 63 and 144). The image of the garden as a metaphor for the Church, which inevitably includes the images of nature and particularly the flower, can be seen repeatedly in Herbert's poems and hymns. Herbert's influence also extends beyond the bee; the final three stanzas of 'The Flower' are echoed in the letter quoted above (L: II, p. 391). In the poem 'Providence,' which there is no evidence for Dickinson having read, but nonetheless proves as an illuminating intertext for her poems, Herbert's bee is emblematic of the harmony and order he perceives through faith in God's design. It appears amidst a long list of 'creatures' which exist harmoniously, side by side, in nature:

> Bees work for man; and yet they never bruise
> Their master's flower, but leave it, having done,
> As fair as ever, and as fit to use;
> So both the flower doth stay, and honey run. (*The Temple:* 'Providence')[42]

Here the bee does not affect the environment it is in, other than to produce honey, and so as a metaphor for the spiritual human, the 'bee' replicates an uncomplicated relationship with God that is spiritually productive. However, Dickinson's use of

---

[41]   N. Shrimpton, 'Hell's Hymnbook: Blake's *Songs of Innocence and Experience* and their Models' pp. 19–35 in B.G. Beatty, and R.T. Davies, (eds), *Literature of the Romantic Period 1750–1850* (Liverpool: Liverpool University Press, 1976) p. 20. Shrimpton traces children's hymns for influences on Blake's poems, citing Watts's *Divine Songs Attempted in Easy Language for the use of Children* (1715). Bruce Woodcock notes in *The Selected Poems of William Blake* (Hertfordshire: Wordsworth Editions, 2000) that lines in Blake's poem 'The Divine Image'; 'And all must love the human form/In heathen, turk or jew' answer Watts's 'Praise for the Gospel'; 'Lord, I ascribe it to thy grace,/And not to chance, as others do,/That I was born of Christian race,/And not a Heathen or a Jew' in *Divine Songs attempted in Easy Language for the Use of Children* (1715) (ed.), J.H.P. Pafford, Oxford University Press, 1971 (p. 157).

[42]   John Tobin, (ed.), *George Herbert: The Complete English Poems* (London: Penguin, 2004) p. 110.

the bee as spiritual actor enacts the design implied in Herbert's use of the image, whilst also conveying ecstatic movement within and beyond the confined space of the garden or church. The productive aspect of the speaker's relationship with God implied in Herbert's use of the bee has strong associations with the production of ecstasy in Dickinson's poetry; in the revery which is derived through bodily pleasure as equally as spiritual connection. Perhaps the most striking allusion to the life of bees in connection with spirituality to be found in Herbert is in 'The Holy Scriptures (1)', where the restorative sustenance that the Bible provides the speaker with is likened to a bee's experience of honey:

> O Book! Infinite sweetness! Let my heart
> Suck ev'ry letter, and honey gain,
> Precious for any grief in any part;
>   [...] thou art a mass
> Of strange delights, where we may wish and take. (*The Complete English Poems*, p. 52)

Not only does the speaker feast on each letter of the Bible as a bee would each flower, but the productive store of the holy book, the 'mass of strange delights,' which provides the speaker with unlimited access to spiritual sustenance is evocative of the beehive, a similar 'mass' with its many strange parts. Herbert's view of holy scripture as restorative can be likened to the effects of poetry in Dickinson, where the bees' access to revery connotes and allows the achievement of an ideal space.

Contemporary uses of the bee image can be gleaned from articles in the *Atlantic Monthly*, which Dickinson read and to which T.W. Higginson frequently contributed. A poem by John Greenleaf Whittier entitled 'Telling the Bees' which appears anonymously in the April 1858 issue of the *Atlantic Monthly*, comes with a footnote explaining a New England custom of covering over the bee hive in mourning:

> On the death of a member of the family, the bees were at once informed of the event, and their hives dressed in mourning. The ceremonial was supposed to be necessary to prevent the swarms from leaving their hives and seeking a new home. ('Telling the Bees', *Atlantic Monthly* 1:6 (1858) p. 722)

Although the custom of 'Telling the Bees' of the death of a family member was perhaps in Dickinson's lifetime a somewhat out-moded custom left over from previous New England generations, it does illustrate the extent to which a belief in a particular quality of consciousness and perception had been invested in the bee. The desire to see the bee as that which seeks a thriving community, and to be an affirmation of life and activity, is attached to this particular meaning of the bee's anticipated flight away from death, and a need to separate itself from the inactivity that death brings. Another anonymous piece from the *Atlantic Monthly* that concerns itself with the notion of 'Individuality' furthers the idea of the bee as social creatures, emblematic of community and city building:

> Bees and ants are, to say the least, quite as witty as beetles, proverbially blind;
> yet they build insect cities, and are invincibly social and city-loving as Socrates
> himself. ('Individuality' *Atlantic Monthly* 9: 54 (1862) p. 428)

Both of these articles serve to demonstrate that bees were certainly part of the
literary consciousness and would also be a familiar talking point at the time that
Dickinson was writing her bee poems.

Advances in science and interest in natural history in mid-nineteenth-century
America no doubt play a part in Dickinson's fashioning of the bee in many of
her poems. The 1828 edition of *Webster's* dictionary[43] includes an entry for 'bee'
that describes the three classes of bees as; female queen bees, male drone bees
and the 'neuters or working bees.' Although this evidences the fact that the sex
of drone bees was known, it is unlikely that Dickinson would have known the
female sex of worker bees. The 'neutrality' of gender which is ascribed to the
worker bee at this point might account for Dickinson's use of it as an image which
frequently disrupts gender stereotypes. One notable influence on Dickinson's
interest in natural history is that of Edward Hitchcock, the Reverend Professor
and President of Amherst College. The work and views of Hitchcock no doubt
informed Dickinson's analysis of the connection between the natural world and
God's design in her incorporation of the life and habits of bees in her poetry,
drawing on both biological/scientific and religious concerns.[44] In her poems the
bee is emblematic of being both 'part' *and* 'process,' that is paradoxically, an
individual, ecstatic part of the productive, communal process.

Bee Imagery: Alternative to Liturgical Symbolism?

The series of changes to the liturgy that took place during the eighteenth century,
such the increased active participation of the laity together with the minimising of
formal rituals, are reflected in Watts's Dissenting hymns. Book Three of *Hymns
and Spiritual Songs* is significantly titled 'Prepared for the Holy Ordinance of
The Lord's Supper' rather than referring to the Eucharist (See *PHSS*, p. 474).
As discussed in Chapter Four, the use of simplified language and the widening
participation of the congregation that Watts's hymns enabled served a communal
response to scripture that deviated significantly from earlier liturgical practices.
If Dickinson's treatment of poetic imagery takes on such a liturgical aspect, what
are the kinds of rituals they are reflecting or enacting? Dickinson's bees are often
celebratory, disruptive and even anarchic; a somewhat surprising hallmark for

---

[43] Dickinson consulted *Webster's* frequently. Consensus suggests that she used the
1844 reprint edition of the 1841 edition, although the 1928 edition was in the Dickinson
library. See Gary Lee Stonum, 'Dickinson's Literary Background', in *The Emily Dickinson
Handbook*, pp. 44–60 (p. 50).

[44] One example is Hitchcock's *Religious Truth, Illustrated from Science, Addresses
and Sermons on Special Occasions* (Boston: Phillips, Sampson and Company, 1857) which
includes an address entitles 'Special Divine Interpositions in Nature' (pp. 98–131).

poems which are frequently concerned with the weight of time, immortality and death. Richard B. Sewall argues in *The Life of Emily Dickinson* (1976) that in many of her poems, Dickinson is concerned with 'the ends of things,' and in this way she displays, what one reviewer of her *Letters* estimated, a 'primitive vision.' Sewall considers the review:

> Primitive, one infers, in the sense of seeing things as if they had just been created, but sophisticated enough to know that all things pass, and possessing the "acute natural sensibility" (again the review) to detect the pathos, or terror, or beauty of the full human cycle.[45]

Although many of her poems which include motifs of nature such as flowers and the sun do indeed explore the idea of conclusions and endings, the image of the bee is arguably Dickinson's most ebullient, conveying life and hope. Moreover, its connection with the regenerative energy of the hive places the bee in opposition to the preoccupation with 'endings' and the turning away from the world ('not on life but on the non-life she saw about her') Sewall identifies in Dickinson's poems (Sewall, p. 719). Her ability to write poems on the other side of an apparently firmly shut door was not a refusal of a 'non-life,' but a direct confrontation with it. Dickinson's poems do not voice a rejection of modernity per se, but a desire for confirmation of what she knew, experientially, of life. This can be seen in a late poem such as Fr 1581, where she looks back upon the certainties of religious conviction, only to find a present absence in comparison:

> Those - dying then,
> Knew where they went -
> They went to God's Right Hand -
> That Hand is amputated now
> And God cannot be found -
>
> The abdication of Belief
> Makes Behaviour small -
> Better an ignis fatuus
> Than no illume at all - (Fr 1581)

The solidity and definiteness of 'God's Right Hand' which is capitalised in the first stanza indicates a place of certainty which she straightforwardly rejects in other poems. In other poems belief is reduced to a mere abstraction, a 'spangled journey' to 'the peak of some perceiveless thing' (THJ 1627). Her interest in the bee image highlights a preoccupation with the *idea* of being a part of an inherent design, whether it be an 'ignis fatuus' or not. Design is integral to the bee image, as it always carries the association of the hive and the design of the bee's work or production.

---

[45]　Sewall, p. 719. Quotes review from the *Times Literary Supplement* (London) May 30, 1958, p. 296.

Dickinson utilises the bee trope to offer a critique of Puritanism and the religious dogma which her age both moved away from and was ultimately still attracted by. However she also aligns herself as poet and her spiritual quest in writing with the image of the bee. Carrying with it a sense of agency and distinctiveness within each poem, Dickinson incorporates in the bee image a sense of autonomy that can be extended to the poet herself. In this way the bee image articulates the tensions Dickinson felt between her own sense of spirituality as against that of her New England Puritan heritage. So on the one hand the bee signals a cacophonous difference, or disruption of the familiar and conventional within her poems and at the same time delineates a pattern of interconnectivity and liberty to which the poems aspire. In a similar way, the use of the trope highlights a tension between the desire to be a female poet, which for her involved being solitary, and the desire to forge in writing a sense of being merely one element of a wider community. This was perhaps a community which did not necessarily require her physical presence, but was one not only composed of other women poets, but also those engaged in spiritual worship. As further analysis of bee imagery in the following chapter will demonstrate, in the imaginative work of the poem Dickinson conjures a congregation of her own and participates in a form of worship that becomes materialised and enacted within the poem itself. In this way her bee imagery delineates her own design also: forging and defining a heterologous space which successfully negotiates the 'I-Thou' model of address in hymn culture.

Connecting Industry and Revery in Dickinson's Use of Bee Imagery

Alexis de Tocqueville's *Democracy in America* (1835–1840) argued that labour was presented to the American people as the 'necessary, natural and honest condition of human existence.'[46] The connection between industry and religion, that is, seeing industry as a form of virtue and religious conviction, was deeply rooted in the American psyche from the Puritan Pilgrim Fathers' emphasis on leading an industrious life to the increasingly 'industrial' and profitable middle America of the nineteenth century. As Bee Wilson observes, the image of the bee was taken up and used as a motif for the American worker in the new republic, and the need to 'sanctify the virtue of labour through bees'[47] was increased with America's fast-moving industrialization. Such a view of industry or the 'religion of work' served to obfuscate the fact that this ethic inevitably benefited those in power over marginalized others and also neglected to pay attention to the idea of pleasure. Dickinson's bee poems offer parodies of the Puritan/Protestant work ethic which connects industry with Christian morality and virtue.[48] However she

---

[46] Alexis de Tocqueville, *Democracy in America,* (ed.), Alan Ryan (London: Everyman, 1994) vol. 2, p. 152.

[47] Bee Wilson, *The Hive: The Story of the Honeybee and Us*, p. 35.

[48] For discussion of the connective elements of ascetic Protestantism and the structure of capitalism, see Max Weber, *The Protestant Ethic and the Spirit of Capitalism* (1930) (London: Routledge, 2004) pp. 102–25.

also uses the image to convey poetic vocation as a form of industry which acquires spiritual significance within her poems (the poet 'gathers' as the bee, as full an experience of life as possible and 'stores' it within the poem). She subverts and re-imagines the Protestant work ethic usually explicitly available to the hymnist, by stressing the connection between industry and 'revery.'

The bees in Dickinson's poems are described as anarchically enjoying their mode of production, representing the ultimate transgressive act which renders their position within a hierarchical social structure dangerously ungovernable. This singular transgression of connecting revery and industry, the forbidden ideal, is described hyperbolically by Dickinson. Her bees are always exaggerated as they indulge in many different forbidden acts and transgressions, from debauched drunkenness and annoying intrusion, to sexual promiscuity and seduction. The fluidity of gender which bee imagery lends also emphasises such transgressions, further perplexing any commitment to defining categories and oppositions as displayed in orthodox religion and Puritanism particularly. Furthermore, playing upon the culturally received connections between the bee and the figure of the Puritan as we have seen in the first part of this chapter, Dickinson emphasises the spiritual dimension of such 'transgressive' behaviour. If the Puritan-bee's 'drunken' pleasure is perceived as a kind of seduction, then the significance of the performing sexual body to spiritual experience in Dickinson's poems is made exaggeratedly apparent. The connection between the body and mystical experience will be discussed here in relation to specific poems where the bee/body is made radically and effectively present. Moreover, oppositional thought, which the 'I-Thou' model of relation to the divine in traditional hymns epitomises, collapses in Dickinson's connection of industry and revery, and a redefinition of space is produced.

References to the role of the poet and poetry found in Dickinson's bee imagery reflect the connections between industry and revery, and community and the individual, which had been made separate by a patriarchally driven religious culture and an increasingly industrialised society. For example:

> Fame is a bee.
> It has a song -
> It has a sting -
> Ah, too, it has a wing. (Fr 1788)

The connections between revery ('wing') and industry (here the combined effect of 'song' and 'sting') made explicit in this poem serve to convey both the transporting effect of poetry and also the dualistic aspects of 'fame'. Dickinson's use of bee imagery describes and makes explicit the connection between experiencing an ideal – a communal 'revery', and the practice of a morally defensible life. Such a connection was necessarily obfuscated for the effective production of a new England, and an increasingly profitable America. Such obfuscation is seen in de Tocqueville's description of how poetic inspiration in a democracy turns *naturally* to an 'ideal' or an all-encompassing, expansive vision of divine design which connects individuals in their daily experience:

[m]en are disposed to conceive a much more vast conception of divinity itself, and God's intervention in human affairs appears in new and brighter light. Seeing the human race as one great whole, they easily conceive that all destinies are regulated by the same design and are led to recognize in the actions of each individual a trace of the universal and consistent plan by which God guides mankind. (*Democracy in America*, p. 486)

Dickinson's concern with connecting revery and industry serves as a critique of the desire for a socially cohesive 'ideal' in which all individuals were clearly not given equal status. The revery connected with her bee imagery is a necessity and not simply equated with ecstasy, or the pleasure of an individual, nor is it simply the self-reflective mode of the Romantic poet, as Roger Lundin argues.[49] He describes Dickinson's use of 'revery' as correlative to the Romantic ideal, and poetry as being for her a 'surrogate for traditional religion' which would lead her 'away from marriage and church into solitude.' (Lundin, pp. 60–62.) While revery in Dickinson's poems is a spiritual and mystical state it is not simply a 'surrogate' for traditional religion; rather, the persistent connection of revery with the life and action of bees connects the ideal of revery with design and pattern. Dickinson's revery in many ways reconsiders and redefines traditional religion, and persistently presents revery as a state in relation to others as opposed to being a form of isolation.

The implicit connection between industry and revery in her bee imagery fully confronts the cultural anxieties about idleness that were implicit in mid-nineteenth-century debates on the work ethic in relation to the woman question.[50] Thus Dickinson challenges the hierarchical ordering and patriarchal versions of the divine within religious culture through her use of bees. In their various ways they serve to interrogate and destabilise the cultural (and social, sexual) divisions between industry and pleasure and between individuality and community. Dickinson's use of bee imagery carries with it a constant reminder of the culturally idiomatic 'busy bee' of Watts's verse and of the 'father' of hymnody himself. It reminds us of the powerful divisions potentially proliferated or destabilised in hymns and that the series of challenges her poetry brings arise from a direct engagement with the central tenets underpinning hymn culture.

---

[49]   Roger Lundin, *Emily Dickinson and the Art of Belief* (Michigan: William B. Eerdmans, 1998) pp. 56–62. Lundin cites the popular *Reveries of a Bachelor* (1850) by Ik Marvell (Donald G. Mitchell) as evidence of the growing approval of 'reveries' as being a suitable mode of inner reflection for young people during the mid-nineteenth century.

[50]   As noted earlier with reference to Harriet Beecher Stowe's treatment of a wife's position in marriage, see Daniel T. Rodgers, *The Work Ethic in Industrial America 1850–1920*, pp. 182–209.

Industry, Idleness and 'divine perdition'

> And that ye study to be quiet, and to do your own business, and to work with your own hands, as we commanded you;
>
> That ye may walk honestly toward them that are without, and ye may have lack of nothing. (I Thessalonians 4.11–12)

The passage above conveys the notion of salvation through 'honest' work which lies at the core of the Protestant work ethic. Much didactic literature of the nineteenth century has this notion of salvation through work as its main focus, with the correlative idea of idleness as a sin. Although she rejected any affiliation with religious orthodoxy, the notion of salvation through work is a paradigm that Dickinson's work fully exploits. It is a particularly apt point of reference for Dickinson as a poet working to articulate and simultaneously perform her sense of vocation *and* belief through poetry. Frequently incorporated in her uses of bee imagery are parodies of the Puritan/Protestant work ethic that is epitomised in Watts's instructive poem for children 'Against Idleness,' which champions the 'busy bee.' The second poem in Franklin's reading edition, this verse introduces a direct parody of Watts:

> Sic transit Gloria mundi,
> "How doth the busy bee,"
> Dum vivimus vivamus,
> I stay mine enemy! (Fr 2)

The Latin phraseology of the Roman Catholic Church ('So the glory of this world passes away') is challenged by its parallel and decidedly defiant response ('Let us live while we live'). It is further undercut by the then idiomatic line from Watts's famous rhyme for children, which Lewis Carroll famously found occasion to parody.[51] Watts exploits the widely-held association of bees with industry to forge a model of virtue for children which is not only colourful but memorable too. He also uses this opportunity to reassert the dangers of being idle, where the figure of 'Satan' loiters to pounce upon 'idle hands' to do his evil 'mischief' for him:

> How doth the little busy bee
> Improve each shining hour,
> And gather honey all the day

---

[51] Carroll's parody of Watts positions a predatory crocodile in the place of the 'busy bee,' to comic effect: 'How doth the little crocodile/Improve his shining tail'. The parody appears in chapter two of *Alice's Adventures In Wonderland* (1865). Martin Gardner provides the full text of the Watts poem in his edition *The Annotated Alice* (London: Penguin, 1965, revised edition 1970) pp. 38–9. Alice's inability to recite the rhyme correctly indicates the change in her which has taken place. This exemplifies both the large extent of children's familiarity with Watts's verse and the way in which his work stood as a benchmark for moral correctness in the nineteenth century.

From every opening flower!
[...]
In works of labour or of skill,
I would be busy too;
For Satan finds some mischief still
For idle hands to do. (*PW*, pp. 340–41)

Watts stresses the industry of the bee, in keeping with his emphasis on leading a useful Christian life. In a similar way the speaker in Herbert's 'Employment (1)' questions his own life's work against the exemplary design of employment and usefulness depicted in the habits and work of bees: 'All things are busy; only I/ Neither bring honey with the bees,/Nor flowers to make that,/nor the husbandry/To water these.' (*The Complete English Poems*, p. 51). The bee is ceaseless in its task of 'gathering' honey from 'every opening flower,' and seems to fit perfectly as an instruction to children to work hard. In emphasising the industriousness of the bees, Watts ignores, or at least obfuscates, the aspect of pleasure implied with the bee's nectar gathering which is exploited to its full in particular instances by Dickinson. Further discoveries about the sex and different functions of bees were being made in the nineteenth century, which might account for Dickinson's association of the bee with pleasure, as found also in both Emerson's 'Humble-bee' who 'leave[s] the chaff and take[s] the wheat,' and Mr Skimpole's 'drone philosophy' in *Bleak House* which emphasises the drone's pleasure-seeking as opposed to the industry of the worker bee.[52] However, Watts's emphasis on industry has less to do with inferior knowledge on the life of bees, than it has with his support and emphasis of the Protestant work ethic which connects productivity with morality. This aspect of the work ethic was particularly attractive to American pioneer sensibilities during the eighteenth and nineteenth centuries. By including Watts's line amongst the antiphonary phrases, the second of which is decidedly secular, Dickinson's poem 'Sic transit Gloria mundi' (Fr2) questions the cognitive connections between traditions and the premises upon which such instructive literature are based.

Although Dickinson's poem does not follow the formal question and answer of versicle and response, the poem echoes it and presents a clear parody. The antiphonary style which Dickinson's poem mimics is similar to poems by Herbert which convey a reciprocal interaction and repetition between a group chorus and individuals made up of both angels and men.[53] However, unlike Herbert's antiphonary poems, the responses in the initial stanza of this poem do not provide agreement or confirmation, but rather represent an inherent conflict in religious doctrine. This poem thus exemplifies the central concerns of this final Section of the book: the realm of the body and material world, and experience as Dickinson felt it, versus the idea of a 'higher' and morally correct way of life; the benefit of

---

[52]   As noted in the previous chapter. Charles Dickens, *Bleak House* (1853) (London: Penguin, 2003) p. 116. Emerson's poem 'The Humble-bee' describes perfect design in the bee's industry which necessarily incorporates pleasure.

[53]   John Tobin, (ed.), *George Herbert: The Complete English Poems*. See poems 'Antiphon (1)' and 'Antiphon (2),' pp. 47 and 85.

which is not felt until this world 'passes away,' as typified in Watts's verse. Both the ideology of the Church and the fact of living one's life 'while we live' are opened to scrutiny in Dickinson's use of the bee trope. She states gleefully in this poem 'I stay mine enemy,' and this can be read as a statement of clear defiance against constraints on the enjoyment of existence as a valuable store of experience not to be missed or misused. However, Dickinson is also quick to convey the notion of one's self being an enemy, just as much as the imposing voice of constraint she characterises so well, with full quotation marks, here. It is interesting to note at this point the editorial choices made by R.W. Franklin and T.H. Johnson. Franklin uses the last fair copy of the poem and does not put quotation marks around the Latin phrases as T.H. Johnson does. This suggests further that Dickinson uses Watts in a specifically dialogic way. Thus, she acknowledges that to challenge orthodoxy is to take the difficult path involving being seen by many as an enemy to the self. Her voice in comparison to Watts is deadpan, the exclamation indicating the poet's desire for surer ground. Surer ground for Dickinson comes from mediating such resonant voices as that of Watts, and working out where the paths of faith and life meet in accordance with her own experience of it. This space is delineated by the arc of the bee's flight in her poems. The bee's flight is both 'ordained' through the fact of its design *and* steeped in embodied revery, in 'ostentation' (Fr 1426). The striking connection between the life of bees and spirituality which this particular poem offers is discussed in further detail in this chapter on pp. 243–5). The bee is an image which permeates a significant part of the corpus of her work, and directly confronts the Wattsian industrious bee. Moreover, Dickinson chooses to manipulate the antiphonary responses used in liturgy to a mockingly dramatic and comic effect in this poem. This illustrates a concern with the nature of liturgy and the effects reached when substituting or replacing traditional religious imagery with one that is self-conceived and also self-acting.

The extent to which the industry/idleness diptych epitomised by Watts's 'How doth the busy bee' was widely recognised can be seen in Dickinson's allusion to Watts in a letter to Mrs J.G. Holland, 1878; 'I am sorry your Doctor is not well. I fear he has "improved" too many "shining hours." Give my love to him, and tell him the "Bee" is a reckless Guide' (L: II, p. 542). She returns to this cultural paradigm again in 1881, in a letter to her nephew Gilbert Dickinson which includes the poem entitled 'The Bumble Bee's Religion'. Gilbert would have been very familiar with the notions of the bee's virtuous industry through Watts's verse for children. Significantly in this poem this paradigm is turned on its head to reconfigure idleness as wisdom and virtue. The 'divine Perdition' which is connected here with 'Idleness and Spring' is a state in which religious constraints are eschewed, and is a necessary prerequisite for spiritual growth and renewal:

The Bumble-Bee's Religion -

His little Hearse like Figure
Unto itself a Dirge
To a delusive Lilac
The vanity divulge

Of Industry and Morals
And every righteous thing
For the divine Perdition
Of Idleness and Spring - (Fr 1547 appears in letter to Gilbert Dickinson, 1881,
L: II, p. 701.)

The bee going about his business of 'Industry and Morals' in this poem is undoubtedly a personified caricature of the Puritan. This active, masculine 'Bumble-Bee' is in contrast with the 'delusive' Lilac which is by comparison static, passive, and through the cultural association of flowers with femininity, it is also feminine. Dickinson draws upon cultural stereotypes on gender to convey a sense of distance between these two central elements of the poem. The static 'delusive' Lilac simply observes the bee before her; his 'Hearse' and 'Dirge' are presented as a show which connotes the slow deadening of life. It also signals the routine and design for life to which the bee is bound. 'Delusive' and 'divine Perdition' both invoke the Lilac's separation from the salvation through work and movement which is available to the bee through virtue of its design. Absurdly, the flower exists in state of potential damnation because of its very existence of being a flower which cannot move in the way that the bee can. The bee's 'design' allows him to move and to be useful. However, the lesson the flower gleans from the bee's movements is also one of vanity.

The Protestant work ethic is placed under scrutiny in this poem. If ability and choice are ignored as factors in this method of achieving salvation then the configuration of industry as morality becomes a form of vanity. The poem highlights the fact that a doctrine that deems the bee's innate design (movement which is also its mode of industry) as a form of morality is not only absurd but vain also. Such doctrine implicitly excludes those (like the Lilac) who cannot move, or whose 'design' does not include movement. If the Protestant moralising of work is unable to accommodate difference, then the 'Bumble-Bee's Religion' (one of the very few titles Dickinson gave to a poem) is, for some, a form of enslavement. Therefore, the state of 'divine perdition' which the Lilac occupies in her exclusion from movement is also one of resistance. The poem privileges this mode of defiant 'idleness' over the culturally ordained 'Religion' or pattern of the bee's industry. This 'divine perdition' connotes an alternative mode of relation to the world altogether. The poem posits the idea that grace and ecstatic pleasure can be achieved through alternative ways of being which orthodox paradigms of salvation do not account for; it is the 'knowledge' which is implicit in the flower. The poem highlights the fact that it is not the design found in nature (as in the action of bees) but rather, the moralising of Puritans, the 'vanity' inherent in the 'Bumble-Bee's religion, which defines 'idleness'. 'Idleness and Spring' are made explicitly concomitant at the end of the poem to fully deconstruct the industry/ idleness diptych and to highlight the alternatives which nature itself offers. Not without irony, Dickinson places 'Idleness' alongside 'Spring' with capitalisation to signal their equal status within the poem, within the reconfigured schema for salvation that the poem presents to Gilbert. This has the effect of conferring the properties of renewal and spiritual growth onto 'idleness' and also points towards its being a part of the natural order of things. 'Spring' is a natural, seasonal pattern which implies design. However, like the kind of 'idleness' Dickinson's speaker recommends and places alongside it, 'Spring' is already in motion; it is the immanent, explosive life-force which can not stop itself.

Dickinson critiques the restrictive doctrines of orthodox religion further in 'The pedigree of honey does not concern the bee' which invokes the Calvinist notions of election and predestination, familiar concepts to be found in revivalist New England:

> The pedigree of Honey
> Does not concern the Bee,
> Nor lineage of Ecstasy
> Delay the Butterfly
> On spangled journeys to the peak
> Of some perceiveless thing -
> The right of way to Tripoli
> A more essential thing. (THJ 1627, version 1)

> The pedigree of Honey
> Does not concern the Bee -
> A Clover, any time, to him,
> Is Aristocracy - (THJ 1627, version 2)

Both versions of this poem appear in Johnson's collection (Franklin includes only the second, final version – Fr1650). The second version broadens this denunciation out to explode all hierarchical distinctions and temporal limitations, including the inherited positions occupied by royalty. One is reminded of Cromwellian rebellion as, through the bee's design, aristocratic status is conferred upon the simple 'clover' at 'any time'. In the first version, the pilgrimage to the apex of 'some perceiveless thing' is quite simply rejected in favour of the 'right of way to Tripoli', which suggests instead, a natural gravitation towards a place (significantly 'Tripoli' also suggests a pun on Trinity.) This is emphasised in the second version, where 'pedigree' is again spurned for the knowledge gained from the bee's everyday experience of clovers. Ecstasy here is accessed at an every day level; it is not static or residing in the sky, but is ecstatic, like the bee, moving constantly from flower to flower. Time pushes us on involuntarily, lending us no space for abstractions of deferred pleasure – and Dickinson's bee is most human in this respect, with the insistence that it has upon variation, upon multiplicity and upon instant gratification as opposed to delayed pleasures. In this way, the bee's undeferred, readily available pleasure invokes a paradoxical transcendence that is dependent upon (inter) action and the dissolution of the hierarchical structures defined by orthodox religion. Paradoxically, by critiquing the Christian notion of riches in heaven, the poem reasserts the example of Christ's humanity in the Gospels.

Dickinson draws upon stereotypical Puritan characteristics with which her culture would be familiar, such as abstemiousness and a cultivation of morality that showed itself in usefulness. Particular attention is placed upon the masculine, ministerial figure who has achieved a vision of God which seems to be absolute.[54] However, in using the bee and its attraction to flowers, she also makes full use of Puritan aesthetics which liked to emphasise the attraction of opposites, (light and darkness, good and evil) in order to highlight the absolutes that they perceived to be necessary for faith. The poem below (Fr 979) exploits the clear distinction Watts makes between 'idleness' and 'labour,' and further highlights the connection between the two modes which the bee's life implies. It describes the bee's mode of existence (his 'labour' *and* his 'idleness') as itself offering a pattern for a critique of the Puritan's rigidly defined notion of 'industry':

> His feet are shod with Gauze -
> His Helmet, is of Gold,
> His Breast, a Single Onyx
> With Chrysophras, inlaid.
>
> His Labor is a Chant -
> His Idleness - a Tune -
> Oh, for a Bee's experience
> Of Clovers, and of Noon! (Fr 979)

The imagery Dickinson uses here is comically evocative of the Puritan who is prepared and ready to defend his faith in battle. Dickinson invokes the biblical metaphor of the breastplate as righteousness and the helmet as salvation which extends from the Old Testament in Isaiah (59. 17) to the New Testament in Thessalonians; 'But let us, who are of the day, be sober, putting on the breastplate of faith and love; and for an helmet, the hope of salvation' (I. 5–8). The 'chant' of the regularised trimeter is swift and compact, conveying an overall sense of symmetry and craftsmanship. However, the mirror-like structure of the poem also implies a scrutiny of the poet's own vocation as a form of such industry or 'honest' work. The first stanza conveys the poet's attempt to depict nature in art. Dickinson uses self-consciously poetic language to construct an image which is decidedly static. In contrast with the view of bees as 'busy', she highlights immovability by employing a lapidarian, gem-like description. By using 'gold', 'onyx' and 'chrysophras' (Johnson's edition uses 'chrysophrase') to describe the bee's armour-like body parts she also suggests the singularity of the poet's vision. The word 'chrysoprase' resonates with the image of the Puritan as the English pronunciation of 'chrys' carries a verbal echo of Christ (from Greek 'khrusos' for gold). In the poem 'chrysoprase' reminds us of Christ, and also the Holy Spirit, as the Puritan's breastplate and protection. It also evokes the word 'praise' and therefore also the act of praising. Onyx and chrysoprase are combined to describe the bee's body because of their colours. Onyx is a precious stone with black and white bands, not unlike the bee's body, and chrysoprase is gold with a green sheen.

---

[54] Dickinson's relationship with Rev. Charles Wadsworth might have provided impetus for such a focus. See Richard B. Sewall, *The Life of Emily Dickinson*, vol. 2, for speculative discussion on Dickinson's relationships with Rev. Charles Wadsworth and Samuel Bowles and the 'master letters' (pp. 512–31).

Gold and chrysoprase are featured amongst many of the precious stones used in the Bible, for example in Exodus 35. 9. They appear most effectively in the Book of Revelations where they are used to describe the foundations of the walls of heaven (especially Rev 21: 18–21). This is undoubtedly the 'gem chapter' which Dickinson used to inspire her poetry and most notably, as this poem evidences, her descriptions of nature.[55] Dickinson connects the colours green and gold with immortality in an earlier letter to Mrs Bowles. Thanking her for a gift, she remarks, 'Why did you bind it in green and gold? The *immortal* colours. I take it for an emblem.' (L: II, p. 358. 26 December 1859).

The second stanza of the poem, by contrast, focuses on the activity of the bee and its casual triumph of experiencing life ('clovers' and 'noon'). This stanza holds a mirror to the first stanza and reflects back to the reader the 'labour' of the poet's self-consciously stylised language. Dickinson highlights for us the excessiveness of her own desire to be equally industrious. The speaker envies the comparative 'idleness' of the bee and his 'tune' ('Oh, for a Bee's experience'). The fixed poetic vision in the first stanza is rendered incomplete, and only secondary to the bee's effortless 'experience' of life in all its fullness. The opposite poles conveyed by 'clovers' (feminine space of morning, shadows) and 'noon' (illumination, sight, masculinity) describe the range of the bee's experience. By comparison the poet's vision labours to capture the experience that the bee's movements delineate. Pleasure and worldly experience are implicit in the design of the bee's life. The 'industry' represented here conveys an ideal state of relation in the world where labour and idleness are necessarily connected. It is an alternative mode of relation in which 'chant' and 'tune' are both produced respectively. In this poem Dickinson considers the ideal of design in the organised community of bees in which pleasure and labour are connected harmoniously. It also conveys an attempt to replicate the pattern of the bee's life in verse. Ultimately, through the existence of the poem itself, we can see Dickinson, the Bee-Poet, creating her own 'tune' (poem) and conferring upon it the status of labour.

The caricatures of the Puritan which are especially evident in some of her shorter, less lyrical poems, also attempt to highlight the contradictions in organised religion:

Partake as doth the Bee,
Abstemiously.
The Rose is an Estate -
In Sicily. (Fr 806)

This poem is almost axiomatic in that it declares the kind of behaviour necessary to obtain the prize of divinity on offer, where the rose is named as a papal-like

---

[55] See SL, p. 242. To Mrs S. Bowles, 1878. Dickinson refers to her discussion with Samuel Bowles of the 'gem chapter', which Johnson supposes is Rev. 21. This is undoubtedly the description in Rev 21:20: 'The fifth, sardonyx; the sixth, sardius; the seventh, chrysolyte; the eighth, beryl; the ninth, a topaz; the tenth, a chrysoprasus; the eleventh, a jacinth; the twelfth, an amethyst.'

'estate' in 'Sicily.' Abstemiousness is connected with the Puritan's simple way of living, where the 'Rose' is paradoxically deemed as the forbidden, Catholic road to indulgences that must be avoided. The word 'abstemious' itself describes avoidance of and restraint from that which can be linked to the Catholic ritual of the Eucharist, being derived from the Latin 'abs,' for 'from' and 'temetum,' for 'strong wine.' 'Rose' and 'Estate,' which symbolise Christ and Heaven respectively, convey a luxuriousness which is held in tension and opposition with the paradoxical instructions of the initial stanza. The bee's very existence is to indulge, to 'partake' of the Rose in order to produce nectar for the collective community, conveying also the notion that human access to the divine must also be necessarily unrestricted if it is to be shared and put into practice. However, the Puritan's example/instruction of abstemiousness is held in conflict with this, as the bee cannot, by its design, be abstemious. Therefore, the poem questions and challenges the connections made between the rituals and instructions of religious orthodoxy and God's design for humanity. If the bee's design means that its productivity and industry is based upon its access to the 'rose' of sweet nectar, then it follows that God's design for humans must necessarily imply a similar access to ecstasy and revery. In many of Dickinson's poems, the bee both symbolises and displays traditionally non-Puritanical qualities, but here, significantly, they are connected with the Puritan way of life, with comical and destabilising effects. In nature's example, industry and revery are necessarily concomitant.

'From Cocoon forth a Butterfly' (Fr 610) includes a similar reflection upon the role of the poet as we have seen in Fr 979. Where the bee's body was reconstructed through the speaker's poetic vision with gem imagery in Fr 979, the speaker in this poem offers a detailed, painterly description of a butterfly emerging from its cocoon:

> From Cocoon forth a Butterfly
> As Lady from her Door
> Emerged - a Summer Afternoon -
> Repairing Everywhere -
>
> Without Design - that I could trace
> Except to stray abroad
> On Miscellaneous Enterprise
> The Clovers - understood -
>
> Her pretty Parasol be seen
> Contracting in a Field
> Where Men made Hay -
> Then struggling hard
> With an opposing Cloud -
>
> Where Parties - Phantom as Herself -
> To Nowhere - seemed to go
> In purposeless Circumference -
> As 'twere a Tropic Show -

The role of the poet is also positioned in this poem within the discourse of the Protestant work ethic; the juxtaposition between 'work' and 'idleness' in stanza five signals this. The butterfly's movements, which the speaker traces, delineate a scene that is laden with existential drama. Dickinson positions herself as the artist, who is at pains to 'trace' the design, the continuity or meaning in the 'scene'. By extension, there is also a search for meaning in life which ends in death, where all life forms are simply 'extinguished':

> And notwithstanding Bee - that worked -
> And Flower - that zealous blew -
> This Audience of Idleness
> Disdained them, from the Sky -
>
> Till Sundown crept - a steady Tide -
> And Men that made the Hay -
> And Afternoon - and Butterfly -
> Extinguished - in the Sea - (Fr 610)

The disappearance of the sun into the sea in this poem conveys also, with a shocking absence of consolation, the inevitability ('steady Tide') of death. The butterfly, the 'Men' and the activity of the 'Afternoon' are all simply 'extinguished' as they sink away with the sun, out the poet's gaze, in the final stanza. However, even more startling is the implied disappearance of the design or pattern that the butterfly usually represents. God's promise of resurrection, and the metamorphosis from a human existence into a heavenly one, which the butterfly symbolises, also slips from view in the poem's final lines.

In contrast with the butterfly, the rather more minor characters in the scene, both 'Bee' and 'Flower', are stripped of any romantic or artistic livery. Markedly, they do not attempt to transcend ('stray abroad') the scene and Dickinson describes them simply as the bee 'that worked - ' and the flower which 'zealous blew - '. They are instead ascribed a tenacity which places them in sharp contrast to the 'Audience of Idleness' which 'Distained them, from the Sky.' Although each life form in the poem occupies a common position, the fact of being below the 'sky' or eye of Heaven, the bee and the 'Men who made Hay' are resolutely connected in their shared capacity for 'work.' Nineteenth-century uses of the terms 'labour' and 'work' carry different associations respectively. For example, 'work' could apply to cerebral and/or spiritual endeavours and 'labour' frequently implies manual labour. However, the speaker's view of the scene encourages an equal reading of all the forms of activity ('trace', 'made' and 'blew') and conveys a disregard for such distinctions. On first reading, the bee's presence in the poem appears to be less significant than it is. However, the use of the word 'notwithstanding' in relation to the bee in this poem is arresting; the tetrameter stretches the word out in order to make it seem adjectival, rather than the qualifier for the poem's final dramatic closure. The figure of the bee highlights the problematic division in the poem between those who act collectively and those who appear to be isolated, as the butterfly, in 'purposeless [c]ircumference'. The work which is part of daily toil for the 'Men' making hay and the bee which symbolises communal industry, appears to subsume the 'struggle' into a larger, discernable 'design'. Gathering hay is equated with gathering honey, and in the speaker's view of the scene this shared process is illuminated only briefly, and then pulled back into the inevitable darkness. The commonality of all life is conveyed in this poem and it is illuminated, standing momentarily apart from the darkness. In this, Dickinson presents for us an alternative idea of design and pattern which goes some way to negate the 'extinguish[ing]' power of darkness and death.

In this poem, as with Fr 979 and Fr 1547, Puritan notions of 'idleness' are reconfigured. The industry and spirit of the bee who simply 'worked' is placed alongside the 'Audience of Idleness' of the 'Sky'. The ability to err, to 'stray abroad/on Miscellaneous Enterprise' is not distinct from Dickinson's notion of industry. The notions of 'work' and 'enterprise' in the poem both point towards Dickinson's sense of her own enterprise as a poet. This is distinct from the decidedly feminine ('Lady'), chaotic, substanceless ('Phantom as Herself') meandering that the butterfly conveys, despite the appearance of design, or promise of fulfilment that its patterned wings symbolize. The critique of idle womanhood found in contemporary novels is also echoed here by Dickinson.

The depiction of the butterfly as 'stray[ing] abroad' 'without design' challenges and confronts the notion of idle womanhood, whilst the poet-onlooker is herself also 'above' the scene being described. In this way the poem conveys a conflicting attitude towards poetic subjectivity. The speaker claims a vision which is capable of registering minutiae ('From Cocoon forth a Butterfly') but is also keen to play down her part as the scene is revealed casually, with a colloquialism ('her pretty parasol be seen'). This has the effect of creating a sense of distance for us as readers, and it thus undermines and minimizes poetic agency. Again there is a paradoxical attitude; the speaker describes her task which is to 'trace' the scene, but what she actually provides is an intense scrutiny of the way in which the 'Sky' controls the movements of the various forms of life and activity below. The speaker's sense of poetic vision is ambiguous and conflicting; she declares non-specificity whilst also conveying a sight of both depth and clarity. The anxieties about poetry which Dickinson makes evident in this poem also echo anxieties about belief itself. The 'Audience of Idleness' possesses the weight of God's omniscient judgement, but it also indicates the speaker herself, who, searching for 'Design' before her, finds only a 'Tropic Show', or accepted ways of thinking about nature. The poet-onlooker wants to invest the summer day with resonant meaning, by 'tracing' symbols of either resurrection or hope. However, these images are emptied of their significance and become merely affectation or 'show'. The emergent butterfly is the traditional symbol of achieved potential, daubed as it is with the evidence of the design implicit in the cocoon. However, it is the butterfly who fails, unable, like the bee, to repair or accommodate for the lack of design apparent in the scene on offer through connected activity. Moreover, the poet's admission of 'trace'[ing] design within the scene serves to overshadow the butterfly's journey for design by observing, casually, the design implied in the bee's 'work' and the flower's 'zealous' tenacity. In this poem, the subjective 'I' is placed at a remove from the stereotypes on gender to which butterfly and bee both refer. Dickinson's persona reaches out in this poem for a sense of purpose and scrutinizes religious certainty. In the absence of that certainty, she is able only to reveal or expose her own 'work' of the poem itself, as conveyed by the industrious role of the worker that the bee in this poem displays.

The use of the industry/idleness diptych fluctuates in this poem from parody and subversion of the Puritan and his ethics to a direct confrontation with ideas of omnipotent design and the poet's subjective desire to impose design, in which she encounters difficulty and struggle. The notion of design remains a fascination with Dickinson and this takes various forms throughout her poems. However, there is also a strong impulse to explode the industry/idleness diptych, and to deconstruct the hierarchies implicit in nineteenth-century assumptions about gender and spirituality that it inevitably includes.

The tension between industry and idleness in 'from Cocoon forth a Butterfly' reflects the cultural association between industry and morality as set out in the popular playwright George Baker's *The Revolt of the Bees* (1826). Its distinction between the idle butterfly and the worker bee is remarkably similar to that depicted in Dickinson's poem. As Wilson observes, Baker's play depicts butterflies which encourage the worker bees to 'sport and flutter in the breeze,' and to lead a 'free and roving life' and to an ultimate rebellion.[56] The didactic tale finds resolution in the Queen Bee's message that the butterflies' 'roving' lasts only a day and conformity and working hard will win in the end:

> Their life they picture as so bright and gay
> Is short and vapid, lasts but for a day.
> While we by labour energy and worth
> Long live and prosper; o'er all the earth. [57]

The motifs of butterfly and bee in Baker's play present a contemporary example of how such associations were culturally resonant and became effectively popularised. However, Dickinson's use of the butterfly and bee in 'From Cocoon forth a butterfly' indicates an uncertainty about, and struggle for, an answer as to which will prosper. It also puts into question whether poetry, as a version of such industry, can offer a form of redemption.

Benjamin Lease has noted that Dickinson's use of the bee trope 'fuses death with deathlessness.' (*RMB*, p. xviii.) The bee, a reminder of spring and of regeneration which we would also associate with the resurrection of Christ,

---

[56] George M. Baker, *The Revolt of the Bees: An Allegory* (1826) (Boston: Lee and Shepard, 1872) p. 83. Cited in Bee Wilson, *The Hive: The Story of the Honeybee and Us*, pp. 35–6. Wilson observes that Baker's play is in many ways a response to Mandeville's *Fable of the Bees* (1714).

[57] Ibid, pp. 35–6.

also becomes emblematic of hope because of its ability to defy gravity with its outsized and awkward body. The 'sublime' sobriety of the Puritan life is made ridiculous when it is compared with the bee's sheer exuberance. The bee's excessive physical presence in Dickinson's poems pushes the boundaries of opposition which govern societal definitions of morality, usefulness, gender, and also representations of the divine.

Getting 'Lost in Balms': Idleness, Subversive Sexuality and Revery

The connection between industry and revery in Dickinson's bee imagery is exemplificative of (and also dependent upon) the connection she explicitly makes between physical and spiritual experience. The 'jaunty' entrepreneur bumblebee Dickinson described and separated from the 'manly, earnest' worker bees in the letter to Graves (L: II, p. 327) cited in the previous part of this chapter is perhaps the best representation of this configuration of her excessive bees. The emphasis on the bee's physical presence in this group of poems is evocative of the emotionality in Puritan preaching as depicted in the figure of the 'rowdy' bobolink in poem Fr1620 who (in the earlier version which appears in Johnson) 'swung upon the Decalogue/ And shouted let us pray - ' (THJ 1591). It also accentuates the gravity assigned to experiential, bodily versions of the divine or 'revery' depicted in the poems. Critics have discussed Dickinson's tendency to portray the 'excessive body' as evidence of her resistance to the mind/body dualism and hierarchical construction of spirit over body which religious doctrine asserts and makes distinct. They have observed that instead, the body and mind/spirit 'draw upon each other for definition'. As Eberwein (1998) summarises, these 'excessive bodies'

> [...] aris[e] from a tension between her typical experience of self and the culture that defines her 'deviant' experiences of self as monstrous. [...] Her society might have sought to repress women's bodies, but the pleasures and complex difficulties of living in a nineteenth-century woman's body live as well in Dickinsons's poetry.'[58]

Similarly pervasive as the human body parts in Dickinson's poetry, the image of the bee also serves to fuse the spirit/body dichotomy and emphasise the connection between bodily, physical experience and spiritual immanence. The excessive bodily 'fuzz' and 'buzz' of the bees, along with their interruptive noises, not only convey dangerous sexuality, but crucially, confuse and disrupt the categories of gender perpetuated by cultural nineteenth century stereotypes. The '*bumblebee*', as Dickinson describes it, displays an 'indefinite', fluid identity that has been adopted through dressing up in 'jaunty clothes'. It is perhaps because of this, and because of the 'implausbility' of the bumblebee's ability to take flight that the image is invoked in Dickinson's depictions of sexuality. Transcendence

---

[58]   Jane Donahue Eberwein, *An Emily Dickinson Encyclopedia* (Connecticut: Greenwood Press, 1998) pp. 25–6.

for the (particularly female) sexualised body is similarly implausible in orthodox religion. The association of the bee with subversive sexuality continues the theme of criminality established in other poems concerning the bee's liberty.

In these poems Dickinson retains the notion of the Puritan way of life and the surety of faith in the structure and design inherent in the bee's life – going to and from the hive in order to collect honey for the collective good. However her description of the bee's movements is decidedly unrestrained. The bee is defiantly errant and has the freedom of choice which flower to visit, how long to stay, and is at points in her poems 'drunken,'(Fr 207) 'debauched,'(Fr 140) or 'lost in balms'(Fr 205). In other words, the bee possesses the freedom that connects it with human free will, despite working within the overall design of its purpose, and relation to the hive. In many ways, this serves as a parallel to the free will given to humans by God, whilst existing within God's design for human life. However, rather than stressing a deferral of pleasure as the manifestation of such design, Dickinson emphasises unrestricted physical experience as the basis for spiritual transcendence (immanence).

This idea can be seen in an earlier poem, where the bee's liberty is described in terms of its ability to 'ride indefinite,' where all possibilities are harnessed in the bee's ecstatic reluctance to settle. The disregard for boundaries and acceptable modes of behaviour which the bee displays is conveyed in terms of criminality, and is mapped onto the speaker's fantasy of freedom:

> Could I but ride indefinite
> As doth the Meadow Bee
> And visit only where I liked
> And No one visit me
>
> And flirt all Day with Buttercups
> And marry whom I may
> Dwell a little everywhere
> Or better, run away.
>
> With no Police to follow
> Or chase Him if He do
> Till He should jump Peninsulas
> To get away from me -
>
> I said "But just to be a Bee"
> Upon a Raft of Air
> And row in Nowhere all Day long
> And anchor "off the Bar"
>
> What Liberty! So Captives deem
> Who tight in Dungeons are. (Fr 1056)

Dickinson conveys with dramatic, comical effect, the ways in which such a desire to transcend societal pressures could be regarded as criminal behaviour.

The speaker's fantasy of deviance from traditionally prescribed roles for the female is depicted here as criminality, which the speaker thoroughly embraces – 'indefinite' being simply another mode of 'revery.' The desire to 'flirt all Day with Buttercups' suggests a sexual identity which is not impinged by externally imposed parameters of time or taste and is not necessarily only a lingering precursor to a conventional 'marriage.' If marriage is on the agenda then the speaker wishes the freedom to marry 'whom I may.' The desire to present an alternative to the constraints of gender is clear in this poem and yet the alternative is presented in meagre terms; 'indefinite,' 'a little everywhere,' 'run away,' 'just to be a Bee,' and to 'row in Nowhere.' The alternative here is presented in terms of a desired absence, of being simply where 'No one' is. However, the poem's leap to the unexpected hyperbole of criminality 'With no Police to follow' in the third stanza, describes the gap between the Captive's expectation of liberty and the sheer force of resistance it is met with. The shifting use of the bee image can be traced from a claim for liberty to articulating anarchic rebellion. The weight of restriction can be measured in this poem against the fact that such small wants are equated with rebellion.

As with many of the poems, this is described with a distance of irony. However, the fact remains that as the sense of a lack of social, sexual, political and spiritual freedom increases, the bees in Dickinson's poems become gradually more disruptive, interrupting the clarity required for an axiomatic faith. In this way, her use of the bee can be seen as being paradoxically axiomatic, carrying with it an implicit design. 'Indefinite' in this poem can be likened to the idea of 'revery,' as the indefiniteness of the bee's movements is also implicit in its design to pollinate flowers, moving industriously, but also pleasurably, from one to the next. So, the mode in which orthodox religion is challenged in Dickinson's poems is not always just a resistance of definition per se, but is rather, an insistence to constantly define what spirituality is not. In attending to that which 'organised' spirituality and religious traditions do not allow and by highlighting the 'absence of what they designate'[59] through a series of disruptions, Dickinson's poems reassert the qualities and behaviour she associates with her own experience of spirituality.

Another striking poem where Dickinson's bee challenges the relation between size and power and disrupts the 'atmosphere' is in poem Fr 622. Here the bee's 'interruption' signals an alternative to the 'clarity' of heaven often expressed in Watts's hymns:

> To interrupt His Yellow Plan
> The Sun does not allow
> Caprices of the Atmosphere -
> And even when the Snow
>
> Heaves balls of Specks, like Vicious Boy
> Directly in His Eye -
> Does not so much as turn His Head
> Busy with Majesty -

---

[59]   Michel de Certeau, 'Mystic Speech' in *The Certeau Reader*, (ed.), Graham Ward, p. 205.

[...]
Yet any passing by

Would deem Ourselves - the busier
As the Minutest Bee
That rides - emits a Thunder -
A bomb - to justify - (Fr 622)

Here, the Sun, the 'Eye' of heaven is aloof, and 'busy' with being at the pinnacle of moral superiority. However, Dickinson playfully suggests on the one hand that such business is a false enterprise, as the bee seems far more engaged in activity, given the impact its noise has on the atmosphere of the sky. She implies that the space of the sky (heaven) is by comparison rather uneventful and insipid. However she implies equally that it is vanity which makes us forget that our actions are indeed futile in comparison to God's 'Plan' which is of a far higher order. The bee, along with the weather, offers an interruption to the beam of the Sun's light and is therefore as 'capricious' as the 'Vicious Boy.' Significantly, it is the Eye that is attacked again, the bee wrangling to obstruct the claim of spiritual vision and clarity as emphasised in Watts's hymns. The bee's presence in the poem is explosive, 'thundering' along the lines as it does, to assert itself, and is in direct contrast with George Herbert's depiction of bees that 'work for man' yet 'never bruise their master's flower'. ('Providence', lines 65–8, from *The Temple* in *The Complete English Poems*, p. 110.)

By alluding to criminality in her depiction of bees, as in Mandeville's *Fable of the Bees*, Dickinson also considers how the ideal of community and of a multiple and open relationality can of course be merely appropriated and exploited for personal or political gain. Although in poem Fr 1078 the 'suit' of the bee refers immediately to his position in courtship as a suitor (as one described in Fr 134 'Did the Harebell loose her girdle / to the lover bee') and conveys the treacherously fickle lover who declares 'troth' and flies off, 'suit' also carries an allusion to a communal identity. In this case the communal identity or 'suit' is cultivated and worn for individual benefit. Written in the same year as poem Fr 979 quoted above (1865), and using a similar formula of describing the bee's features, there is a connection to be drawn between the two poems. The earlier poem describes the bee's features as a Puritan defender of the faith; the later poem reconsiders the connection between those Puritan values and theology with the support political activities. It is no surprise that towards the end of the Civil War, Dickinson would consider the connection between religious ideals and political gain, when so many hymns were used to support social cohesion during war time.[60] Her use of 'terms' such as 'traitor', 'troth', 'propoundeth' and 'divorce' each echo the rhetoric of

---

[60] For discussion on Dickinson's use of military and theological tropes during the Civil War years, see Shira Wolosky, *Emily Dickinson: A Voice of War* (New Haven: Yale University Press, 1984) (pp. 32–63). Also reference for the distribution of one million hymnals and books of psalms during the war in 1864 (p. 57).

the law. The opening alliteration and repetition of an 's' sound in the first stanza underscores the hint and hiss of deception:

> Of Silken Speech and Specious Shoe
> A Traitor is the Bee
> His service to the newest Grace
> Present continually
>
> His Suit a chance
> His Troth a Term
> Protracted as the Breeze
> Continual Ban propoundeth He
> Continual Divorce. (Fr 1078)

In this instance, the freedom and expansiveness of 'breeze' available to the bee is described as being a tool of verbal obfuscation for the 'traitor'/lover, whose promises and loyalties are 'protracted as the Breeze'. The bee is personified, and is described as displaying a permanently fickle attitude towards not only his lover but by extension religion also, 'continually' swearing allegiance to the 'newest Grace'. Moreover, far from invoking the ideal multiple relationality and community, the bee represents exclusion and separation ('Continual Ban' and 'Continual Divorce'). However, Dickinson's estimation of the disingenuous ('specious') member of a community, in turn, mimics the suspicion and disdain for 'inauthentic' or cultivated religiosity prevalent in her own community.[61] The collective identity ('suit') of the bee in this poem is acquired only by 'chance' as opposed to a pre-ordained identity such as that of the Calvinist notion of the chosen, 'elected' minority. Evangelical revivals created divisions as much as they aimed to convert and promote cohesion and community. Dickinson's use of bee imagery in this poem conveys a struggle with the ideal of relationality that the bee represents but also the manifestation of such an identity in organised religion, and the hierarchical barriers that such claims to spiritual authenticity generate. Ultimately, the 'Continual Ban,' and 'Continual Divorce' can be read, not as a statement of the benefits of separation per se (or from the ideal of a multiple and open relationality which the bee in other poems represents) but of the necessary separation from organised religion which proliferates such divisions. Moreover, the poem also underscores the differences between the state of multiple and open relationality as traced and enacted in Dickinson's poetics, and the definitive versions of God in orthodox religion and the problematic hierarchies such versions project.

---

[61]   See *MWL*, p. 143. Habegger notes the division in Amherst between a 'cultivated Episcopalian' (member of Anglican Community in America governed by Bishops) and the egalitarian, Evangelical 'orthodox scheme of things' which the educational texts Dickinson would have used at Amherst Academy reflected, such as Watts's *The Improvement of the Mind* (1741).

The connection between physical pleasure and spiritual transcendence, and the association of it with transgression in Dickinson's bee imagery, is noted by Judith Farr (2004). Farr argues that Dickinson frequently employs the bee as a rape metaphor, where flowers are ravished and the bee is unruly, drunken, taking his nectars in.[62] There are a number of closely related poems in which the bee image can be associated with sexuality and exuberance, of which Fr 205, Fr 134 and Fr 207 are examples. As we have seen, the excessively fuzzy body of the bumblebee and its interruptive noises and movements can be seen as articulating sexual desire in the connection they illustrate between physical pleasure and ecstatic transcendence. This configuration of the bee trope allows Dickinson to highlight the sterility and comparative silence of 'official' religious and literary culture. John B. Pickard observes the 'erotic expectations' in poems where Dickinson is 'employing the bee-flower image to convey physical desire' and gives examples of the poems 'Come slowly-Eden!'(Fr 205) and 'A Bee his burnished Carriage,'(Fr 1351), describing them as her 'most sentimental and derivative love poems.'[63] However, the resistance of gender that the bee allows, provides a wider interpretation which takes the poetic imagery beyond such aesthetics of heterosexual procreation and accusations of sentimentality. The range of fluctuation with regard to gender which is available within bee imagery means that it is at different times, and even all at once, the 'manly, earnest bee,' the solitary Queen bee, the chaste, asexual bee and the delirious rapist. In poem Fr 1351 for example, the 'erotic expectation' of the courtship between a 'male' bee and 'female' rose is subverted as the rose receives the bee, not with rapture, but with a decidedly measured, anti-climactic 'frank tranquillity:'

> A bee his burnished Carriage
> Drove boldly to a Rose -
> Combinedly alighting -
> Himself - his Carriage was.
>
> The Rose received his Visit
> With frank tranquility,
> Withholding not a Crescent
> To his cupidity.
>
> Their Moment consummated
> Remained for him - to flee -
> Remained for her, of Rapture
> But the Humility. (Fr 1351)

Rather than appearing as a rapist, the stereotypical power relation between genders is reversed. The bee's anticipation and exuberance is quashed somewhat

---

[62] Judith Farr, *The Gardens of Emily Dickinson* (Cambridge, MA: Harvard University Press, 2004) pp. 184–5.

[63] John B. Pickard, *Emily Dickinson: An Introduction and Interpretation* (New York: Holt, Rinehart and Winston, 1967) p. 87.

by the automated response of the rose. Although part of the bee's repeated pattern and industry, his 'boldness' is paradoxically indicative of an action that has been performed on numerous previous occasions, and conveys endlessly renewable vitality. The notion of romantic courtship is parodied by the capitalisation of 'Moment' for dramatic effect. If sexual intercourse is not a pleasurable exchange in this poem then the metaphor for the procreative, generative imagery is also undermined. The bee's vitality is present before the 'Moment,' and is seemingly not increased after the encounter, where his action is simply to 'flee;' thus furthering the idea that the bee is itself an instant of self-generative ecstasy.

The 'fainting' bee in the often quoted 'Come slowly - Eden!' (Fr 205) is representative of physical, experiential ecstasy. Its movements represent to the speaker a sense of abandon which is fleeting, but also considered. The recommendation here is that paradise should be reached 'slowly'; the experience of life should be savoured before reaching 'Eden', which is also the realm of the unknown. The bee in this poem is 'ecstatic' in the sense that it roves from flower to flower, collecting nectars and thus being 'late' getting to the next one. However, bee's delay is also the moment of anticipation which allows for full recognition of the transcendent moment. The poem highlights this space of contemplation of ecstasy. Ecstasy should be experienced 'slowly,' as the bee who considers his rosary-like 'nectars' before giving himself up to being 'lost in balms.' This point is emphasised by the use of an exclamation mark. The metaphor of the bee entering the flower is extended here beyond generative imagery to include the idea of a congregation member who considers the moment of spiritual renewal before entering a place of worship. The bee takes stock, considers his 'nectars', and counts his blessings. Unheeding of both time and production, the bee is detained ('reaching late his flower') by the multiple opportunities for pleasure which nature affords him. In this poem the connection between spiritual and physical ecstasy rests easily. The poem explodes the idleness/industry paradigm by privileging a decentred simultaneity, where the bee is both lingering and on course, both aimless and in pursuit. The teleological premises of the Puritan's spiritual journey, where pleasures are postponed for the afterlife, are deconstructed in this poem to incorporate a series of seeming impossibilities. Thus the bee is used in this poem to signal an alternative poetics and alternative mode of relation.

In poem Fr 1562 ('His oriental heresies/Exhilirate the Bee'), the bee's exuberance is exaggerated even further, to the level of heresy and 'gay apostacy'. 'Oriental heresies' might mean exotic flowers from the East or simply the bee's line of motion, his orientation, with the various flowers pulling him this way and that, controlling his path. The poem conveys the multiplicity available to the bee and it is overtly sexualised. However, the bee is eventually allured by the plainness of clover much in the way that the puritan's disapproval of catholic luxury is oriented towards plain living; 'Fatigued at last, a Clover plain/Allures his jaded Eye'.

A variant on 'idleness', drunkenness is often used by Dickinson to convey the ecstatic pleasure and 'revery' of bees. In poems where drunkenness occurs, she also presents a series of parodies on the rhetoric of temperance literature. For example, in poem Fr1630, as in 'The Pedigree of Honey/Does not concern the

Bee' (Fr 1650), the bee is upheld as knowing the right way to 'delight' and 'joy'. Here the idea of excess is championed over abstemiousness and the Bumble Bee is the chief 'consultant' in such matters:

> A Drunkard cannot meet a Cork
> Without a Revery -
> [...]
> The moderate drinker of Delight
> Does not deserve the spring -
> Of juleps, part are in the Jug
> And more are in the Joy -
> Your connois[a]eur in Liquors consults the Bumble Bee - (Fr 1630)

Both poems (Fr 1650 and Fr 1630) are placed alongside each other in Johnson's collection (THJ) and the dominant ideas of physical pleasure and spiritual ecstasy evident in both are clearly linked, as are other poems in which the bee represents this anti-temperance mode. (For example, poems Fr 207 and Fr 244 are closely related in their representation of the bee as 'Debauchee of Dew' and 'revel[ling]', 'First - at the Vat - and latest at the Vine -', and are both dated 1861.) The bee is linked with physical pleasure and spiritual ecstasy in this poem by the virtue of his innate connection with nature and the dictates of 'Spring'. 'Joy' is a necessary element of 'Juleps'; materiality is abstracted and then reshaped into a definite and tangible form. Any knowledge that the speaker may have about joy is referred to the consultant-drunkard Bumble Bee. However, Dickinson's Bumble Bee is instinctive and anarchic and in this respect is distinct from Emerson's elevated 'yellow-breeched philosopher'. The bee in this poem by Dickinson would openly frown at 'moderation' as being non-conducive to 'Revery'. Dickinson uses 'Revery' to convey a state of 'joy' connected with spirituality in this poem. This state is also inextricably connected in her work with poetry and writing, and the mystical immanence it enabled her to express. Therefore, Dickinson's excessive and rebellious bees represent not only the physical transgression and blurring of the hierarchical, social and sexual boundaries which are represented in hymn culture through the 'I-Thou' model of relation to the divine, but also, subsequently, they delineate a space in which spiritual immanence might be experienced.

Revery in Relation and Ideal Space

> To make a prairie it takes a clover and one bee,
> One clover, and a bee,
> And revery.
> The revery alone will do,
> If bees are few. (Fr 1779)

The connection between industry and revery, and between physical and spiritual experience in Dickinson's bee poems generates a space in which 'excessive' bodies can perform and access 'revery'. Revery is therefore always experienced through relation. The emphasis on the bee's connection to the hive is associated with the ideal space in which 'revery' can occur, the ideal state which many of the bee poems illustrate a desire for. This element of the bee image correlates with the systematic resistance to orthodox religion in Dickinson's poems and projects meaning which is not compatible with postmodernist readings of Dickinson's evasive quality. The association of the bee with the idea of community, relation and faith, is important as it replaces and reconfigures elements of orthodox religion within her own poetics. Analysing the image of the bee in terms of community and relation radically repositions Dickinson's poetics within theological debates on spirituality and gender. This is because Dickinson uses bee imagery in a way which carries many correlative connections between the shape of community and the shape of God in contemporary feminist theology. Further, it also aligns the shaping spaces which Dickinson's poetics create with the alternative values of 'multiplicity of perspectives [...] and a community of voices [...]' over unitary or monologic identity, [...] narratives of persistence rather than conversion or transformation' which Scheinberg suggests are necessary to counter the androcentric 'generic patterns' in Victorian poetic theory (Scheinberg, p. 236).

In this late poem (above) 'reverie', a term usually connected with dreaming or imagination, is pointedly reconfigured ('revery') by Dickinson as a trope for mystical immanence, as well as for writing, in its relation with the bee. It displays what is almost an emblematic formula for the spiritual dimension that is circumnavigated in her bee imagery poems. With its economical display of language, it dissects and lays bare the mechanism of 'revery', and effectively encapsulates the interconnection between writing and spirituality that her bee imagery implies. Here 'revery' is exposed as being the creative force that exists in relation, as an interconnected element of a trinity.

The poem utilizes procreative imagery – one of each (clover and bee) – to multiply and produce 'revery'. Taking it further, the analogy also stretches to a minister and a congregation, that is, the bee that provides the vehicle for worship, and the clover, the receptacle who receives the divinely inspired words. However, her assertion at the end of the poem, which also reads axiomatically, is to use imagination ('revery') if 'bees are few'. Thus rendering a reading of the metaphor of heterosexual procreation insufficient, and also exploding the active/passive oppositions in favour of an in-between mode of connectivity. Here, she urges for a worship that does not rely upon clergy (or the necessary attraction of opposites), but is freely available to those who employ their own active engagement as the vehicle for spiritual ecstasy. The association of 'revery' with singing and hymn-like verse is important, as this denotes a comparatively sacred space which transcends the boundaries between the divine and the speaker (here also between gender) that are laid out in conventional hymns. Here, the 'I-Thou' model of relation dissolves as each element of the trinity collapses into each other endlessly. The absence of capitalisation so favoured by Dickinson in other poems is notable, upsetting the reader's impulse to distinguish nouns from verbs and vice versa. 'Revery' is a noun which describes an act which connotes dream-like passivity and yet it is described in the poem as a vital, active ingredient for the production of a 'prairie.'

The components of 'prairie' are explosive with meaning; Dickinson parodies 'Father, Son and Holy Ghost' whilst conferring such creative power upon nature and human imagination, using examples from nature and the romantic notion of 'revery' for poetic inspiration. 'Prairie' itself invokes the pun on the word prayer, but it also connotes an expansive, ideal space, the logical resultant form created by connecting the three elements described. Thus, the connection between 'revery' and an ecstatic state can be drawn.

The production of this space in the poem is connected with the vocation of the poet, as poetry is also the method of praise here, indicated by Dickinson's pun on 'prairie' and 'prayer.' The Blakean location of 'Heaven in a Wild Flower' ('Auguries of Innocence') does not depend upon the communication of it from the bee, that is, the mechanism of divine inspiration from preacher to congregation, but can be accessed directly through imagination. Imagination here is assessed in terms of re-evaluating what spiritual ecstasy means, and the method of achieving it in relation to traditional forms of worship. The poem places emphasis upon the act of praise, that is, the song or revery of the subject herself: 'Revery alone will do', but even this is not satisfactory ('will do') in isolation.

Crucially, this poem challenges the reader's urge to separate the elements that combine to make a 'prairie', that is, a prayer or ideal space in which the divine is experienced. The poem posits, in a prescriptive manner, the fact that to engage with spiritual worship one must also be able to rest with opposition ('bee' and 'clover', male/female, God/human), and allow a third element of (imagination, mystery or 'revery') to occur. The poem presents difficulty because satisfactory substitutions cannot be made adequately, nor can one permutation of the triune connection (of 'clover', 'bee', or 'revery') be rationalized as being preferable to the other. The triune pattern, which invokes the Trinity (seen elsewhere, for example in Fr 1788 and Fr 610) serves to fuse together the received notions of religious faith and morality against the flux of human experience that pulls ideology into a space which signifies its contradictions, incompletenesses and absences. This is tradition versus experience; it is also Dickinson at her perplexing best, teasing the reader with the formulated phrases of religious orthodoxy versus the potentially liberating space of poetry. The triune relation in this poem is indicative of the intimate connection between poetry, subjectivity and spirituality; the dynamic relation which drives much of Dickinson's poetics. It is also central to the generation of space at work in Dickinson's bee imagery.

In describing 'revery' in this way, Dickinson explodes the need for boundaries between gender, extracting the spiritual dimension of the Trinity as the genderless element that is the mode of prayer for her. This mode of prayer is the process which is *both* the source of, *and* route towards, the divine. There is a gesture towards a rejection of the heterosexual model for procreation and access to the divine which 'clover' and 'bee' invokes, and yet 'revery' cannot be isolated or fully chosen by the speaker. The endless interplay between the three elements at work in this poem constructs divine immanence which is both within the 'prairie' and within the process of the poem itself, conveying what feminist theologians such as Mary Daly have termed 'God the Verb.' In this way, Dickinson's poetics of revery reconfigure an ideal space of relation and community in hymn culture without reinscribing an oppositional 'I-Thou' model of relation to the divine.

'Fuzz Ordained': Bees and Poetic Baptism

The notion of 'revery' in Dickinson's bee poems articulates a third space, of possibilities and relation, in which oppositional thinking is at once both suspended and collapsed. The production of this space is connected with her own industry as a poet. For Dickinson, to be useful is to gather and capture experience of life as she felt it, rendered 'amber-like' in the poem, like the bee who travels from flower to flower, gathering honey. It is also to reach out to others with her 'revery,' a real and/or anticipated community, and in doing so to actively participate in Watts's notion of a useful life. 'I dwell in possibility' (Fr 466) is a good example of where images we would associate with the bee's life are used without explicit reference to the bee itself. Notions of 'gathering' Paradise with 'narrow Hands' and having innumerable and multiple 'chambers' which we would associate with the work of a bee are utilised by Dickinson in this poem to convey the work or 'occupation' of a poet:

> For Occupation - This -
> The spreading wide my narrow Hands -
> To gather Paradise - (Fr 466)

Significantly, such an occupation is valued in terms of its many opportunities for openness and expansiveness, of possibilities. The bee, like the speaker-poet, is able to dispense with restriction (roof is replaced by 'Sky') and inhabit an airy space. The work of the poet is to represent imaginative spaces and openings ('more numerous of windows/Superior - for Doors - ') which can accommodate multiple and different 'visitors' and visions of 'Paradise'.

The ideal space of interconnectedness which the speaker in Dickinson's poems wishes to achieve is often conveyed in a poem by associating the bee with the idea of riding, thus describing the enjoyment and ease implied by a bee's access to revery. The freedom of the bee's flight indicates the speakers' desire to acquire a similarly available access to revery. It not only delineates a trajectory for the speaker to follow but also represents the vehicle or transport to ecstasy for the speaker to take. Significantly, in this poem, revery is equated with being able to make a sound that is a form of praise, an alternative hymn, indicated here by the bee's 'hum:'

> Because the Bee may blameless hum
> For Thee a Bee I do become
> List even unto me.
>
> Because the Flowers unafraid
> May lift a look on thine, a Maid
> Alway a Flower would be.

Nor Robins, Robins need not hide
When Thou upon their Crypts intrude
So Wings bestow on Me
Or Petals, or a Dower of Buzz
That Bee to ride, or Flower of Furze
I that way worship Thee. (Fr 909)

The bee's humming and buzzing, which is indicative of singing (a variant perhaps on Blake's 'singing' bees at the beginning of *The Marriage of Heaven and Hell (1794)*) is described as a form of worship in the final line of the poem, thus connecting the poem with hymn singing and congregational worship. The metre is irregular, only further highlighting the speaker's distance from traditional or acceptable ('blameless') devotional poetry or conventional hymns. The mode of the poem is coy, and the noises of the bee are 'blameless' because they are non-linguistic, and therefore also potentially non-threatening within the context of nineteenth-century religious traditions which either silence and subordinate women or offer specifically defined and limiting roles. The domestic 'angel at the hearth' is one such version of this. Combining the diminutive/coy mode with boldly assertive directions, 'List even unto me,' the qualifier of 'even' denoting the 'lowest place' of subordination is modified by the initial, insistent directive of 'List.' The poem surveys the various strereotypical roles or guises on offer for women and it is the bee which is most acceptable here, ironically, because of its ability to 'hum,' but also perhaps because of the association with the Puritan notion of industry which Dickinson utilises in other bee poems. The parameters of 'acceptable' female relation to the divine is parodied in the 'Dower of Buzz' and 'flower of Furze.' The former invokes a widower, a legally connected person to the essence of spirituality ('Buzz') and therefore a 'legitimate' speaker, and the latter describes the small yellow flowers of spiky gorse, again reiterating a relatively diminished, humble position, as it would not be esteemed highly for its aesthetic value. Furze is resilient and known for withstanding an inhospitable environment, a quality which is both inevitably required of the pious woman but is simultaneously unrecognised as strength or independence in patriarchal religious culture, a double standard which Dickinson's poem highlights.[64]

Gilbert and Gubar have discussed Dickinson's tendency to create acceptable covers or masks through which to speak in a 'ventriloquist' fashion. They argue that this tendency in Dickinson highlights the woman poet's problematic relation to language and the dubious legacy of Romanticism's gendering of nature. They describe her various 'child masks;' 'a tiny person, a wren, a daisy, a mouse, a child,

---

[64]   Tennyson uses 'furze' to connote a calm place of morning and dew in *In Memoriam* (1850). See Alfred Lord Tennyson, *In Memoriam* , XI, lines 5–6: ' Calm and deep peace on this high wold,/ And on these dews that drench the furze'. Dickinson parodies the association of these qualities with femininity in letters to Susan Gilbert. (See L: I, p. 210. Letter dated June 1852.)

a modest little creature easily mastered by circumference and circumstance.'[65] The insect is a guise Dickinson favours as it accommodates her tendency to portray the self as diminutive, coy and unobtrusive. However, the bee image, which might also be placed in this 'child mask' category cannot be regarded as being like the other guises as it is neither 'modest,' nor 'mastered by circumference and circumstance.' The Classical association of bees with poets means that Dickinson's bees are more significantly aligned with the poet-speaker in her poems than other insects. The position the bee's transport allows the speaker to potentially achieve in this poem is one that makes the bee (and therefore also the speaker) bold, hubristic and heretical. In this poem, the speaker dares, ironically, to 'intrude' both within the scene of nature's perfection and also the position of a worshipping objective onlooker. The 'crypts' invoke here the hierarchical structure of the church, being placed both below the choir ('robins') and providing a link or passage to connect the martyrs grave beneath the high altar.

And yet, 'intrude' is assigned to 'Thou,' the God-like figure being addressed in this form of poetic praise/worship, therefore describing the speaker's desire to be in the same position as the transcendent God figure. In order to be at least at equal height with 'Thou' in the poem, the speaker wishes to achieve transcendence by 'riding' a 'bee' and singing like one. Although this poem critiques acceptable forms of worship which the distance of the speaker from the bee's path describes, it also articulates an alternative mode of worship where the bee's noises are instructive because of their non-linguistic quality. They exist in a self-cultivated state of 'buzz' which is akin to the ideal space of revery. Revery would be achievable in this poem if transcendence is 'bestowed' upon the speaker, as 'wings' invokes. And yet the bold desire to be on equal terms with God is described in terms of the poetic flight the image of the bee allows the speaker, therefore enacting and creating an alternative mode of worship and a self-bestowed/created mode of spiritual transcendence. The final statement confirms this; 'That way I worship thee.' Worship has been asserted within the poem and redefined as the expression of the speaker's ability to access transcendence through following the example of the bee in nature, which is both outside of linguistic/patriarchally defined expectations of worship and praise and within it. The bee is therefore an example of both non-threatening articulated subjectivity and also powerfully subversive subjectivity precisely because of this position. The traditional 'I-Thou' model of relation to the divine in hymns is destabilised and renegotiated in this poem as the nature and whereabouts of 'Thou' and 'Thee' is essentially non-consequential to this act of asserting subjectivity.

Dickinson's use of the industry/idleness diptych in Protestant doctrine highlights an anxiety about poetic vision (as evident in the speaker's desire to

---

[65]   Sandra M. Gilbert and Susan Gubar, *The Madwoman in the Attic*, p. 581–91. They describe Dickinson's technique of disguise or dramatisation of a 'supposed' self (p. 587). Dickinson famously remarked in a letter to T.W. Higginson (July 1862) that the 'I' in her verse was not herself, but a 'supposed person' (SL, p. 176).

'blameless hum' in the poem above, or the attempt to 'trace' 'design' in Fr 610 above) as much as a scepticism about religious doctrine. It also, equally, provides an unexpected trajectory, a design of sorts, for reaching towards and reconfiguring belief through writing. The ecstatic bodily excess that the bee often conveys in her poems also delineates a strong subjectivity which negotiates the confines of gender, and which feminist literary theory has connected with the 'horizon' of spirituality. The reconfiguration of gender stereotypes and the connection Dickinson makes between this refusal to settle and spirituality goes some way to negotiate a powerful alternative to the religious revivals that inspired her to grow 'careless' and rebel. Moreover, the bees in Dickinson's corpus signal a 'becoming space' and can be seen as an alternative liturgy which, as we have seen, takes its mode of dissent from the examples she found in contemporary hymn culture. In this space of becoming, signalled by the bee (historically associated with the poet figure), Dickinson self-baptises and confers upon herself a poetic identity, her own 'Title Divine'.

In *Aurora Leigh* (1856), a text which Dickinson almost certainly read (SL, p. 172, 214), Elizabeth Barrett-Browning describes the awakening of the biographical speaker's senses and renewed perception. This runs parallel to her development and awareness as a writer, and is a baptism of 'seeing' which takes place within an enclosed garden setting. The scene invokes both the 'garden' of traditional male devotional poetics (as epitomised by Herbert), where communication with the divine is apprehended, and also the enclosed nature of woman's position as a caged bird within a privet-hedge/nest:

> I had a little chamber in the house,
> As green as any privet-hedge a bird
> Might choose to build in
> [...]
> You could not push your head out and escape
> A dash of dawn-dew from the honeysuckle,
> But so you were baptized into the grace
> And privilege of seeing... (*Aurora Leigh*, I, p. 382)[66]

Furthermore, the catalyst to such 'seeing' is described as an interruption which is precipitated by the humming of bees in the lime trees which awakens the speaker from her sleep:

> First, the lime
> (I had enough there, of the lime, be sure, -
> My morning-dream was often hummed away
> By the bees in it)

---

[66] Elizabeth Barrett-Browning, *The Poetical Works of Elizabeth Barrett Browning* (London: Henry Frowde, 1904) p. 382. Aurora Leigh, Book One.

And again, the life of bees is referred to when describing the speaker-poet's self-'crowning' or self-baptism of her poetic vocation directly. She prefaces the self-baptising fantasy monologue with a comparison of the bee's self-affirmative humming with her own 'murmuring':

> Meanwhile I murmured on
> As honeyed bees keep humming to themselves,
> 'The worthiest poets have remained uncrowned
> Till death has bleached their foreheads to the bone;
> And so with me it must be unless I prove
> Unworthy of the grand adversity,
> And certainly I would not fail so much.
> What, therefore, if I crown myself to-day
> In sport, not pride, to learn the feel of it,
> Before my brows be numbed as Dante's own
> To all the tender prickling of such leaves?
> Such leaves! What leaves?' (*Aurora Leigh*, II, p. 393)

Such self-baptising is evident in Dickinson's poems and the bee is connected directly to this act, with the emphasis on producing a self-affirmative song and 'humming.' Paul Ricoeur's assertion that 'the symbol gives rise to thought'[67] describes the powerful reversal of the process where thought becomes language, where the symbol itself elicits thought and therefore also language. Dickinson's use of bee imagery presents an alternative liturgy because its repeated presence suggests structure, both communion and participation, whilst being itself an image of ecstatic erring which resists structure. The imagery exploits the reader's prior knowledge of bees and also literary and cultural usage of bee imagery in order to produce a dialogic interplay between 'known' meanings of community and industry, and traditional paths to the divine, and the new 'ecstatic' ones being produced both within the poem and within the reading process.

The image of the bee has a history of being connected with the rite of baptism in Christian liturgy. Although the practice was not retained after the sixth century, the concluding rituals involved the baptised person being given milk and honey to take, as a symbol of their entrance into the promised land. Isaiah 7.18 includes the Assyrian bee as an image of God's power and forgiveness; those who do not choose evil are provided with honey. The bee is also associated with rebirth, renewal and spring, and this is reflected in Carmelite liturgy for Easter, which features a 'Eulogy of the Bee'.[68] The transformational quality of the bee imagery in Dickinson's poems invokes a similar association of rebirth and renewal and suggests notions of self-baptising. Dickinson's tendency to wear only garments of white from middle age onwards conveys perhaps a dramatic outward show of

---

[67] Paul Ricoeur, *The Symbolism of Evil* (Boston: Beacon, 1967) pp. 347–57.

[68] The 'Eulogy of the Bee' is performed on Holy Saturday, during Easter. See Archdale A. King, *Liturgies of the Religious Orders* (London: Longmans, 1955) p. 267.

this baptism, as white garments are also associated with baptism in the Christian tradition. By using the bee, Dickinson creates an ecstatic metaphor that effectively redefines the self as poet as well as experience of the divine. We have seen the desire to self-baptise elsewhere in Dickinson, in poems such as Fr 194 ('Title divine, is mine.'), Fr 411 ('Mine - by the Right of the White Election!'), and Fr353 ('I'm Ceded - I've stopped being Theirs'), where she states 'But this time - Adequate - Erect/With Will to choose, or to reject/And I choose, just a Crown - '. Here she invokes the rhetoric of Calvinist election in order to both reject the mode of hierarchy which spurns her self-defined position as heretical, and also to confer status upon this position, which is itself depends upon the collapse of such hierarchical definitions of self and God.

Defiant self-definition is conveyed in poems which also allude to the act of writing. They also invoke the bee to signal an alternative liturgy in which defiant, noisy subjectivity triumphs over the stasis of doctrine. Dickinson tackles religion's failure to represent and accommodate the freedom and chaos of nature and humanity explicitly in 'Safe in their Alabaster Chambers,' where the bee in this earlier version of the poem 'babbles' into a 'stolid ear:'

> Light laughs the breeze
> In her Castle above them -
> Babbles the Bee in a stolid Ear,
> Pipe the Sweet Birds in ignorant cadence -
> Ah, what sagacity perished here! (THJ 216, 1859 version)

The deafness of the dead many, the unseeing, unhearing congregation, signals a triumph of nature and life over death. The poem asserts that the ear should be attuned to the sounds of life - which the laughing breeze and the babbling bee represents here. The 'noise' of life is in full resonance, brought into sharp contrast against the deathly silence of the poem's first stanza which depicts the coldness of the grave. Dickinson takes the Wattsian notion of the afterlife and heaven as the palatial 'courts above' ('Come, let us lift our joyful eyes/ Up to the courts above' *HSS*, II, 108: 440) and turns death into the abstraction, life being the 'Castle' here, the place to reside in the present life of activity and noise. Dickinson berates the death of 'sagacity' in the Puritan meditation on death, and denial of life, as depicted in the poem's first stanza. The bee in this poem is aligned with 'sagacity' - that is foresight, wisdom and even reward. Although the bee 'babbles,' its noise symbolises the way in which the message of life cannot seep through to those who, in Dickinson's view, remain 'dead to the world,' as it were. In a situation akin to that of dead bodies, life cannot reach those who are ignorant of life and the elements, or those who are not alert to sensory experience. A notable precedent for connecting bees with sagacity can be seen in Dryden's translation of Virgil's *The Georgics*. In his translation, which Dickinson may have read, Dryden uses 'sagacious' to describe Virgil's use of bees in Book IV of *The Georgics*: 'last, he singles out the bee, which may be reckoned the most sagacious of them, for his subject.' (*The Works of Virgil* Vol. 3, 1822). The metaphor of the tomb in Dickinson's poem extends not only to the 'members' of the Church, but to the very foundations of the Church itself – cold, lifeless and devoid of light in its 'alabaster' and 'stone' construction: signalling the extent of her criticism of the Church as an institution. Bees symbolise the strength and goodness which comes out of death, but also, in Dickinson's poem, a sagacious and triumphant transcendence above it.

In the second, revised version of this poem (a revision prompted by Susan Gilbert's criticism of the poem in 1861) she draws her criticisms of orthodox religion together and relates them explicitly to writing as her vocation:

> Safe in their Alabaster Chambers -
> Untouched by Morning -
> And untouched by noon -
> Lie the meek members of the Resurrection -
> Rafter of Satin and Roof of Stone -
>
> Grand go the Years,
> In the Crescent above them -
> Worlds scoop their Arcs -
> And Firmaments - row -
> Diadems - drop -
> And Doges - surrender -
> Soundless as Dots,
> On a Disc of Snow. (Fr 124, later version)

In this version it is significant that the freedom of the first version's second stanza (indicated by the bee's presence) is absent. It has been replaced with time's delineation ('Grand go the years' and 'Firmaments - row - ') which the freedom that writing offers her ('Soundless as dots - on a disk of Snow') serves to conquer. Therefore the bee, and the freedom and triumph over death which it represents in the first version, is explicitly interchangeable with, and connected directly to, the act of writing in the later version.

The idea of bees occupying an ideal space is returned to and developed in poem Fr 1426 where the state of 'Buzz' is connected with the sustenance provided by the variant 'Fuzz ordained.' The idea of riding is associated with the bee once again (see Fr 1056 above), who is in this poem described as a 'Buccaneer', wearing 'Gilt Surcingles':

> Bees are Black, with Gilt Surcingles -
> Buccaneers of Buzz.
> Ride abroad in ostentation
> And subsist on Fuzz.
>
> Fuzz ordained - not Fuzz contingent -
> Marrows of the Hill.
> Jugs - a Universe's fracture
> Could not jar or spill. (Fr 1426)

Perhaps the most striking example of Dickinson's use of the bee to describe spirituality, this bee appears at first to be a parody of the Puritan. The ineffable spiritual agency which 'Fuzz' connotes in the first stanza simultaneously undermines the notion of God as sustenance and spiritual strength with its flippant invocation of frothiness or excess. 'Marrows of the Hill' invokes a comparison between the nectar of many flowers (perhaps red) in a landscape and the blood of Christ ('Hill' reminds us of Calvary), reminding us at once of the sustenance of bees and of the Puritan. However, 'Fuzz' playfully undercuts the gravity of such a metaphor. 'Gilt' and 'ostentation' also convey an inauthentic, almost fraudulent mode, where the (perhaps stolen) paraphernalia of the Puritan-like 'buccaneer' is boldly on display and unnecessarily opulent. The outward show of their position which is highlighted in the first stanza appears to undermine the remarkable quality of their actions of 'riding abroad'. These actions are described in the second stanza; the bees collect nectar from flowers ('Jugs') which, because of their size, will not spill and can withstand the full force of the Universe if it should 'fracture.' Such remarkable ability is both questioned by the speaker in the poem, but also presented as a rare and special feature. The smallness of the bee's receptacles also makes their prized nectar paradoxically unspillable, rendering their ability to pollinate and produce honey virtually infallible and therefore also part of a perfect, 'ordained,' design:

> Fuzz ordained - not Fuzz contingent -
> Marrows of the Hill.

The distinction between 'ordained' and 'contingent' in the initial lines of the second stanza is crucial as it separates the steadfast word of God from the idea of contingency. Contingency and faith are oppositional as the latter does not depend upon anything else for its existence, it simply is there or it is not. Equally, however, the poem allows for readings in which 'ordained' might not necessarily be correlative to negative associations of religious doctrine, but rather an alternative, positive state that is beyond the realm of religion and therefore human conceptions of 'Fuzz,' or spirituality. Moreover, 'ordained' is likely another variant of the self-baptism which poetry affords her. 'Marrows of the Hill' describes an essential quality in nature, not a man-made concept, as providing the sustenance, the 'Fuzz,' of the bee. Marrow being the essential life force and sustenance for the body is a striking metaphor which connects the figure of the bee in this poem to the human body, and therefore also to humanity. 'Marrow' is evocative of Watts's diction and the emphasis which he places upon the humanness of the body in order to convey the speaker's wretchedness and separation from God. However, here human physicality is invoked to convey the bee's (that is, the spiritual human's) inherent connection with the essence of God (as 'Marrows of the Hill' reminds us) which provides sustenance and resides in the core of all things.

Although the poem parodies the Puritan figure in a similar manner to some of the other bee poems, and in many ways the existence of such a faith is questioned and gently mocked by the comical depiction of the bee/Puritan riding the currents of ecstasy whilst wearing 'gilt surcingles,' the existence of the ideal space indicated by 'buzz' is still a real consideration. The fact that the bee is described as a Buccaneer, with its association of piratical, plundering activities, suggests the idea that such a paradisal space has been similarly plundered or hijacked by orthodox religion, which attempts to 'ordain' and therefore impose limitations upon the spiritual ecstasy which 'Buzz' and 'Fuzz' convey in this poem. This being so, the ideal space where revery can occur still exists within the poem, within the speaker's gaze, as the example from nature ('Marrow of the Hill') conveys.

The pointed repetition of 'Fuzz' in this poem (the repetition of words being itself a rare occurrence for Dickinson) accentuates, as in many other of Dickinson's bee poems, the excessiveness of the bee's body, and suggests that it is perhaps a bumblebee. Again, it is an example of impossibility made possible and actual, where the sheer volume of the bee's body in comparison with its wing power renders it miraculous in scientific terms. A connection between the implausibility of the bee and the implausibility of Christian salvation and immortality is implied. Dickinson exploits this remarkable fact by alluding to the bee's precarious position in the air with its need for surcingles, which aid balance, as it rides upon the currents of the air, plundering 'Buzz.' The fact that the bee image in this poem allows the reader to observe both a critique of religious faith, with its apparent implausibility (as indicated by the bee's implausibly excessive body) and also what is essentially a reassertion of faith in an ideal space of revery, indicated by 'Buzz,' suggests further that in connecting industry and revery, the bee image serves (like Virgil's bees) as a bridge between faith and doubt and between life and death. It connotes an ideal space where both, impossibly, could exist, escaping the 'contingency' of human thinking on spirituality and also on the potential of women poets. The fact that the bees in Dickinson's poems are often described as 'riding' the air is suggestive of angels on horseback, riding the unseen, spiritual currents, delineating the arc of such an ideal space of possibilities. Significantly, the bees are themselves, their own method of 'transport,' and transcendence, where 'surcingles,' 'wings' or 'carriages' are also their bodies. In this way the bee is an automaton and an example of the self-'ordained', and also of the self-defined woman poet, giving expression to this self.

Despite this autonomy, the mode of relation and destabilised oppositions which this self-baptism draws from in her poems works against reinscribing self-centredness and interiority. However, Benjamin Lease cites Thomas à Kempis (Of the Love of Solitude and Silence') and Sir Thomas Browne ('Christian Morals': 'Be able to be alone. Lose not the advantage of solitude'), both read by Dickinson, to support the emphasis of interiority he places upon her mode of spirituality: 'Emily Dickinson was engaged in a life that reflected Browne's vision of simultaneous solitude and deep involvement' (*RMB*, p. 58). There is a difference between Dickinson's rejection of orthodox rules of salvation, and the damnation associated with traditional forms of religion, particularly Puritan and even revivalist, evangelical Christianity with which she would be familiar. Her inclination to not assent to the majority or accepted patterns implicit in such orthodox religions must not be mistaken for privileging interiority and isolation over a desire to connect with the world and partake in a 'communion'. Lease himself notes the connection between the bee (an image of relation) and spiritual vision in Dickinson, when he cites 'These are the days when Birds come Back' (Fr 122) as evidence of her direct engagement with Thomas à Kempis's *Imitation*, reading it as an extrapolation of the emphasis on childhood in Kempis:

> The *Imitation* dwells on the central importance of the Lord's Supper – and the need for simplicity and purity in everyday life ('By two wings, a man is lifted up from things earthly, namely, by Simplicity and Purity.') [...] In the dying season, there is for the child – and for the child in spirit – the possibility and promise of eternal life. The lesson of the undeceived bee is that the season is indeed dying; the bee is not cheated in *this* false season. But they who become as little children partake in a celebration of cyclical death and life, of life in death – and are not cheated in any season. (*RMB*, pp. 54–5)

Lease observes the apparent special immunity to 'fraud' that Dickinson imparts to the figure of the bee in this poem, and highlights the emphasis she places upon being 'as little children.' However, the bee's immunity to the 'fraud' of appearances in this poem does not 'induce' the poet speaker's child-like belief in, and acceptance of, Christian redemption and immortality through Christ ('Almost'), but rather invokes a communion with nature and its cyclical, immortal seasons, in which all things are inextricably related:

> These are the days when Birds come back -
> A very few - a bird or two -
> To take a backward look.
>
> These are the days when skies resume
> The old - old sophistries of June -
> A blue and gold mistake.
>
> Oh fraud that cannot cheat the Bee -
> Almost thy plausibility
> Induces my belief.
>
> Till ranks of seeds their witness bear -
> And softly thro' the altered air
> Hurries a timid leaf.
>
> Oh Sacrament of summer days,
> Oh last Communion in the Haze -
> Permit a child to join.
>
> Thy sacred emblems to partake -
> Thy consecrated bread to take
> And thine immortal wine! (Fr 122)

The bee in this poem is the objectified, observed participant in the 'summer communion,' but acting as it does as an intermediary between the scene on display and the speaker in the poem, it becomes itself a 'sacred emblem' within Dickinson's poetic liturgy. The bee, dependent upon the nectar of blooming flowers, cannot be cheated by the appearance of a summer day because the absence of flowers for it provides proof of the seasonal change to autumn. Its relation to the hive and the industry *and* revery it must continue dictates the objective 'truth' of the season for it. It is the bee who communicates the gap between faith and doubt and the collapsing division between the 'I' ('my') of the speaker and the inherent divinity 'Thou' ('Thy') of the scene. If, then, we trust the bee, whose proof against fraud has been proved by its innate relation to the world, then so, perhaps, we must trust in that pattern of relation but also, and just as importantly, in the individual vision of the poet who sees the truth of the sacrament of 'Communion' laid out in the 'haze' of late summer days. And so in this way, the bee provides the evidential, relational truth of the existence of a design in which industry and revery are *always* connected, the circumference of which, for Dickinson, is traced through her own poetic work.

Treatments of Dickinson's use of nature which have contributed to a dismissal of her as a 'nature poet' have also diverted us away from her radical revisionings of theology and self-awareness as a mystical poet. Dickinson's bee poems, with their erratic flight, create a new notion of space and rely on a constant exchange between 'I-Thou' which defies and collapses models of hierarchy. She exploits and ruptures the culturally idiomatic connection between industry and morals (as epitomised by Watts's 'busy bee') to connect industry and revery in her bee imagery. Thus, giving voice to the erring other who dares to 'ride indefinite' and willingly get 'lost in balms', and who demonstrates the 'impossible' flight which is at once non-linear, erratic and ecstatic. This mode of being allows 'revery' to come to the fore, which is also an 'impossible' state, a state of possibilities, in which oppositional thought can not rest and in which social hierarchies can not be reproduced. This particular use of bee imagery explodes divisions and delineates an ideal space in which the shapes, and shaping, of spirituality are articulated.

Dickinson's use of the bee image thus both critiques and utilises familiar modes of religious ideology and also offers one way of perceiving the shape or design of her industry and license as a poet, and ultimately, her own connection with belief and 'illume' or 'revery'. In this way, Dickinson's use of the bee image can be seen as being emblematic of an ideal space and thus performing an alternative symbolism for spirituality within her poetics. Ultimately it is the transportive power of poetry that offers Dickinson a mode of revery which is both an ecstatic experience and also a form of industry. Her version of industry delineates a spiritual life by constantly redefining and simultaneously destabilising the force of oppositions which stifle it. In using bee imagery to parody or subvert Puritan values Dickinson creates a new aesthetic response to religious orthodoxy and in doing so articulates an alternative mode of belief.

Chapter 7
'Why Floods Be Served to Us in Bowls - /
I Speculate No More -':
Reading Dickinson's Strategy

> One blessing had I than the rest
> So larger to my Eyes
> That I stopped gauging - satisfied -
> For this enchanted size -
> [...]
> I knew no more of Want - or Cold -
> Phantasms both become
> For this new Value in the Soul -
> Supremest Earthly Sum - (Fr 767)

By reassessing Emily Dickinson's hymn culture it is clear that her engagement with hymns goes beyond metrical subversion of Isaac Watts's hymn patterns, broadening out to a wider theological engagement. This engagement renegotiates the hierarchical 'I-Thou' model of relation to the divine in hymns and an alternative version of spirituality, a 'new Value in the Soul', is asserted. That engagement can be seen by reading Watts primarily as a model for dissent, by identifying a tradition of contemporary women hymnists and by going further to analyse and develop theories of hymnic space. In this way the representation of spirituality in Dickinson's poetry can be traced against 'tradition' and experience. Thus this book has demonstrated that Dickinson's relation to hymnody can provide one way of examining the representation of apparently contradictory, fluid and multiple spirituality in her poetry. Hymn culture provides a 'bowl' into which Dickinson's expansive spiritual vision can be poured, where her series of challenges to, and creative reconstructions of, the divine can be measured against both the oppositional 'I-Thou' model of address and notion of cohesive 'community' which are associated with hymns. The representation of spirituality in Dickinson's poetry can be traced through an engagement with hymn culture; from the influence of Watts and the example of Dissent and autonomy that his hymns demonstrate, through the challenges to teleological representations of the divine found in the work of contemporary women hymnists, to the knowledge of the self and assertion of subjectivity which are performed through metaphors of relation in Dickinson's poetics.

Analysing Dickinson's use of the hymn in terms of a heterologous space in which to articulate an individual's relation to community provides a paradigm for the version of the female divine which is described in twentieth and twenty-first century feminist theology and feminist literary theory, particularly that of

Daphne Hampson and Luce Irigaray. Although the echoes of hymns in Dickinson's work serve to highlight her dislocation from the religious communities and the particular versions of social cohesion and of the divine which she found to be antagonistic to her own experience of self and spirituality, her interaction with hymn culture is not based exclusively upon recalcitrance. The poetics of relation which Dickinson's writing constructs belies a commitment to the ideas of *community* and *relation* which the hymn form encodes. However, these aspects of hymn culture are reworked and transformed in Dickinson's poetics and evade oppositional models that do not accommodate her own experience. In this way they have affinity with the alternative models for the divine considered in current feminist theology. By arguing that Dickinson's engagement with hymn culture goes beyond formal concerns of metre, this study seeks to move Dickinson studies forward, beyond a simple perception of her interaction with hymnody as being limited to the disruption of regularised metre and subversion of biblical tropes in the hymns of Isaac Watts. Rather, it shows that Dickinson's hymns can be seen as positive responses to and expansions of the tropes of dissent, flight and spiritual community instigated by Watts and developed by other women hymnists. Thus re-visioning Dickinson as radically engaged with the politics of theology and the voices of hymn culture.

It has been necessary to provide a context for Dickinson's relation to hymnody, not least because 'tradition' must always be interrogated, but also because such a context provides new ways of seeing how her theology and poetics merge. Her use of an anti-teleological, anti-hierarchical mode of writing can be seen as both looming out of and operating within a culturally prescribed and acceptable form for nineteenth-century women. The hymns of Isaac Watts, Phoebe Hinsdale Brown and Eliza Lee Follen demonstrate that the hymn is a form of expression which inherently allows limitation to become visible. Highlighting the ways in which each hymnist engages with the expectations of a hymn and also its limitations, provides an important context for Dickinson's engagement with the hymn and hymn culture in a period when the use of patriotic hymns during war to reassert social cohesion, together with the emergent proliferation of female hymnody, made the genre a particularly potent form of expression for the poet to use.

The evidence of hymnody being used by Watts and antebellum era women hymnists as a form of Dissent and protest, as well as expression of spirituality, serves to shed light upon Dickinson's use of bee imagery. Her use of bee imagery carries particular resonance with both Puritanism and the Protestant work ethic and aspects related to hymns and hymn culture, such as singing (the bee's noises and interruptive presence within the poem), relationality and community. Analysis of Dickinson's particular uses of this imagery illustrates how she exploits the connection with industry and morals in hymn culture to give voice to her ecstatic and erring self, and to express her own divine 'revery'. A triune pattern of industry, revery and relation can be traced in the bee motif. This combination, and particularly the notion of relation, can be brought into critical focus by comparing it to the notions of community and relation in feminist theology and also with the mode of the mystical writings of Irigaray and Certeau, as examined in Chapter Three in relation to the redefinition of hymnic space.

By engaging with hymn culture and cultural associations of the bee, and primarily the idiomatic connection between industry and morality, Dickinson radically transforms the image into a trope of multiple, *diverse relationality* which also becomes an image associated with poetry and the poet. By highlighting the connections between labour and pleasure in nature and by connecting this with her own industry as a poet, Dickinson's bee imagery delimits a *heterologous space*, where individuality is given freedom and movement within a structure. This is also, by implication, a reworking of hymn culture as it repositions the 'I' in hymn address into a diverse relationality, thus escaping the linear, teleological relation to the divine which is exclusionary. Both centripetal and centrifugal forces come together in Dickinson's bee imagery, signaling again a reconfiguration of the outwards but also centralising movement of address in hymns. Dickinson holds the inwards/outwards movement in tension, the 'centre' of God is not pursued, but is replaced instead with the mystical and Dissenting mode of tracing the margins, Dickinson's 'Business' of 'Circumference' (SL, p. 176). In this way, the reconfiguration of the 'I-Thou' model in Dickinson's poetry which this book has demonstrated, displays qualities which are comparable with the 'alternative values' of 'multiplicity' and 'community' which Scheinberg suggests are necessary to counter the androcentric 'generic patterns' in Victorian poetic theory (Scheinberg, p. 236). Dickinson's bee imagery, like Virgil's, bridges the gap between death and life, between old traditions and new hopes.

Ultimately, this book has shown that the hymn is a form of expression which makes its limitations visible; and by doing so is able to take spiritual discourse some way beyond those limitations, leaving space for an openness which cannot be 'contained'. The ways in which Dickinson's poems probe the limitations of the hymn genre serve to make hymn culture an endlessly rejuvenating and self-regenerative source of inspiration within her poetics. Rather than reading Dickinson's poetry as the meditations of a spiritual isolate, her mystical 'alternative hymns' convey the expression of a radically engaged mind, pushing the boundaries of a traditional and patriarchally defined form to create a new mode of expression for the a-temporal divine space in human, temporal relation.

'instead of getting to Heaven, at last - '

Dickinson's poetics work against the linearity and fixity associated with the depiction of the speaker's relation to the divine to be found in traditional hymns. Whilst the vestiges of hymnic metre in many of Dickinson's poems suggest that such linearity and fixity is available, the speaker's vision is always deferring, open, and engaging with an alternative which is much more explosive. By choosing transgression of traditional hymnody's boundaries as the basis of her poetic style, Dickinson provides an open space for herself and for her version of the divine to become animated through a method that is both a response *and* a non-saying.

Moreover, like the mystic, Dickinson's hymnic space remains new, and as such is a space for the reader to make cognitive connections that are suggested but not final. In this, Dickinson's language is placed in relation to the reader, but that relation is paradoxically (and crucially) without ties. This paradoxical sense of connection is explored by feminist theologians in relation to qualities of a female divine and the problematic negotiation of hierarchical structure in traditional religious culture.

The idea of received knowledge, or as Graham Ward writes, 'a response to the reception of what is given' (*Christ and Culture*, p. 185) requires a horizon, a barometer against which to measure itself as similar or to be recognised. Watts's hymns convey the points at which his 'describable' knowledge of God seems to fail him, which are articulated in terms of sight/blindness or closeness/distance in many instances. Dickinson's poems, on the other hand, describe a journey of relation with the unsayable, whilst also challenging the view of traditional hymnody as representing and enacting social cohesion. In this way, they work against the 'act of naming' in traditional hymnody whilst both deconstructing and renegotiating the premises of community and interconnectedness proliferated by hymn culture. Traditional hymns are sites in which the speaker's relation to God, and the naming of the divine which they (re-) produce can be articulated. Dickinson's poems allow space for experience which is both unexpected and unbounded, as the initial and penultimate stanzas from poem Fr 483 exemplify:

> Most she touched me by her muteness -
> Most she won me by the way
> She presented her small figure -
> Plea itself - for Charity -
> [...]
> I supposed - when sudden
> Such a Praise began
> 'Twas as Space sat singing
> To herself - and men - (Fr 483)

In generating this space Dickinson allows for the possibilities of self and spirituality which can be experienced through writing. She depicts the surprise event of bursting out of 'muteness', which in this poem is anticipated by the poet-onlooker, or paternal 'Benefactor'. The occupation of multiple positions in Dickinson's poems (as the speaker's role of onlooker and the implied connection between the bird singer and the poet herself in this poem demonstrates) serves to highlight but also blur distinctions between 'I' and 'Thou' and thus collapse the model of relation in traditional hymn address. This book has demonstrated that this relation is a feature which permeates Dickinson's work and signals her engagement with hymn culture.

'Heterologous space' has been used to describe the forms of relation to hymn culture and also to the divine which Dickinson's poems display. Certeau's notion of mystical writings as delineating absences and ruptures, whilst also operating within a heterologous space of relation to the historicity of discourses which produced them is instructive. In applying this idea we can see not only how Dickinson's relation to hymn culture delineates absences in traditional hymnody's 'I-Thou' model of address, but also that the 'open' shape of her poetics is connected with this relation to hymn culture. It is this relation to hymn culture which results in a redefinition of the divine within hymnic space. Dickinson's hymnic spaces open out the 'I-Thou' model to incorporate a multiple relationality in which the linear relation between 'I' and 'Thou' is replaced with multiplicity and mobility with regard to the divine. Through this, Dickinson's 'alternative hymns' also create an alternative space in which the divine and self can be endlessly re-imagined and reborn. Therefore, the contradiction and fluidity which characterises Dickinson's work does not delimit absence per se, but instead, a space in which possibilities can inhabit.

In forging a poetics in which difference is incorporated, and in which an alternative to the 'I-Thou' model of relation in hymns is persistently considered, Dickinson articulates both a 'female divine' and 'mystical discourse' in which the premises and assumptions of traditional religious culture are invoked to make them 'say the absence' of 'what they designate'.[1] It is the moments at which traditional religious culture fails the woman writer who searches for a way to express the divine which she experiences that furnish Dickinson with the architecture of her poetics. Through dissent, doubt and discontent, Dickinson spins a poetics of an alternative faith; an optimism for, and faith in, ideas of relation and community which are reconfigured to connote immanent experience:

> God preaches, a noted Clergyman -
> And the sermon is never long,
> So instead of getting to Heaven, at last -
> I'm going, all along. (Fr 236)

Dickinson claims in this poem to have direct access to God as she defines him, a definition which is itself hinged upon understatement and irony because of her rejection of God as 'Father' (25 April 1862, SL, p. 173). Here she parodies but also dismisses the need for formalised worship and the 'noted clergym[e]n' of her social milieu. She rejects formalised religious experience and does not address a 'Thou' to answer the 'I' in her poem, as would be the case in traditional hymnody. However, she does not dispense with the claim to spiritual experience but charts an alternative way, in which relation to the divine is reached immediately through the self, paradoxically, without the interposing hierarchy which 'noted clergyman' invokes and without the 'interposing days' found in Watts (*HSS*, II, 145: 458–9). Relation to the divine is not defined through a telos ('Heaven, at last - ') but in relation to the present, with its chaotic multiplicity ('*all* along'). This, the poem's final line ('I'm going, all along') voices ironic surprise at the autonomy of her journey, however, it also encapsulates the mode of Dickinson's relation to the divine which is within both self and world, both immediate and all encompassing.

---

[1]   Michel de Certeau, 'Mystic Speech' in *The Certeau Reader* (ed.), by Graham Ward, p. 205.

This mobile and fluid relationality is inscribed and enacted poetically by Dickinson, thus reconstructing the symbolic values of the hymn whilst negotiating hierarchical models of address. Dickinson's words form themselves, congregationally around the circumference of her own experience; the communion with nature and also the journey of her own life. They do not define nor are constricted by a demand for a telos, but instead simply express Heaven through and within present experience. Therefore, the product of Dickinson's experience of and engagement with the tradition of hymn culture does not merely offer a parody of the modes of expression and metrics of the popular hymnody of her day; it actively shapes a new kind of theology.

Bibliography

Primary Sources

Anon., 'Individuality' *Atlantic Monthly* 54:9 (1862) 424–30

Anon., 'Telling the Bees' *Atlantic Monthly* 6:1 (1858) 722–24

Baynes, Rev. Robert. H., ed., *Lyra Anglicana: Hymns and Sacred Songs* (London: Houlston and Wright, 1867)

Brown, Mrs P.H., *The Tree and Its Fruits, Or, Narratives from Real Life* (New York: Ezra Collier, 1836)

Bryant, Mark, ed., *Literary Hymns: An Anthology* (London: Hodder and Stoughton, 1999)

Burnap, George, *Popular Objections to Unitarian Christianity Considered and Answered*, 5th edn (Boston: Crosby, Nichols and Company, 1855)

Cleveland, Charles Dexter, ed., *Lyra Sacra Americana: Or, Gems from American Sacred Poetry* (London: Samson Low, Son and Marston, 1868)

Duffield, S.W., *English Hymns: Their Authors and History* (New York: Funk and Wagnalls Co., 1886)

Follen, Eliza Lee, *Hymns, Songs and Fables for Young People*, 2nd edn (1831;Boston: W.M. Crosby and H.P. Nichols, 1851)

———. *The Life of Charles Follen* (London: John Chapman, 1844)

Franklin, Ralph W., ed., *The Poems of Emily Dickinson: Reading Edition* (Cambridge, MA: The Belknap Press of Harvard University Press, 2005)

Gray, Janet, ed., *She Wields a Pen: American Women Poets of the Nineteenth Century* (London: J.M. Dent, 1997)

Griswold, Rufus, ed., *Sacred Poets of England and America* (New York: D. Appleton and Company, 1848)

Hitchcock, A.P., 'Hymns and Hymn-Tinkers,' *The Atlantic Monthly* 46:3 (1882) 336–46

Hitchcock, Edward, *Religious Truth, Illustrated from Science, in Addresses and Sermons on Special Occasions* (Boston: Phillips, Sampson and Company, 1857)

Holy Bible: King James Version (New Jersey: Thomas Nelson Inc, 1972)

Johnson, Thomas H., ed., *Emily Dickinson: Selected Letters*, eleventh printing (Cambridge, MA: The Belknap Press of Harvard University Press, 2002)

———. *The Complete Poems of Emily Dickinson*, 2nd edn (London: Faber and Faber, 1975)

———. *The Letters of Emily Dickinson*, 3 vols (Cambridge, MA: The Belknap Press of Harvard University Press, 1958)

Julian, John, ed., *A Dictionary of Hymnology: Setting Forth the Origin and History of Christian Hymns of All Ages and Nations*, rev. edn (1892; London: John Murray, 1907)

Nason, Elias, ed., *The Congregational Hymn Book, For the Service of the Sanctuary* (Boston: John. P. Jewett and Co., 1857)

Nettleton, Asahel, ed., *Village Hymns for Social Worship Selected and Original: Designed as a Supplement to Dr Watts's Psalms and Hymns* (Hartford: Printed by Goodwin and Co., 1824)

Pafford, J.H.P., ed., *Isaac Watts: Divine Songs attempted in Easy Language for the Use of Children* (1715) (Oxford University Press, 1971)

Pitman, Mrs E.R., ed., *Lady Hymn Writers* (London: T. Nelson and Sons, 1892)

Tocqueville, Alexis de., *Democracy in America*, 2 vols, 13th edn, ed., J.P. Mayer, trans. by George Lawrence (1848; London: Fontana Press, 1994)

Virgil, *The Works of Virgil*, trans. by John Dryden (Chiswick: C. Wittingham, 1822)

Watts, Isaac, *The Psalms and Hymns of Isaac Watts* (no ed.; combined repr. of *The Psalms of David* [1719] and *Hymns and Spiritual Songs* [1707]) (Pennsylvania: Soli Deo Gloria Publications, 1997)

———. *Philosophical Essays on Various Subjects: With Some Remarks on Mr Locke's Essay on the Human Understanding* (1742; Bristol: Theommes, 1990)

———. *The Poetical Works of Isaac Watts, With a Memoir* (Boston: Little, Brown and Company, 1866)

———. *The Psalms, Hymns and Spiritual Songs of the Rev. Isaac Watts*, D.D. To which are added Select Hymns from other Authors; and Directions for Musical Expression (Boston: Samuel T. Armstrong and Crocker and Brewster, 1832)

———. *Horae Lyricae* (London: John Hatchard and Son, 1834)

———. *The Poems of Isaac Watts* (London: C. Whittingham, 1822)

———. *The World to Come: Or Discourses on the Joys or Sorrows of Departed Souls at Death and the Glory or Terror of the Resurrection to which is Prefixed an Essay toward the Proof of a Separate State of Souls after Death* (1738; London: Richard Evans and Edinburgh: John Bourne, 1814)

Secondary Sources

Allen, Michael, *Emily Dickinson as an American Provincial Poet* (Brighton: BAAS, University of Sussex, 1985)

Armstrong, Isobel, and Angela Leighton, eds, *Victorian Women Poets: An Anthology* (Oxford: Blackwell, 1995)

Armstrong, Isobel, *Victorian Poetry: Poetry, Poetics, and Politics* (London: Routledge, 1993)

Arseneau, Mary, *Recovering Christina Rossetti: Female Community and Incarnational Poetics* (Houndmills: Palgrave Macmillan, 2004)

Bakhtin, Mikhail, *Rabelais and His World* (Bloomington: Indiana University Press, 1984)

Barney, William L., ed., *A Companion to Nineteenth-Century America* (Oxford: Blackwell, 2001)

Barrett-Browning, Elizabeth, *The Poetical Works of Elizabeth Barrett Browning* (London: Henry Frowde, 1904)

Barry, Peter, *Beginning Theory: An Introduction to Literary and Cultural Theory* (Manchester: Manchester University Press, 1995)

Beatty, B.G., and R.T. Davies, eds, *Literature of the Romantic Period 1750–1850* (Liverpool: Liverpool University Press, 1976)

Belsey, Catherine and Jane Moore, eds, *The Feminist Reader: Essays in Gender and the Politics of Literary Criticism*, 2nd edn (London: Macmillan, 1997)

Bennett, Paula, *Emily Dickinson: Woman Poet* (New York: Harvester Wheatsheaf, 1990)

———. *My Life a Loaded Gun: Dickinson, Plath, Rich and Female Creativity* (Urbana: University of Illinois Press, 1990)

Bercovitch, Sacvan, ed., *The American Puritan Imagination* (Cambridge: Cambridge University Press, 1974)

Berry, Philippa and Andrew Wernick, eds, *Shadow of Spirit: Postmodernism and Religion* (London: Routledge, 1992)

Bishop, Selina L., ed., *Isaac Watts: Hymns and Spiritual Songs 1701–1748: A Study in Early Eighteenth-Century Language Changes* (London: The Faith Press, 1962)

Blake, William, *The Marriage of Heaven and Hell* (1794) (New York: Dover Publications, 1994)

Blanch, Brenda, ed., *Heaven A Dance: An Evelyn Underhill Anthology* (London: SPCK, 1992)

Bond Stockton, Kathryn, *God Between Their Lips: Desire Between Women in Irigaray, Bronte and Eliot* (Stanford: Stanford University Press, 1994)

Boswell, Jeanetta, *Emily Dickinson: A Bibliography of Secondary Sources, with Selective Annotations, 1890 through 1987* (Jefferson, North Carolina: McFarland and Company, 1989)

Bradbury, Malcolm and Richard Ruland, *From Puritanism to Postmodernism: A History of American Literature* (London: Routledge, 1991)

Bradford Bedingfield, M., *The Dramatic Liturgy of Anglo-Saxon England* (Woodbridge: The Boydell Press, 2002)

Brett, R.L., ed., *Poems of Faith and Doubt: The Victorian Age* (London: Edward Arnold, 1965)

Brewer, E. Cobham, ed., *A Dictionary of Phrase and Fable* rev. edn (London: Cassell and Company, 1958)

Buber, Martin, *I and Thou* (1937), trans. by Walter Kaufmann, 3rd edn (Edinburgh: T and T Clark, 1970)

Cameron, Sharon, *Lyric Time: Dickinson and the Limits of Genre* (Baltimore: The Johns Hopkins University Press, 1979)

Capps, Jack L., *Emily Dickinson's Reading 1836–1886* (Cambridge: Harvard University Press, 1966)

Carper Thomas and Derek Attridge, *Meter and Meaning: An Introduction to Rhythm in Poetry* (London: Routledge, 2003)

Certeau, Michel de., *Heterologies: Discourse on the Other* (1986) trans. by Brian Massumi, 6th edn (Minneapolis: Minneapolis University Press, 2000)

Claghorn, Charles Eugene, *Women Composers and Hymnists: A Concise Bibliographical Dictionary* (London: Scarecrow, 1984)

Clarke, Graham, ed., *Emily Dickinson: Critical Assessments Vol. IV* (Mountfield: Helm Information Ltd., 2002)

Clarke, Norma, *The Rise and Fall of the Woman of Letters* (London: Pimlico, 2004)

Cooper, Helen, *Elizabeth Barrett Browning: Woman and Artist* (Chapel Hill: The University of North Carolina Press, 1988)

Cosslett, Tess, ed., *Victorian Women Poets* (Harlow: Longman, 1996)

Couzyn, Jeni, ed., *The Bloodaxe Book of Contemporary Women Poets: Eleven British Writers* (Newcastle: Bloodaxe, 1998)

Cunningham, Valentine, 'The Sound of Startled Grass', *The Guardian*, October 19, 2002. From *The Guardian* website archive, accessed on 14/11/02. http://arts.guardian.co.uk/features/story/0,,814836,00.html

Daly, Mary, *Beyond God the Father: Toward a Philosophy of Women's Liberation* (1973) (London: The Women's Press, 1995)

Daly, Peter M. and others, eds, *Andreas Alciatus: (1) The Latin Emblems Indexes and Lists* (Toronto: University of Toronto Press, 1985) Reprint of the Padua 1621 edn

Davie, Donald, *The Eighteenth Century Hymn in England* (Cambridge: Cambridge University Press, 1993)

————. ed., *New Oxford Book of Christian Verse* (Oxford: Oxford University Press, 1981)

Davies, Horton, *Worship and Theology in England: From Watts and Wesley to Martineau, 1690–1900* (Cambridge: William B. Eerdmans Publishing Company, 1996)

Dickens, Charles, *Bleak House* (1853) (London: Penguin, 2003)

Diehl, Joanne Feit, *Dickinson and the Romantic Imagination* (New Jersey: Princeton University Press, 1981)

D'Monte, Rebecca, and Nicole Pohl, eds, *Female Communities 1600–1800: Literary Visions and Cultural Realities* (London: Macmillan, 2000)

Dobson, Joanne, *Dickinson and the Strategies of Reticence* (Bloomington: Indiana University Press, 1989)

Eberwein, Jane Donahue, ed., *An Emily Dickinson Encyclopedia* (Connecticut: Greenwood Press, 1998)

Emerson, Ralph Waldo, *Essays* (1841) (London: J.M. Dent and Co., 1904)

England, Martha Winburn, and John Sparrow, *Hymns Unbidden: Donne, Herbert, Blake, Emily Dickinson and the Hymnographers* (New York: New York Public Library, 1966)

Erikson, Kai T., *Wayward Puritans: A Study in the Sociology of Deviance* (New York: John Wiley and Sons, 1966)

Farr, Judith, with Louise Carter, *The Gardens of Emily Dickinson* (Cambridge, MA: Harvard University Press, 2004)

Farr, Judith, ed., *Emily Dickinson: A Collection of Critical Essays* (New Jersey: Prentice Hall, 1996)

————. *The Passion of Emily Dickinson* (Cambridge, MA: Harvard University Press, 1992)

Flanagan, Sabina, *Secrets of God: Writings of Hildegard of Bingen* (Shambala Publications: Boston and London, 1996)

Foote, Henry Wilder, *Three Centuries of American Hymnody* (Connecticut: Shoe String Press, 1961)

Foucault, Michel, *Discipline and Punish: The Birth of the Prison* (1975) (London: Penguin, 1986)

Fountain, David G., *Isaac Watts Remembered* (Harpenden: Gospel Standard Baptist Trust Ltd., 1974)

Francis, Emma Jane, *Poetic Licence: British Women's Poetry and the Sexual Division of Poetics and Culture – 1824–1889, Letitia Landon, Amy Levy, Emily Bronte* (Unpublished PhD thesis, University of Liverpool, 1995)

Frye, Northrop, *The Eternal Act of Creation: Essays 1979–1990* (Bloomington: Indiana University Press, 1993)

Galvin, Mary. E., *Queer Poetics: Five Modernist Women Writers* (Connecticut: Greenwood Press, 1999)

Garbowsky, Maryanne M., *The House Without the Door: Emily Dickinson and the Illness of Agoraphobia* (London: Associated University Press, 1989)

Gardner, Martin, ed., *The Annotated Alice* rev. edn (London: Penguin, 1970)

Garraty, John A., and Mark C. Carnes, eds, *American National Biography* vol. 3 (Oxford: Oxford University Press, 1999)

Gaustad, Edwin Scott, *Dissent In American Religion* (Chicago: University of Chicago Press, 1973)

Gelpi, Albert, *Emily Dickinson: The Mind of the Poet* (Cambridge, MA: Harvard University Press, 1966)

Gelpi, Barbara Charlesworth, and Albert Gelpi, eds, *Adrienne Rich's Poetry and Prose*, 2nd edn (New York: Norton, 1993)

Gilbert, Sandra M. and Susan Gubar, *The Madwoman in the Attic: The Woman Writer and the Nineteenth Century Literary Imagination* (1979) rev. edn (New Haven: Yale University Press, 2000)

Grabher, Gudrun, Roland Hagenbuchle and Christanne Miller, eds, *The Emily Dickinson Handbook* (Boston: The University of Massachusetts Press, 1998)

Graham, Elaine L., *Making the Difference: Gender, Personhood and Theology* (London: Mowbray, 1995)

Graves, Robert, *The White Goddess* (1948) 4th edn (London: Faber and Faber, 1999)

Griffin, Jasper, ed., *Virgil: The Aeneid* trans. by C. Day Lewis (Oxford: Oxford University Press, 1998)

Habegger, Alfred, *My Wars Are Laid Away in Books: The Life of Emily Dickinson* (New York: Random House, 2001)

———. 'Evangelicalism and its Discontents: Hannah Porter versus Emily Dickinson,' *The New England Quarterly* vol. 70: 3 (1997) 386–414

Hampson, Daphne, *Theology and Feminism* (Oxford: Blackwell, 1990)

Hobbs Hadden, June, *I sing for I cannot be Silent: The Feminization of American Hymnody, 1870–1920* (Pittsburgh: University of Pittsburgh Press, 1997)

Hogan, Anne and Andrew Bradstock, eds, *Women of Faith in Victorian Fiction: Reassessing the Angel in the Home* (Houndmills: Macmillan, 1998)

Hollander, John, ed., *American Poetry: The Nineteenth-Century* (New York: Library of America, 1996)

Holquist, Michael, ed., *The Dialogic Imagination: Four Essays by M.M. Bakhtin* (Austin: University of Texas Press, 1981)

Homans, Margaret, *Women Writers and Poetic Identity: Dorothy Wordsworth, Emily Bronte and Emily Dickinson* (New Jersey: Princeton University Press, 1980)

Howe, Daniel Walker, *The Unitarian Conscience: Harvard Moral Philosophy, 1805–1861* (Cambridge, MA: Harvard University Press, 1970)

Hoyles, John, *The Waning of the Renaissance 1640–1740: Studies in the Thought and Poetry of Henry More, John Norris and Isaac Watts* (Netherlands: Martinus Nijhoff, 1971)

Hughes, Ted, ed., *A Choice of Emily Dickinson's Verse* (London: Faber and Faber, 1968)

Hunt, Tristram, *Building Jerusalem: The Rise and Fall of the Victorian City* (London: Phoenix, 2004)

Inge, M.Thomas., ed., *Handbook of American Popular Culture*, vols. I-II (Connecticut: Greenwood Press, 1980)

Ingram, Tom and Douglas Newton, eds, *Hymns as Poetry* (London: Constable, 1956)

Irigaray, Luce, *Sexes and Genealogies*, trans. by Gillian C. Gill (New York: Columbia University Press, 1993)

———. *Speculum of the Other Woman*, trans. by Gillian C. Gill, 5th edn (New York: Cornell University Press, 1992)

———. *This Sex Which Is Not One*, trans. by Catherine Porter, 4th edn (New York: Cornell University Press, 1988)

Jackson, Gordon, ed., *Isaac Watts: Selected Poems* (Manchester: Carcanet, 1999)

Jackson, Virginia, *Dickinson's Misery: A Theory of Lyric Reading* (Princeton: Princeton University Press, 2005)

Janzen, Grace M., *Becoming Divine: Towards a Feminist Philosophy of Religion* (Manchester: Manchester University Press, 1998)

Johnson, Elizabeth, *She Who Is: The Mystery of God in Feminist Discourse* (1992) tenth anniversary edn (New York: Herder and Herder, 2003)

Johnson, Thomas H., *Emily Dickinson: An Interpretative Biography*, 3rd edn (New York: Atheneum, 1976)

Jones, Cheslyn, and others, eds, *The Study of Liturgy* (London: SPCK, 1979)

Joy, Morny, Kathleen O'Grady and Judith L. Poxon, eds, *French Feminists on Religion* (London: Routledge, 2002)

Juhasz, Suzanne, ed., *Feminist Critics Read Emily Dickinson* (Bloomington: Indiana University Press, 1983)

Juster, Susan, *Disorderly Women: Sexual Politics and Evangelicalism in Revolutionary New England* (London: Cornell University Press, 1994)

Juster, Susan, and Lisa MacFarlane, eds, *A Mighty Baptism: Race, Gender and the Creation of American Protestantism* (Ithaca and London: Cornell University Press, 1996)

Kaplan, Cora, *Sea Changes: Essays on Culture and Feminism* (London: Verso, 1986)

Keller, Karl, *The Only Kangaroo Among the Beauty: Emily Dickinson and America* (Baltimore: John Hopkins University Press, 1979)

King, Archdale A., *Liturgies of the Religious Orders* (London: Longmans, 1955)

Kramnick, Isaac, ed., *Thomas Paine: Common Sense* (Harmondsworth: Penguin, 1984)

Ladin, Jay, "So Anthracite to Live:' Emily Dickinson and American Literary History,' *The Emily Dickinson Journal* (13:1) (2004) 19–50

Landow, George P., *Victorian Types, Victorian Shadows: Biblical Typology in Victorian Literature, Art and Thought* (Boston: Routledge and Kegan Paul, 1980)

Lease, Benjamin, *Emily Dickinson's Reading of Men and Books* (Houndmills: Macmillan, 1990)

Leder, Sharon and Abbott, Andrea, *The Language of Exclusion: The Poetry of Emily Dickinson and Christina Rossetti* (New York: Greenwood Press, 1987)

Lerna, Gerda, *The Creation of Feminist Consciousness: From the Middle Ages to Eighteen-Seventy* (Oxford: Oxford University Press, 1993)

Lewis, Linda, *Elizabeth Barrett-Browning's Spiritual Progress: Face to Face with God* (Columbia: University of Missouri Press, 1998)

Livingstone, E.A., ed., *Concise Oxford Dictionary of the Christian Church*, 2nd edn (Oxford: Oxford University Press, 2000)

Lonsdale, Roger, ed., *Eighteenth Century Women Poets* (Oxford: Oxford University Press, 1989)

Lundin, Roger, *Emily Dickinson and the Art of Belief*, 2nd edn (Michigan: William B. Eerdmans Publishing Co., 2004)

Maddocks, Fiona, *Hildegard of Bingen: The Woman of Her Age* (London: Review, 2001)

Makins, Marian, and others, eds, *Collins English Dictionary*, 3rd edn (Glasgow: Harper Collins, 1991)

Manning, Bernard. L., *The Hymns of Wesley and Watts* (London: Epworth Press, 1942)

Marks, Elaine and Isabelle de Courtivron, eds, *New French Feminisms: An Anthology* (Brighton: Harvester Wheatsheaf, 1981)

Marshall, Madeline Forell, ed., *The Poetry of Elizabeth Singer Rowe (1674–1737)* (Lewiston: Edwin Mellen Press)

Martin, Wendy, ed., *The Cambridge Companion to Emily Dickinson* (Cambridge: Cambridge University Press, 2002)

———. An American Triptych: Anne Bradstreet, Emily Dickinson, Adrienne Rich (Chapel Hill: University of North Carolina Press, 1984)

Marty, Martin. E., *The Infidel: Freethought and American Religion* (New York: World Publishing Co, 1961)

McIntosh, James, *Nimble Believing: Dickinson and the Unknown* (Ann Arbour: The University of Michigan Press, 2004)

McIntosh, Mark A., *Mystical Theology* (Oxford: Blackwell, 2000)

McNeil, Helen, *Emily Dickinson* (London: Virago Press, 1986)

Melnyk, Julie, *Christianity, Community and Subjectivity in Victorian Women's Hymns* (Forthcoming)

Miller, Cristanne, *Emily Dickinson: A Poet's Grammar* (Cambridge, MA: Harvard University Press, 1987)

Montefiore, Jan, *Feminism and Poetry: Language, Experience, Identity In Women's Writing,* 3rd edn (London: Pandora, 2004)

Morgan, Victoria and Clare Williams, eds, *Shaping Belief: Culture, Politics and Religion in Nineteenth-Century Writing* (Liverpool: Liverpool University Press, 2008)

Mott, Wesley T., ed., *Dictionary of Literary Biography: The American Renaissance in New England*, third series (Boston: Gale Group, 2001)

Munns, Jessica and Gita Rajan., eds, *A Cultural Studies Reader: History, Theory and Practice* (Harlow: Longman, 1995)

Murray, J., and others, *Oxford English Dictionary*, 2nd edn, vols 1–13 (Oxford: Clarendon Press, 1989)

Myerson, Joel, ed., *A Historical Guide to Ralph Waldo Emerson* (Oxford: Oxford University Press, 2000)

Mynors, R.A.B., ed., *Virgil: Georgics* rev. edn (Oxford: Clarendon Press, 1994)

Noll, Mark A., and Edith L. Blumhoffer, eds, *'Sing them Over Again to Me:' Hymns and Hymnbooks in America* (Alabama: The University of Alabama Press, 2006)

Nye, Russell Blaine, *Society and Culture in America, 1830–1860* (New York: Harper and Row, 1974)

Oberhaus, Dorothy Huff, *Emily Dickinson's Fascicles: Method and Meaning* (University Park: Pennsylvania State University Press, 1995)

O'Gorman, Francis, ed., *Victorian Poetry: An Annotated Anthology* (Oxford: Blackwell, 2004)

Paglia, Camille, *Sexual Personnae: Art and Decadence from Nefertiti to Emily Dickinson* (London: Penguin, 1991)

Palazzo, Lynda, *Christina Rossetti's Feminist Theology* (Houndmills: Palgrave, 2002)

Petrino, Elizabeth, 'Late Bloomer: The Gentian as Sign or Symbol in the Work of Dickinson and Her Contemporaries,' *The Emily Dickinson Journal* 14: 1 (2004) 104–125

Philips, Elizabeth, *Emily Dickinson: Personae and Performance* (University Park: Pennsylvania State University Press, 1988)

Pickard, John B., *Emily Dickinson: An Introduction and Interpretation* (New York: Holt, Rinehart and Winston, 1967)

Podhradsky, Gerhard, ed., *New Dictionary of the Liturgy* (London: Geoffrey Chapman, 1967)

Pollak, Vivian R., ed., *A Historical Guide to Emily Dickinson* (Oxford: Oxford University Press, 2004)

Porter, David, *Dickinson: The Modern Idiom* (Cambridge, MA: Harvard University Press, 1981)

———. *The Art of Emily Dickinson's Early Poetry* (Cambridge, MA: Harvard University Press, 1966)

Prince, F.T., ed., *Milton: Paradise Lost, Books I and II* (Oxford: Oxford University Press, 1962)

Ramsey, Paul, ed., *Freedom Of the Will: The Works of Jonathan Edwards Vol. I* (New Haven: Yale University Press, 1957)

Rhoades, James, trans., *The Georgics of Virgil: Translated into English Verse* (London: Paul Kegan and Co., 1881)

Rodgers, Daniel, T., *The Work Ethic in Industrial America 1850–1920* (Chicago: The University of Chicago Press, 1974)

Rosenbaum, S.P., ed., *A Concordance to the Poems of Emily Dickinson* (New York: Cornell University Press, 1964)

Ross, Christine, 'Uncommon Measures: Emily Dickinson's Subversive Prosody,' *The Emily Dickinson Journal* (10: 1) (2001) 70–98

Rowbotham, Sheila, *Hidden From History* (1973) (London: Pluto, 1992)

Ruland, Richard and Malcolm Bradbury, *From Puritanism to Postmodernism: A History of American Literature* (London: Routledge, 1991)

Sanchez-Eppler, Karen, *Touching Liberty: Abolition, Feminism and the Politics of the Body* (Berkeley: University of California Press, 1993)

Scheinberg, Cynthia, *Women's Poetry and Religion in Victorian England: Jewish Identity and Christian Culture* (Cambridge: Cambridge University Press, 2002)

Sewall, Richard B., *The Life of Emily Dickinson*, 2 vols (London: Faber and Faber, 1976)

Shepherd, Emma Ladd, ed., www.monsonhistoricalsociety.org/emilydickinson. htm (website accessed on 12/04/06)

Shoobridge, Helen, "Reverence for each Other being Sweet Aim:' Dickinson Face to face with the Masculine,' *The Emily Dickinson Journal* 9:1 (2000) 87–111

Showalter, Elaine, *Sister's Choice: Tradition and Change in American Women's Writing* (Oxford: Clarendon, 1991)

————. ed., The New Feminist Criticism: Essays on Women, Literature and Theory, 4th edn (London: Virago Press, 1993)

Sielke, Sabine, *Fashioning the Female Subject: The Intertextual Networking of Dickinson, Moore, and Rich* (Ann Arbour: The University of Michigan Press, 1997)

Skeggs, Beverley, *Class, Self, Culture* (London: Routledge, 2004)

Sowerby, Robin, ed., *Alexander Pope: Selected Poetry and Prose* (London: Routledge, 1988)

Spiro, Lisa, 'Reading with a tender Rapture: 'Reveries of a Bachelor' and the Rhetoric of Detached Intimacy' Book History 6 (2003) 57–93

Stannard, David E., *The Puritan Way of Death: A Study in Religion, Culture and Social Change* (Oxford: Oxford University Press, 1977)

St. Armand, Barton Levi, *Emily Dickinson and Her Culture: The Soul's Society*, 3rd edn (Cambridge, MA: Cambridge University Press, 1989)

————. 'Paradise Deferred: The Image of Heaven in the Work of Emily Dickinson and Elizabeth Stuart Phelps,' *American Quarterly* 29: 1 (1977) 55-78

Stocks, Kenneth, *Emily Dickinson and the Modern Consciousness* (Houndmills: Macmillan, 1988)

Stonum, Gary Lee, *The Dickinson Sublime* (Madison: The University of Wisconsin Press, 1990)

Storey, John, ed., *Cultural Theory and Popular Culture: A Reader* (Hertfordshire: Harvester, 1994)

Sutherland, James, *A Preface to Eighteenth-Century Poetry* (Oxford: Clarendon Press, 1948)

Taylor, Mark. C., *Erring: A Postmodern A/theology* (Chicago: University of Chicago Press, 1987)

Tobin, John, ed., *George Herbert: The Complete English Poems* (London: Penguin, 2004)

Tucker, Herbert F., *A Companion to Victorian Literature and Culture*, rev. edn (Oxford: Blackwell, 2004)

Turner, T., *Without God, Without Creed: The Origins of Unbelief in America* (Baltimore: Johns Hopkins University Press, 1985)

Underhill, Evelyn, *Mystics of the Church* (1925) (London: James Clarke, 1975)

Walker, Cheryl, *The Nightingale's Burden: Women Poets and American Culture Before 1900* (Bloomington: Indiana University Press, 1982)

Ward, Graham, ed., *The Certeau Reader* (Oxford: Blackwell, 2000)

————. *Christ and Culture* (Oxford: Blackwell, 2005)

Ward Jouve, Nicole, *Female Genesis: Creativity, Self and Gender* (Cambridge: Polity Press, 1998)

Watson, J. R., *The English Hymn: A Critical and Historical Study* (Oxford: Clarendon Press, 1997)

Watts, Michael R., *The Dissenters: From the Reformation to the French Revolution* (Oxford: Clarendon Press, 1978)

Weber, Max, *The Protestant Ethic and the Spirit of Capitalism* (1930) (London: Routledge, 2004)

Webster's *Dictionary* (1828) from: http://65.66.134.201/cgi-bin/webster/webster.exe?firstp=17671 managed by Christian Technologies, Inc. 2002 (date accessed 5/06/07)

Welch, Sharon D., *A Feminist Ethics of Risk* (Minneapolis: Fortress Press, 2000)

White, L.E., *The Imagery of the Hymns of Isaac Watts* (Unpublished MA thesis, University of Liverpool, 1964)

Wilson, Bee, *The Hive: The Story of the Honeybee and Us* (London: John Murray, 2004)

Williams, Peter W., ed., *Perspectives on American Religion and Culture* (Oxford: Blackwell, 1999)

Williams, Raymond, *Culture and Society: 1780–1950* (Harmondsworth: Penguin, 1971)

Wolosky, Shira, 'Rhetoric or Not: Hymnal Tropes in Emily Dickinson and Isaac Watts,' *The New England Quarterly* 61 (1988) 214–32

———. *Emily Dickinson: A Voice of War* (New Haven: Yale University Press, 1984)

Wolters, Clifton, trans., *The Cloud of Unknowing and Other Works* (London: Penguin, 1978)

Woodcock, Bruce, ed., *The Selected Poems of William Blake* (Hertfordshire: Wordsworth Editions, 2000)

Wright, Thomas, *The Life of Isaac Watts* (London: CJ Farncombe & Sons, 1914)

Wu, Duncan, ed., *Romanticism: An Anthology*, 2nd edn (Oxford: Blackwell, 1998)

Zim, Rivkah, English Metrical Psalms: Poetry as Praise and Prayer 1535–1601 (Cambridge: Cambridge University Press, 1987)

Zizek, Slavoj, *On Belief* (London: Routledge, 2001)

Index